International
Library of the
Philosophy of
Education

**Values,
education
and the
adult**

International
Library of the
Philosophy of
Education

General Editor

R. S. Peters
Professor of Philosophy of Education
Institute of Education
University of London

Values, education and the adult

R. W. K. Paterson

Lecturer in Philosophy
Department of Adult Education
University of Hull

Routledge & Kegan Paul

London, Boston and Henley

First published in 1979
by Routledge & Kegan Paul Ltd
39 Store Street,
London WC1E 7DD,
Broadway House,
Newtown Road,
Henley-on-Thames,
Oxon RG9 1EN and
9 Park Street,
Boston, Mass. 02108, USA
Printed in Great Britain by
Redwood Burn Limited, Trowbridge & Esher

British Library Cataloguing in Publication Data

Paterson, Ronald William Keith
  Values, education and the adult – (International
  library of the philosophy of education).
  1 Adult education – Philosophy
  1 Title
  374'.001   LC5219   79-40680
  ISBN 0 7100 0102 9

Contents

LC
5215
P39

General editor's note

There is a growing interest in philosophy of education
amongst students of philosophy as well as amongst those
who are more specifically and practically concerned with
educational problems. Philosophers, of course, from the
time of Plato onwards, have taken an interest in education
and have dealt with education in the context of wider
concerns about knowledge and the good life. But it is
only quite recently in this country that philosophy of
education has come to be conceived of as a specific branch
of philosophy like the philosophy of science or political
philosophy.

To call philosophy of education a specific branch of
philosophy is not, however, to suggest that it is a
distinct branch in the sense that it could exist apart
from established branches of philosophy such as episte-
mology, ethics, and philosophy of mind. It would be more
appropriate to conceive of it as drawing on established
branches of philosophy and bringing them together in ways
which are relevant to educational issues. In this respect
the analogy with political philosophy would be a good one.
Thus use can often be made of work that already exists in
philosophy. In tackling, for instance, issues such as the
rights of parents and children, punishment in schools, and
the authority of the teacher, it is possible to draw on
and develop work already done by philosophers on 'rights',
'punishment', and 'authority'. In other cases, however,
no systematic work exists in the relevant branches of
philosophy - e.g. on concepts such as 'education',
'teaching', 'learning', 'indoctrination'. So philosophers
of education have had to break new ground - in these cases
in the philosophy of mind. Work on educational issues can
also bring to life and throw new light on long-standing
problems in philosophy. Concentration, for instance, on
the particular predicament of children can throw new light

on problems of punishment and responsibility. G.E.Moore's
old worries about what sorts of things are good in
themselves can be brought to life by urgent questions
about the justification of the curriculum in schools.

There is a danger in philosophy of education, as in any
other applied field, of polarization to one of two
extremes. The work could be practically relevant but
philosophically feeble; or it could be philosophically
sophisticated but remote from practical problems. The aim
of the new International Library of the Philosophy of Education is to build up a body of fundamental work in this
area which is both practically relevant and philosophically competent. For unless it achieves both types of
objective it will fail to satisfy those for whom it is
intended and fall short of the conception of philosophy
of education which the International Library is meant to
embody.

'Continuing education' is very much a subject of
'practical relevance' that is supported fervently -
though, in this country at any rate, more by sentiment
than by cash. It is appropriate, therefore, that whatever
philosophical issues it raises should be discussed in a
volume of the International Library of the Philosophy of
Education. Dr Paterson's 'Values, Education and the
Adult', which deals with the philosophy of adult education, is the first book in the Library to be published
in this field.

Dr Paterson's book is distinctive not only because it
pioneers new ground but also because the positions which
he takes up are controversial and likely to be unpopular
both with many of his colleagues in adult education and
with many philosophers of education. He is, for instance,
uncompromising in his refusal to harness education to
practical or social purposes. Education, he claims, is
concerned with the development of 'the person in his
person-hood'. He vigorously defends the importance of
subject-matters and their intrinsic criteria of worth.
And he deals with moral education from a point of view
that owes much to Max Scheler.

In dealing with adult education Dr Paterson deals with
a great many issues within philosophy of education that
have been dealt with by other philosophers. The richness
of his book, as well as the heterodox character of many
of his views, should make it a book arousing both interest
and irritation amongst those working both in adult education and in philosophy of education alike.

R.S.P.

The concept of 'adult education'

Part I

Adulthood and education   1

It is significant that we distinguish adult education from
other forms of educational provision by reference to the
nature of its clients. Primary, secondary, further, and
higher education are differentiated from one another in
terms of notional stages in the unfolding of the educational enterprise. Technical, physical, and moral
education are differentiated from one another and from
legal or medical education in terms of their distinctive
contents and objectives. But, if nomenclature is any
guide, the vast assortment of activities which are collectively styled 'adult education' derive whatever common
character they have from the character of the clients,
actual and potential, on whose behalf they are initiated.
Naturally, within this heterogeneous collection of activities different levels of operation are recognized, and the
multitude of programmes of study evince a multitude of
distinguishable objectives and spheres of concern.
However, if for most purposes we marshal this astonishing
miscellany of activities under the generic name of 'adult
education', this is solely because they are felt to
partake of a common identity rooted in the characteristic
needs, claims, and circumstances of adults as a distinct
genus of educational beneficiaries. To elucidate the
concept of 'adult education', then, we require to elucidate the concept of an 'adult'.

This is by no means as straightforward as it may seem.
We use the term 'adult', as noun or as adjective, in
different contexts with differing overtones and emphases.
Thus, when an anthropologist speaks of the average height
and weight of the adults in some society, he does so in a
context where the accent is on processes of physical
growth and development. When a critic refers to an adult
novel or play, he is claiming that it solicits a certain
maturity of response from the reader or spectator. When

a newspaper advertisement promises that a forthcoming
pantomime will be heartily enjoyed by adults, it is
acknowledging that the entertainment is principally
devised for the benefit of children. When a man tells
his sixteen-year-old son that he is not yet an adult, he
may be reminding him that some of his claims and expectations are inappropriate because premature. And in a
wide variety of contexts the term 'adult' is put to a wide
variety of uses, with continuously changing implications
and readily discernible shifts of emphasis.

Common to all these uses, of course, is the focal
contrast of the adult with the child. What is adult is
contrasted, in this or that respect and for this or that
purpose, with what is adolescent, juvenile, or infantile.
An adult has been a child but is no longer one. Adulthood
is a state into which he has passed, from a state of
childhood which he has quitted. His passage into
adulthood is not conceived as a bare movement through
time, however, for central to the concept of an adult is
the idea that this state is attained by a process of
growth. Adults are what children grow up to become. To
be an adult is to have reached a certain stage of development, and, moreover, to have reached a stage which
is thought of as in some sense final, an end-stage of a
process of development which confers meaning and direction on the earlier stages of the process. Within the
state of adulthood, as within the state of childhood,
there may be earlier and later phases, from young
adulthood to senility, but one does not pass from
adulthood into some altogether distinct and novel state,
at least within the bounds of our natural lives. 'Second
childhood' is a condition which only adults can suffer.
Once an adult, in short, always an adult.

Although in recognizing that someone is an adult we
are recognizing that he has reached a certain stage of
development, it does not follow that the concept of an
adult is a straightforwardly empirical concept. In saying
that someone is an adult we are not simply saying that his
physical development is complete, or that his mental
capacities and attainments, his qualities of character,
and his social awareness and skill have developed to some
given degree, for we might say all this of a precocious
child. Indeed, we are not necessarily saying anything
about his degree of physical, mental, and social development, for we acknowledge that many adults are physically
stunted, mentally retarded, or socially backward. The
stage of development which the adult has reached cannot
be equated with any particular stage of physical, mental,
or social development. In calling someone an 'adult' we

are not claiming that he has any one empirical characteristic or set of empirical characteristics. We are not
describing, however vaguely, his appearance, state of
mind, or behaviour. In calling someone an 'adult' we are
rather ascribing to him a certain *status*, a status which
derives its significance from contrast with the status of
a child and which he gains only after relinquishing the
status of a child. If adulthood represents an end-stage
of development, this is because it unalterably revokes
the previous status of the individual who has now attained
adulthood, and it can never itself be revoked in favour of
any higher status into which the individual may pass from
adulthood.

Now, the concept of 'status' (while it may need
empirical criteria for its correct application) is pre-
eminently a *normative* concept. It enshrines valuations,
priorities, estimates of regard. Enfolded within the
concept of 'status' there are all kinds of prescriptions
and prohibitions, licences and requirements. In particular, a person's status comprises the ethical requirement
that he act in certain specific ways and be treated by
others in certain specific ways - and indeed the precise
specification of these ways in large measure yields the
precise specification of the status he enjoys. To be an
adult, then, is to possess a certain status, with inherent
proprieties and forms of comportment, inherent obligations
and rights. When we consider someone an adult, we
consider that there are distinctive compliances, modes of
respect, which he may rightfully demand of us, and that
there are natural dispositions, qualities of concern,
which we may rightfully demand of him.

Among the various rights and duties of adults, there
are some which have little direct relevance to the adult
as a participant in education. A man has a duty to keep
any promises he has made, and he has a right to choose his
own friends, but it can hardly be claimed that the application of either of these principles seriously affects the
scope and character of his educational needs and interests. There are other rights and duties of the adult
which are of more direct relevance to his participation
in education, but which he has in common with children
and which therefore have no special implications for adult
education in particular. It is in virtue of his general
status as a moral agent, not in virtue of his special
status as an adult, that he has a duty to tolerate the
expression of opinions different from his own, and that
he has a right to equality of consideration along with
others.

However, inherent in the status of adult there are

numerous valuations and requirements which do have
considerable significance for the adult as a participant
in education and which do not apply in anything like the
same degree to children. Thus an adult is expected to
take a full share in the tasks of the society to which he
belongs, and to bear some measure of responsibility for
the internal life and external acts of his society. He is
expected to play his part in actively bettering his
society, in raising its quality of life and in making it
a wiser and more just society. It is to the adult that we
ascribe the duty of recognizing and caring for those
things which are enduringly valuable in our civilization
and in the natural environment, for we rightly believe
that natural beauties and works of art, bodies of
knowledge and insight, economic and technological
advances, social institutions and freedoms, in short
everything worthwhile that can be preserved and transmitted by intelligence and care is held by the present
generation of mature men and women in trust for future
generations. The adult, moreover, is in an important
sense charged with caring for himself: we ascribe to him
the duty to be mindful of his own deepest interests, to
cultivate whatever talents he may possess, and to accept
responsibility for his moral character and conduct and
for the development of his qualities as a person.

The adult is also distinguished from the child by his
enjoyment in high degree of various entitlements and pre-
rogatives, many of which also have the greatest significance for his participation in education. An adult has
a right to share in the making of decisions which affect
his wellbeing. As a full member of the community, he has
a right to share in the making of many decisions which
affect the wellbeing of others, even when his own
wellbeing is not directly involved. He is entitled to
frame his life and conduct his personal affairs as he
alone thinks fit, provided only that his obligations to
others are met and that in his free initiatives he does
not injure other men's legitimate interests or infringe
their spheres of liberty. An adult is entitled to consult
with whom he chooses, on whatever topics are of moment to
him; he is entitled to seek opinions from whatever
quarters he pleases, and to accept or ignore these
according to his own free decision.

Unlike many of the 'rights' which are ascribed to
children, the rights of adults are fully rights: they
are discretionary claims, which he may choose to exercise
or not to exercise according to his own unconstrained
wishes and judgment. The fact that in some societies
many adults are prevented from exercising their rights,

and perhaps in addition absolved from performing some of
the duties which rightly pertain to their status as
adults, in no way affects the character or limits the
scope of these rights and duties, which depend solely on
certain proprieties inherent in the status of adulthood,
not on the contingent circumstance of these proprieties
being recognized. And the fact that in our own society
individual adults may be debarred from exercising certain
rights or exempted from performing certain duties, usually
on grounds of incapacity, in no way diminishes their
validity, which like the validity of all norms is always
subject to a variety of relevant conditions being satisfied.

When we characterize someone as an 'adult', then, we
are ascribing to him various prima facie rights and
duties, which may in exceptional circumstances be rescind-
ed but which are normally operative, just as a debtor may
sometimes be released from his debts or a creditor denied
his rights of recovery if good cause can be shown,
although this by no means impairs the prima facie duties
and rights inherent in the status of 'debtor' or
'creditor' as such. The proprieties which reside in the
status of adult qua adult may and do lapse in individual
cases, when they are overridden by more fundamental
ethical considerations, but this does not in the slightest
alter the general requirements which we hold to be intrinsic to the status of an adult as such.

On what grounds, however, do we feel it necessary to
distinguish and identify these proprieties, these rights
and duties, which constitute the status of the adult? We
distinguish some men as 'debtors' and others as 'creditors' in virtue of an actual economic relationship, involving the objective exchange of money, goods, or
services, and we identify individual debtors and creditors
by reference to observable transactions which have taken
place, from which their status as 'creditors' or 'debtors'
flows. By reference to what actual characteristics do we
distinguish those individuals on whom we correctly confer
the status of 'adult'? In virtue of what objective qualities or relationships do we correctly ascribe to some
human beings, but not to others, those rights and duties
which are intrinsic to 'adulthood'?

Adults are not held to be adults because they have
larger bodies than children, or because they have greater
intelligence, since this is often not in fact the case.
Nor is it because their bodies and intelligences have
ceased developing: physical and intellectual growth
commonly ceases before adulthood is reached, and in any
case we would continue to consider someone aged thirty or

forty an adult even if at that age he made a belated spurt of physical or intellectual development. It is not because a man has wider knowledge than a child that he is considered to be an adult, for some children are more knowledgeable than some adults. Nor is it because he makes a more tangible contribution to society: elderly or disabled adults make little or no tangible contribution to society, while some adolescents may be doing hard and dangerous work or performing essential services.

Perhaps, since adulthood is a status, with inherent ethical requirements, we should expect to locate the criteria justifying the conferment of this status a little nearer to the realm of the ethical. Perhaps our judgment that someone is an adult rests on our judgment that he possesses certain moral qualities, certain qualities of character, which coalesce to form a distinctive body of claims to adult status: to evince such qualities as prudence, self-control, patience, fortitude, tolerance, and objectivity, is, we might think, to have good claims to the dignity of adulthood. Kindred to these moral qualities there are deeply personal qualities which have an undeniable cognitive dimension but which are intimately interwoven with the individual's capacities for emotion and feeling - mature human insight, the perceptiveness of compassion, the imaginative understanding of another's situation, an unembarrassed responsiveness to the needs of others, a capacity for forming meaningful, stable, and realistic relationships: we might well judge that such personal qualities of balanced concern and involvement, when manifested in sufficient degree, constitute excellent grounds for the ascription of adulthood. No doubt our recognition of these moral qualities and personal capacities depends in part on valuations, appraisals, normative judgments, but equally there is no doubt that these qualities and capacities are objective characteristics discernible in the observable character and conduct of actual men and women. We might well want to take into account, also, the network of responsibilities - in the family, in the community, at work - which the individual has undertaken to carry, for we expect an adult to be able and willing to shoulder many different types of responsibility and to discharge them efficiently and without fuss. Finally, we might consider that an individual's title to adulthood rests in part on his length and breadth of experience, not in the sense of a mere catalogue of passively received impressions, but 'experience' in the sense of actively lived experience which has refined and at the same time strengthened the individual's relations with the world and with his fellows.

The trouble is that very many people who are unquestionably adults do not come anywhere near to satisfying these criteria. Many adults are foolish, weak,
impulsive, self-deluding, or egotistical, and by comparison with many adolescents and even quite young children
their qualities of character are meagre and inglorious.
By the side of some perceptive and sympathetic children,
who may show surprising quickness and depth of understanding, many adults appear emotionally obtuse, lacking
in insight and sensitivity, and neither self-aware enough
nor self-forgetful enough to make real connections with
other people. They may shrink from responsibility, or
prove woefully inadequate to discharge the responsibilities they have reluctantly incurred. And in too many
cases age may not even bring instructive experience, but
merely an increasingly mute mass of repetitive and undif-
ferentiated commonplaces.

Yet we are surely right in surmising that the status
of adulthood is very closely connected with these moral
qualities and personal capacities, with the acceptance of
responsibilities and the building-up of a meaningful body
of experience. It is not so much that an adult must
actually possess attributes and competencies of these
various kinds. It is rather that an adult is someone
whom we may *justifiably presume* to possess them. If we
treat our neighbour as an adult, with the rights and
duties intrinsic to that status, this is because we feel
entitled to presume, for example, that in appropriate
circumstances he will show restraint and impartiality,
concern and understanding in some sufficient degree, and
that he will accept a certain amount of responsibility
and prove capable of drawing on his relevant experience
with some measure of sense and skill. We do not normally
feel entitled to presume any such attributes and competencies on the part of our neighbour's young child. Unless
we have reasons to the contrary, that is, we shall form
one set of expectations of the father and a quite different - and much more limited - set of expectations of the
child. In the event, we may be disappointed in the father
and pleasantly surprised by the child, but unless there
are good reasons obviously annulling our original expectations of the father (an exonerating handicap, for
example, or perhaps his exceptionally adverse circumstances) we shall feel and be *justifiably* disappointed
in him. We do have justifiable presumptions concerning
the attributes and competencies of different categories
of people, and although we are often disappointed or
surprised in individual cases, those cases in which our
disappointment or surprise is justifiable at least demon-

strate the justice if not the accuracy of our original
presumptions. We may in the event be mistaken about
individual soldiers, policemen, or doctors, but we are
justified in expecting soldiers to be alert and cou-
rageous, policemen to be helpful and fair-minded, and
doctors to be skilled and solicitous, all in their
characteristic ways and in appropriate degrees. Similarly, we are justified in expecting a very much larger
category of people to exhibit certain very basic moral
and personal attributes and competencies, and it is
because these very basic expectations are just (whether
in individual cases they are accurate or not) that we are
justified in ascribing to this large and assorted body of
people all the rights and duties which are intrinsic to
the status of adulthood.

An adult, then, may not *be* morally and emotionally
mature, but we are entitled to expect him to be so, and
he is an adult *because* he is a rightful object of such
expectations. We are still left, however, with the
unanswered question: on what *grounds* are we entitled to
form these expectations of one individual, the father, but
not of another, the child?

The answer to this question is, I think, deceptively
obvious. It is, quite simply, because the father is older
than the child. Adults are adults, in the last analysis,
because they are older than children. For legislative
purposes, of course, most modern states use age as the
criterion for distinguishing adults from children, and it
might seem as if age is used merely because it is administratively the easiest criterion to apply on a large scale
though in itself purely arbitrary as a criterion of
adulthood. This would be erroneous, however. In point
of fact, age is not administratively the easiest of
criteria to apply (height would be considerably easier),
and while no doubt there is a margin of arbitrariness in
adopting a particular age for the criterion of adulthood
and applying it right across the population, the choice
of age as such is completely in tune with what we intui-
tively perceive to be the permanent human realities underlying and underwriting the concept of an adult. If it is
on grounds of age that we rightly form one set of expectations of the father and a different, more limited, and
less demanding set of expectations of his son, ascribing
to one the status of adult and to the other the status of
child, this is because we correctly deem their difference
of age to have *in itself* the greatest ethical and existential relevance.

Of course, we do in fact observe a fairly close
correlation between a person's age and his degree of

actual moral and emotional maturity, and our general
experience that older people do in fact tend to be in
varying degrees more mature leads us to 'expect' them to
be more mature in that purely descriptive sense of
'expect' in which we expect it to snow in January. However, there is a normative sense of 'expect', the sense
in which even known liars are expected to tell the truth
and are only blamed because we rightly expect them to do
what we anticipate they will probably not in fact do; and
it is above all in this normative sense that we expect
moral and emotional maturity from older people, justifiably ascribing to them the status of adults in this legitimate expectation. In and of itself, we feel, age *ought* to
have recruited an appropriate combination of those moral
and personal attributes and competencies in presumption of
which we consider older people to merit the status of
adulthood with all its intrinsic proprieties.

There is nothing arbitrary or paradoxical in our
judgment that a person's age, the mere fact that a certain
period of time has elapsed since his birth, should of
itself generate fresh dimensions of moral identity. In
human life the mere passage of time may create new situations, making new demands and offering changed potentialities. As conscious selves, we are aware of our being
as mediated by time, we are aware of our being as inescapably rooted in time, and it is across time that we
necessarily seize the meaning of any human eventuality or
project. Brute objects, physical things, may be *in* time,
but there is no time *for* them. Whether changing or
unchanging, things simply *are*; it is persons who *act*,
and in acting announce their consciousness of temporal
transition. A conscious self, a person, is a fount of
action as well as a centre of consciousness, and of course
consciousness itself is essentially an activity, an
ongoing and ceaseless manifold of conscious acts. While a
wholly static and eternally unchanging physical universe
is perhaps conceivable, the irruption of consciousness
into such a universe would necessarily import a principle
of change merely by virtue of the successive (and
consciously successive) acts of the scrutinizing
consciousness. The mode of existence of conscious selves,
personal existence, is fraught with the recognition of its
own temporality, and it is across the horizon of our
temporality that we grasp and disclose ourselves and the
world. The passage of time both encloses and liberates
us; time limits as it frees; but in all its workings it
is a primordial and overarching condition of human
existence.

A person's age states his relationship to time. It

states that a certain time has elapsed since his birth
and that the time of his death is in that measure nearer.
Only with the passage of time can there come use, habitu-
ation, inurement, for it takes time to get used to anything, and it takes the arriving consciousness time to
get used to the structures and possibilities of existence.
Only with the passage of time can there come real urgency,
deepening seriousness, more intense concern, for it is as
the hour of departure wings nearer that we become
conscious of necessarily lessening opportunities and
unavoidably altering priorities, and as the time remaining
grows shorter we become increasingly alert to what remains
of significance and value.

Quite apart from the changing circumstances it brings
in its train, then, the mere passage of time in itself is
of central importance to the life of a conscious being,
critically affecting our key valuations and transforming
our attitudes and expectations at their focal points.
Thus we consider the postponement of a benefit to be in
itself a deprivation, and the deferment of an evil to be
in itself a grace. The duration of a friendship or of any
relationship profoundly affects its inner quality, for
better or worse. The length of a man's service, his
seniority, confers upon him changing rights and responsibilities. Priority in time may establish moral entitlement, as in the principles of 'first come, first served'
and the 'right of the first occupant'. We see periods of
time as requiring division and distribution on principles
of justice, as when we judge that a man has enjoyed some
benefit for long enough and it is time he made way for
others. The passage of time may in turn be a factor
influencing the application of other principles of
justice, as when the lapse of a considerable time between
an offence and its punishment is adduced as a ground for
merciful treatment. We consider the attainment of a great
age - not only in human beings but also in the case of
many inanimate objects, such as buildings or manuscripts -
to be a proper theme of wonder, awe, reverence. And in
general the past, qua past, comes before us as a dimension
with which we are forced to come to terms; while we are
conscious of the future, qua future, as the indefinite
dimension which awaits us but which will not await us
indefinitely.

Thus there is nothing arbitrary or paradoxical in our
judgment that a person's age, his objective relationship
to time, of itself engenders objective presumptions of
moral and emotional maturity. If a child's transition to
adulthood is always more than a bare movement through
time, this is because the mere passage of time, the very

process of growing older, in itself creates new validities
and altered expectations. Whereas we rightly expect a man
of forty to display qualities of prudence, self-control,
and perseverance, it would be quite unfair to expect a boy
of ten to possess these qualities in anything like the
same measure. We are entitled to expect people above a
certain age to show tact and self-awareness in personal
relations, and to respond with understanding to the
emotional needs of others. We are entitled to expect them
to assume a measure of responsibility in several different
spheres. We are entitled to expect them to be in possession of an adequate body of experience, ready to use
it, and capable of modifying and extending it. There is,
in short, a wide but recognizable spectrum of moral qualities and personal capacities, habits of outlook and modes
of conduct, which we consider to be distinctive of
'maturity' because we consider that the passage of time,
and therefore the attainment of a certain age, is peculiarly relevant to the degree and manner in which a
person may be expected to exhibit them. After reaching
a certain age, a person who fails to show a sufficient
degree of mental, moral, and emotional maturity is rightly
regarded as blameworthy (unless there are exonerating
circumstances), for we rightly judge that a person of
this age *ought* to be thinking, feeling, and acting in
ways appropriate to his age.

It is, then, because we may justifiably presume in
someone of a certain age a sufficient measure of those attributes and competencies distinctive of maturity that we
correctly ascribe to him the various rights and responsibilities which constitute the status of 'adulthood'. To
say that someone is an adult is to say that he is entitled, for example, to a wide-ranging freedom of life-
style and to a full participation in the taking of social
decisions; and it is also to say that he is obliged,
among other things, to be mindful of his own deepest
interests and to carry a full share of the burdens involved in conducting society and transmitting its benefits. His adulthood consists in his full enjoyment of
such rights and his full subjection to such responsibilities. Those people (in most societies, the large majority) to whom we ascribe the status of adults may and do
evince the widest possible variety of intellectual gifts,
physical powers, character traits, beliefs, tastes, and
habits. But we correctly deem them to be adults because,
in virtue of their age, we are justified in requiring them
to evince the basic qualities of maturity. Adults are not
necessarily mature. But they are supposed to be mature,
and it is on this necessary supposition that their
adulthood justifiably rests.

Although we initially distinguish adult education from
other forms of educational provision by reference to the
nature of its clients, we may well surmise that from this
initial distinction there flow other distinguishing
features, shaping the profile of adult education into
something immediately recognizable as an educational
enterprise acknowledging special objectives, favouring
characteristic styles of teaching and learning, and
carrying distinctive consequences for the life of the
individual and for society. These other distinguishing
features are not logically intrinsic to the concept of
'adult education', inasmuch as they are not literally part
of what we mean by the term. Rather, they represent the
normative implications of the concept which become visible
as soon as we try to work out how in practice the education of adults is bound to differ from the education of
children and adolescents in terms of its concrete aims,
inner proprieties, and ethical or social relevance. Whatever the differences dividing adult education from the
education of children and adolescents, however, their
logical kinship is of the most intimate, for the concept
of 'adult education' is wholly and exclusively the concept
of an *educational* enterprise, and the concerns of adults
to which it ministers are wholly and exclusively their
educational concerns. Before the concept of 'adult education' can be fully elucidated, therefore, some preliminary elucidation of the concept of 'education' in general
will obviously be required.

The concept of education is clearly the concept of a
certain kind of *purposive activity*. It is an activity
because, as we shall see, education is not the kind of
thing which can just happen to a person: it postulates
some degree of deliberate contrivance by the educator and
conscious participation by the educand. And it is purposive both in the sense that it sets out to attain certain
essential objectives and in the further and principal
sense that it is these objectives that furnish the main
grounds on which we pick out 'educational' activities from
the many other activities which may outwardly resemble
them. There is no single empirical activity or group of
activities which is in itself educational. There is
nothing inherently educational about reading, writing,
talking, listening, carving, stitching, drawing, singing,
or any of the countless other activities which we may
observe going on in educational situations, for we may
engage in these activities for a whole host of reasons
quite unconnected with education. The term 'education',
as R.S.Peters says, 'refers to no particular process;
rather it encapsulates criteria to which any one of a

family of processes must conform'. (1)   If reading a short
story or carving a piece of wood is to count as an educational activity, it must be undertaken as part of a
strategy for the attainment of those essential objectives
in terms of which the category of 'the educational' is
defined.

What, then, are these essential objectives, in the
pursuit of which an activity for the first time assumes
the character of education? They may best be stated, I
think, in relation to our nature as persons, as conscious
selves, moving centres of action and awareness, whose
being is the radically finite being of individuals
conscious of the shifting but ever-present limits placed
upon their being by time, space, and matter, but conscious
also that these limits exist to be surpassed. An educational activity, we may say, is one which is intended
to foster, and in fact does foster, the highest development of individuals as persons. Education is intended to
enable people really to *be* - to live more intensively and
extensively, to manifest in themselves a higher quality of
life, to live more abundantly. Education is essentially
concerned with our growth as persons, and with our ultimate stature as persons. In short, an educational activity is one which is intended to bring about in its participants a greater fullness of personal being, and which in
some measure succeeds in doing so.

Of course, there are numerous other activities - social
work, medical care, even many industrial and commercial
activities - whose practitioners might also describe themselves as enabling people to lead fuller lives and realize
their highest potentialities as persons. Indeed, probably
most human activities enrich our lives in some way and so
may contribute to our growth in stature as persons: it is
reasonable to suppose that a man has a better opportunity
of attending to his personal development if he is
adequately fed, clothed, and housed, if he is in good
health, and if he is not under strain in his family and
social life. However, the contribution of these economic
and social activities to the development of persons is
chiefly of an instrumental and indirect kind. They remove
some of the barriers to personal development, they
establish the physical and social conditions in which
personal development may take place, but they do not of
themselves augment our stature as persons. Education, on
the other hand, directly touches us in our personal being,
tending our identity at its roots, and ministering
directly to our condition as conscious selves aspiring
in all our undertakings to a greater fullness and
completeness of being. Whatever the detailed ways in

which the concept of education be given practical
currency, it is not with the means but with the *ends* of
personal existence that education is essentially concerned.

At this stage it may be objected that some forms of
personal existence are worthless or positively evil, and
that it cannot possibly be the purpose of education to
enable men to realize their potentialities for destruction
or bestiality, for example. Since some of our potentialities are deeply undesirable, surely it cannot be the
purpose of education to bring about in its participants
mere fullness of being, mere self-realization, without
regard to the quality and value of the self which is
supposed to emerge enlarged and quickened from the
process? To this the answer is, I think, that there are
many different faces of being, and it is indeed not the
purpose of education to foster any and every potentiality
of men's being, but only their being as *persons*. An
activity which nourished the daemonic forces in man, or
pandered to the brutish in our nature, could not possibly
be described as an 'educational' activity, for inherent in
the concept of education is the requirement that its
purposes should be benign. When we judge that an activity
is 'educational', we are in part making a judgment of
value: we are judging that the fullness of being which it
fosters comprises only those qualities which are *desirable*
and which, moreover, are *intrinsically,* not just instrumentally, desirable or useful. But in fact to state this
evaluative element in the meaning of 'education' is not to
qualify, rather it is to elaborate and expound, our
earlier statement that education promotes in its participants a greater fullness of personal being, since the
concept of a 'person' (in contrast with demons, brutes,
or things) is itself suffused with evaluative meaning.
To the extent that someone is really a person, he has
transcended the grosser and darker elements in our
compound nature and has made some advance towards making
himself a being worthy of existing in his own right, a
being of whom we can truly say that it is intrinsically
good that he should exist. There is an ontological and
an axiological dimension to the concept of a 'person',
and therefore to the concept of 'education'; education
is essentially concerned with being, and essentially
concerned with values; but not with being in separation
from values, or with values as a simple appendage to
being: the fullness of being which education promotes is
a fullness of personal being, and as such education serves
as a midwife of values *in and through* its service as a
midwife of being.

A recipient of education, then, is someone whose
potentialities of becoming a full person are being
developed and who is therefore being treated, by those
responsible for his education, as immanently a being whose
existence is worthwhile in his own right.   In being educated, he is being treated as an independent centre of
value, and his development is being regarded as a matter
of objective significance.   It must be noted, however,
that from the concept of education so analysed it does not
follow that any particular individual or group will
actually receive education or be entitled to receive it.
A society (perhaps from deep instinctive fear of the
responsibilities of personhood) might rule that no one
should be educated; or that certain privileged individuals or sections of society only should be given education,
or that everyone should receive education.   While no doubt
it is wrong that anyone should be excluded from education,
the concept of an exclusive education does not embody any
formal contradiction.   If education is restricted to the
rich or the aristocratic, it remains perfectly self-
consistent to say that it is 'education' which is so
restricted.   Indeed, if exclusive education were not
counted as education, there could never logically be any
inequity in the distribution of education, and this all
too common type of educational injustice could logically
never occur.   The notion of 'universality', then, is not
built into the concept of 'education'.   The case for universal education needs to employ ethical reasoning;   it
cannot be proved by conceptual analysis alone.
When we say that education is the development of
persons as independent centres of value whose development
is seen to be an intrinsically worthwhile undertaking, it
might be thought that this account of the meaning of 'education' is excessively individualistic.   To correct this
erroneous impression, perhaps two points need to be emphasized.   First, there is an immense difference, which needs
to be marked by the words we use, between teaching a man
something solely because it is good in itself that he
should learn what is being taught, and teaching a man
something solely because his acquisition of the knowledge
or skill being taught will help to produce some extrinsic
social or economic benefit;   in the former case, the
learning to be done is something inherently worth doing
(and therefore something which ought to be done, unless
it seriously conflicts with some other thing which is also
inherently worthwhile), whereas in the latter case the
learning to be done is not something inherently worth
doing (and therefore not something which ought to be done,
if the social or economic benefit sought can be encompass-

ed in some more direct or efficient way); no doubt the
two cases often overlap in practice, but they are con-
ceptually distinct, and it is reasonable to confine the
term 'education' to the former case only, since the term
'education' does connote something worthwhile in its own
right. But this is of course a distinction between the
intrinsically valuable and the instrumentally valuable or
useful, not between something of use only to the individuals on whom it is conferred and something of use to
society in general. Given that education is a benefit of
intrinsic value, how could this benefit possibly be
conferred on society without conferring it on the individuals of whom society is composed? In forming educated
individuals, we are forming an educated society. It is
thus a complete misunderstanding to suppose that there is
anything specially 'individualistic' about our analysis
of the concept of education so far. Second, the full
development of a person as a person undoubtedly includes
his development as a member of society. If the pejorative
force of 'individualistic' flows from the insinuation that
an individualistic activity somehow divides people from
one another or at least fails to promote fruitful
interpersonal relations based on mutual concern and shared
responsibility, then it must be emphatically asserted that
education cannot possibly be individualistic in this
narrow sense. An activity directed to the full development of persons is pre-eminently an activity which, among
much else, is bound to nourish our potentialities for
creative and responsible social living and our capacities
for realistic fellowship.

However, this last point has taken us beyond what is
strictly contained in the concept of 'education' as such.
Up to now we have been focusing on what is logically
involved in any correct use of the term 'education'. Up
to now, that is, we have been concerned with analysing the
meaning of 'education'. It is a further, and quite
different, task to determine those characteristic activities to which the description 'educational' can be
properly applied. We have seen that the term 'education'
signifies an activity which intentionally develops those
intrinsically desirable qualities which we deem to be
constitutive of personhood. What those intrinsically
desirable qualities *are* is a further and distinct
question, which cannot be answered by logical analysis
alone. Mere analysis of the notion of 'desirable quality'
cannot of itself show that sociability and co-operativeness, for example, either are or are not desirable
qualities. The concept of 'desirable quality' does not
logically contain the quite distinct concepts of

'sociability' and 'co-operativeness'. While no doubt we
are right in believing that these qualities are in fact
desirable, the statement, 'sociability and co-operativeness are desirable qualities', is clearly not an analytic
statement, and the statement that 'sociability and co-
operativeness are undesirable qualities' is clearly not
self-contradictory. Thus we are not strictly entitled to
say, on grounds of logic alone, that education necessarily
develops a person as a member of society. The most that
we are strictly entitled to say, on grounds of logic
alone, is that education does not necessarily develop a
person in ways inimical to his membership of society,
since obviously the concept of 'desirable quality' does
not logically contain such quite distinct concepts as
'unsociability' or 'unco-operativeness', for example.
The concept of education is simply the concept of fostering in people a greater fullness of personal being with
all its inherent values, but as such the concept does not
state what these values specifically are and thus far it
is strictly neutral as between the claims of the individual and those of society. The full development of personal
being undoubtedly does include, among much else, the
development of our social being, our being-with-others,
but this assertion can only be justified by exhibiting
the distinctive character of personal being, by tracing
its formative modalities, and by identifying its key
ethical and existential demands. Only when this has been
done can we hope to glimpse the rich texture of living
commitments which are needed to give flesh and blood to
the formal definition of education in the abstract.

Our chief question, then, must ultimately be this. To
what are we committed when we commit ourselves in education to the full development of persons as persons? The
rest of this book will largely be an attempt to answer
this question, in its particular application to the education of adults, and obviously so fundamental a question
needs pretty well the scope of a whole book if it is to be
given any kind of satisfactory answer. However, at this
stage at least some kind of preliminary and general answer
may rightly be expected. Let me therefore suggest that in
education we are in general and of necessity committed to
the enlargement of awareness. A person is essentially a
centre of awareness, for we should not count any wholly
unconscious entity as a person, or dignify it as an
aspirant to personhood, whatever degree of external
resemblance it bore to the real, living, perceiving,
thinking, judging, desiring, choosing, and acting unities
which we recognize ourselves and others essentially to be.
In the measure that we are alert, wakeful, intensely

experiencing and aware of what is going on around us and within us, in that measure we sense ourselves as really *being*, and as being real. And chief among those things which we know to be of great worth are certain states of awareness - love, happiness, knowledge, the contemplation of beauty, moral conviction, religious adoration - since, whatever the intrinsic value of the external objects of these states of awareness, the fact that these objects are appropriately loved, enjoyed, known, admired, obeyed, or worshipped is undoubtedly something of very much greater value and importance. To grow as persons we need to grow and advance in awareness.

Of course, it by no means follows that any and every extension of our awareness is worth promoting as a fit object of educational endeavour. We certainly cannot divorce the quality of our awareness from the quality of the object *of* which it is the awareness, since there is no awareness in a vacuum: to be aware is always to be aware *of* this or that physical thing, person, concept, proposition, state of affairs, or other object to which our awareness is directed and in virtue of which it really is 'awareness'. There certainly are things scarcely worth noticing, truths scarcely worth knowing, states of affairs it is scarcely worth troubling about. Clearly, the educator needs an educational axiology. He must settle what classes of things have objective value and in what degree, before he can settle the relative educational importance of, for example, knowledge of the physical world, the purely formal knowledge of mathematics and logic, understanding of the past, understanding of other people, or the acquisition of various mental and physical attitudes and skills. One very fundamental point can be made here, however. The awareness of the educated man should be marked both by *breadth* and by *perspective*. Education has to develop in the educand a sense of per-spective, since we can be sure that any flat equation of the value of one piece of knowledge with another, or of the value of one skill with another, will blur contrasts and distinctions which it is the nature of awareness to keep sharply in focus; and thus education needs to develop the educand's capacity for making valid judgments about what is relatively important and what is relatively trivial. It is hard to see how this can be done if the educand is not equipped with a considerable breadth of knowledge and experience, embracing many radically differ-ent kinds of thing and mirroring the rich diversity of the world into which he is being initiated. In any case, these qualities of awareness are plainly of high value in their own right: no one could possibly consider, for example, that to describe a judgment as narrow and lacking in perspective was in any way to commend it. Among the grounds on which we correctly deem someone to be worthy of the regard due to a person (still more, the regard due to an adult person) is his manifestation of these qualities of breadth and perspective in his judgments and in his range of experience and feeling. Among the grounds on which we correctly deem someone's conduct to be 'daemonic' or 'brutish' there often figures a typical and sinister narrowing of vision, a failure of response except within certain obsessive patterns of hatred or lasciviousness, a rigidity of motives which results in a total loss of perspective and insight, all surely justifying our refusal to dignify such conduct by favouring it with the categories of personhood. As the development of persons in their personhood, education is bound to promote forms of awareness through which the educand is given access to reality at many different points and by many different routes, and through which he is shown not a mere panorama but a luminous landscape meaningfully structured on objective principles of order and proportion.

It is no accident that the communication of knowledge is right at the centre of all education deserving of the name. If 'education' is correctly defined as 'the making of persons' (to borrow an apt phrase of Archbishop Beck's); (2) and if we are right in our claim that the making of persons means the building up and enlargement of their awareness; then we should expect that the communication of knowledge, the initiation of the educand into rationally organized and objectively validated systems of publicly shared belief, would play a central part in any truly educational undertaking, since a body of knowledge enshrines our most sustained and thorough attempts to grasp and penetrate some meaningful reality of which we seek enlarged awareness. And of course it would be quite wrong to regard the communication of knowledge as essentially a detached, impersonal operation. On the contrary, as Peters reminds us, 'it must involve the kind of commitment that comes from being on the inside of a form of thought and awareness'. (3) To be truly educated, a man must care profoundly about the bodies of knowledge into which he has been initiated - about the manner in which they have been arrived at and the manner in which they will be preserved and transmitted. He must not only be at home within a form of thought or awareness; he must show fidelity to its standards and concern for its advancement. The educated must come to see knowledge as something of deep intrinsic value. Education, in enlarging his awareness, should enlarge his awareness of the value of awareness.

It was stated earlier (4) that education was clearly a
'purposive activity'. We have now seen what the purpose
of any activity properly styled 'educational' must be, and
we have seen to what we essentially commit ourselves when
we embrace that purpose. The purpose of education is the
development of persons in their personhood. And as this
'making of persons', education is essentially committed to
the enlargement of our awareness, the building up of our
stature as conscious selves whose being is a being-in-the-
world and who are fully alive to the manifold constituent
interiorities of the world within which we may achieve a
meaningful identity. (5)

However, the terms 'purpose' and 'purposive activity'
are somewhat ambiguous, and it may be opportune here to
clarify the precise sense in which education can be correctly described as a purposive activity. Leaving aside
purely private mental activities such as daydreaming, we
can I think say that an activity always involves at least
some kind of intentional bodily movements, and that these
bodily movements are commonly intended to bring about some
result, usually some change in the external world. Thus a
signaller may wave his arms with the intention of causing
a passing ship to come alongside. Now, the concept of the
intended *result* may or may not form part of the concept of
the *activity* in question. In the case of activities like
'drumming one's fingers', 'scowling', 'running', or
'waving one's arms', the concept of the activity is simply
the concept of certain characteristic bodily movements,
without reference to any results which these are intended
to accomplish. Of course, such activities may in fact be
intended to accomplish definite and obvious results
(drumming one's fingers in order to gain attention, for
example), but because the concept of the results is
logically quite distinct from the concept of the activity
we can characterize the results aimed at by such activities as *extrinsic* to the activity. However, there are
many activities directed towards results which are logically *intrinsic* to the activity, in the sense that the
concept of these results forms part of the very concept
of the activity in question. 'Ploughing' would not be
ploughing if it were not intended to result in a field
having been ploughed; 'washing' would not be washing if
it were not intended to result in something having been
washed; 'haircutting' would not be haircutting unless it
were intended to result in hair having been cut. Indeed,
in the case of most activities to which we annex names,
the name of the activity signifies *both* a set of bodily
movements (whether precisely specified or not) *and* an
intended result (however vaguely designated). In these

cases the concept of the activity is logically inseparable
from the concept of the result, and therefore of necessity
any reference to the activity contains an inbuilt
reference to its intended result.

Now, the concept of 'education' is the concept of an
activity which belongs logically to the latter of the two
foregoing kinds. To speak of 'educating' someone is to
acknowledge that some sort of overt operations are going
on (although as yet completely unspecified) and it is also
to acknowledge that these operations are intended to bring
about a definite result (the development of the educand as
a person). Yet there is a crucial difference between
education and most other activities incorporating logically intrinsic results. In the case of most other such
activities, the logically intrinsic results are themselves
simply means to the attainment of some *further* purpose,
and it is in terms of this further, logically extrinsic
purpose that the activities in question are thought to be
justified. The activities of 'haircutting' or 'filling a
tooth', for example, would indeed be unintelligible
without some understanding of the result to which the
physical movements of the barber or the dentist are
intrinsically intended to lead; but nearly always the
hair is cut or the tooth filled as a means to some further
purpose - comfort and beauty, or health and freedom from
pain - which indeed we may not need to know in order to
understand what 'haircutting' or 'filling a tooth' is, but
which we do need to know if we are attempting to *justify*
these activities. These are, then, examples of essentially instrumental activities, since the justification for
engaging in them is to be found, not in the results
intrinsic to the activities, but in some quite distinct
state of affairs to which the activities are supposed to
lead. However, education is not an activity of this
essentially instrumental kind. Whereas we can fully
describe the activity of 'filling a tooth' without making
any reference to the value of the results produced, since
the concept of 'filling a tooth' does not logically
include the concept of 'producing desirable results', we
cannot fully describe the activity of 'educating' without
some reference to the value of its intrinsic objectives,
since the concept of 'education' logically does include
the concept of 'fostering desirable qualities' (viz. those
constitutive of personhood). Because at least a very
general commendation of its intrinsic objectives is logically included in any designation of an activity as
'educational', then, we can say that 'educating' - like
'reforming', 'curing', and 'rescuing', but unlike
'haircutting', 'filling a tooth', or 'changing a burst

tyre' - is the kind of purposive activity which (whatever
the value of any extrinsic results it may also happen to
produce) is deemed to be justified in the sufficient light
of those distinctive purposes intrinsic to the very nature
of the activity itself.

It is now, I hope, clear in what sense education is a
'purposive activity'. The concept of 'education' is the
concept of a range of operations directed towards a very
general and intrinsically worthwhile purpose, the purpose
of building up in people a greater fullness of personal
being. 'Education' is defined in terms of its inherent
purpose, and thus a logically necessary condition which
any activity must satisfy if it is to be deemed 'educational' is that it be aimed at the development of
persons as persons. This is not yet a logically sufficient condition, however. There could be activities which
intentionally developed someone as a person but which we
refused to consider 'educational' because we felt that the
means used (although efficacious) were in some relevant
respect *improper for this purpose*. The concept of education has a 'task' aspect as well as an 'achievement'
aspect; (6) it involves the following of procedures, the
mounting of operations, the taking of measures, as well as
the general objective to which all these are directed:
and just as activities which fail to attain the appropriate objective cannot be counted as 'educational', so we
must also rule out activities which attain the appropriate
objective but in educationally unacceptable ways. If by
the judicious administration of some drug a man could be
helped to grow in understanding and insight, in his range
of sympathies and in the quality of his perceptions, we
should be willing to acknowledge that he had developed as
a person, but we should not be prepared to describe the
process by which he had developed as an 'educational' one.
People may acquire knowledge, good taste, intellectual
honesty, and all the other attributes of an educated
person by many of life's processes, not only by educational processes. Whether we are prepared to call a man
'educated' if he has all the attributes of an educated
person, but has acquired these by the accidents of living,
is a terminological matter of slight importance; but what
we surely cannot say of such a person is that he 'has been
educated', for this would be to treat the haphazard,
intermittent, and unintentional (if in this case felici-
tous and opportune) ministrations of life as if they were
in no relevant way different from the studied, purposeful,
and clear-sighted ministrations of the concerned and
responsible educator - and this would be to obliterate a
difference which is surely as palpable and momentous as
the difference between any two things can be.

The logic of the concept of 'education', then, requires us to acknowledge proprieties which any activity must observe if it is to count as an educational activity. However, this is as far as logical analysis alone can take us. Analysis of the concept of 'education' cannot of itself tell us what these proprieties *are*. The development of persons in their personhood by the taking of measures which are proper for this purpose - this is what the term 'education' *means*, but we can determine to which activities the description 'educational' can be *properly applied*, and to which activities it cannot be properly applied, only by scrutinizing and evaluating the measures they involve in the light of the ethical and existential goal of personhood which they are designed to promote and which they are therefore bound, in their own nature, to respect and uphold. In Chapter 7 of the present book we shall examine the particular ways in which the educational processes engaged in by mature men and women call for a special recognition of the proprieties governing all education properly so called. Here, however, it may be expedient to give at least a preliminary and general account of the chief proprieties which any educational activities must observe, if they are to count as dis- tinctively 'educational' activities, and of the basis on which these proprieties rest.

There are numerous activities which, like education, involve the taking of measures designed to secure logi- cally intrinsic ends esteemed to be of value in their own right, and which therefore, again like education, need no justification in terms of any extrinsic results they may happen to produce. Thanking a benefactor, for example, involves the uttering of words and perhaps the doing of deeds intended to assure the benefactor that the benefits he has conferred, and his goodness in conferring them, are adequately appreciated by their recipient. No further result may be contemplated, it may be that no further result is desirable, and certainly no further result is required in order to justify the act of giving thanks for benefits received. As a matter of logic, if the words and deeds of the recipient fail in their intention, the benefactor has not been thanked and thanks have not yet been given; equally, as a matter of logic, if some chance word or deed by an ungrateful recipient causes his bene- factor mistakenly to believe that his benefaction has been appreciated, the benefactor has not really been thanked and thanks have still not been given. But consider now a man who thanks his benefactor by a few mumbled and cursory words or by some grudging and hastily performed gesture. As a matter of propriety we are bound to say that 'this is no way to thank someone'; we are bound on grounds of propriety to judge that the benefactor has not been 'properly thanked'; and, *given this basis in the proprieties* governing the words and actions used in conveying thanks, we are then entitled to conclude as a matter of logic that the benefactor has not yet been thanked and thanks have not been given, since thanking which is not proper thanking is not thanking at all. Logic alone tells us that the activity of thanking involves the observance of proprieties; but logic cannot tell us in what these proprieties consist; it is not by logical analysis, but by attentive reflection on the values implicit in gratitude and the manner in which these should inform the conduct of him who is beholden, that we correctly judge that thanking a benefactor should be done with candour, openness, and pleasure, and that it should be done as something worthy of the time and effort expended on it. Similar considerations apply to the activities of worshipping, loving, rewarding, punishing, eulogizing, and countless other activities where the manner of their performance is fraught with inherent proprieties, any violation of which immediately renders the activity in question null and void. Worshipping would not be worshipping, for example, if it were done under compulsion, or by mechanical means, or by a hired proxy. Punishment would not be punishment, if for example a trivial pain were inflicted as retribution for a grave offence, or if physical pains were inflicted on someone very dear to the offender in an attempt to make the offender suffer the psychological pains of sympathy or shame.

Similarly, an activity which developed someone in his personhood would not be an *educational* activity if it violated certain inherent proprieties which are inseparably connected with the values implicit in personhood itself. Thus we rightly require that the educand shall be aware of the nature of the process in which he is participating; in some degree at least, we feel, he should understand that the situations in which he finds himself, the demands to which he is exposed, and the new experiences to which he is submitted, all have as their ultimate objective his development as a person; he need not put it to himself in these terms, but unless he is in some sense aware that he is participating in an educational activity, we insist, one important criterion which an educational activity must satisfy is not in fact being met. We rightly require, too, that the educand's participation should be ultimately based on his own free consent, that it should partake of the character of a voluntary action, even ideally that it should express the educand's

conscious choice unconstrained by extrinsic influences;
for we consider that a man's participation in education
should be at least to some extent based on his recognition
of, and assent to, the intrinsic value of personhood as an
end which he therefore willingly pursues. (Clearly, this
second requirement cannot be satisfied unless our first
requirement is satisfied.) Closely associated with these
two requirements is a third. We demand that an educational situation be at least in some minimal sense 'formal',
that is, subjected to some degree of conscious planning
and contrivance, not left completely to the mercy of
whatever chances to occur; it cannot be just a theatre
for the unfolding of indiscriminate 'natural' processes
(including the random interaction of fortuitous human
motives); as a project of developing personhood, an
educational activity must finally be subject - at whatever
distance - to direction by the personal, and so we can
demand that it be clearly under the ultimate sovereignty
of conscious educational intentions. We can demand, also,
that it involve an encounter between persons, at some
stage and in some form; however remote and attenuated,
personal relations can never be completely absent, for
an educational activity is essentially an interpersonal
enterprise and an educational situation is nothing if not
a meeting-place of free conscious selves. Lastly,
therefore, we can demand that it involve some kind of
activity, some kind of independent exertion and outgoing
self-commitment, on the part of the educand, since an
enterprise in which one of the partners was a wholly inert
and passive recipient would not be the collaborative,
interpersonal enterprise which we have seen education must
essentially be, and it could hardly hope to favour the
emergence of those free, choosing, acting, responsible
persons in whose development the intrinsic purpose of
education essentially consists.

These requirements, then, - that the educand's participation should be witting and voluntary, and that the
processes in which he is participating should be under
conscious control, should involve interpersonal encounter,
and should engage him as an active partner - these are the
requirements which any process of teaching or learning
must satisfy if it is to count as a process of *education*.
If these requirements are mandatory on the educator, this
is because they enshrine values ultimately rooted in that
ideal of personhood which education by definition promotes
and because we rightly judge that an activity aimed at the
development of personhood should itself evince those
values which it is concerned to foster. To processes
which failed to respect and uphold these values we might

attach various names, depending on the exact character of
the process and the circumstances in which it took place -
'propaganda' for example, or 'conditioning', or even
simply 'growth' - and of course some of these processes
might make a useful and perfectly honourable contribution
to our lives. But because they failed to evince the
paramount qualities distinctive of personhood and inseparable from it, we should in every case be obliged to
refuse to dignify them by the name of 'education'.

We have now, I think, sufficiently elucidated the
concept of education and sufficiently sketched its chief
normative implications. To speak of education at all is
to speak of the development of persons in their personhood
by the taking of measures which are proper for this
purpose, since this is what the word 'education' means.
As a purpose-directed activity (a range of tasks as well
as a characteristic achievement), any process of education
is necessarily both *intentional* and *efficacious*. It would
be self-contradictory to assert that someone was being
educated - except in a metaphorical sense - by people who
had no interest in his development as a person, even if as
a result of his experiences at their hands he in fact
manifested some increase in personal development. And it
would be self-contradictory to assert that someone was
being educated if in fact the efforts of his teachers
quite failed to elicit any increase in his development as
a person (just as it would be self-contradictory to assert
that a man was being cured of some ailment if in fact the
efforts of his physicians quite failed to produce any
improvement in his condition): what we ought to say in
this case is that his teachers are *trying* to educate him.
Education, moreover, is the kind of purposive activity
which necessarily requires the observance of inherent
proprieties. It would be self-contradictory to assert
that someone was being educated but in a way which violated the inherent proprieties of all education (just as
it would be self-contradictory to assert that someone was
worshipping God but in a way which violated the inherent
proprieties of all worship): the most we can say in this
case is that the teachers *think* they are educating their
pupil.

As an activity observing inherent proprieties, I have
suggested, an educational activity must be marked by the
qualities of wittingness, voluntariness, conscious
control, interpersonal encounter, and active participation
by the educand. The truth of this proposition, however,
cannot be established by conceptual analysis alone. It is
not self-contradictory to assert, for instance, that
someone is being educated without his knowledge and

consent. This is a perfectly meaningful assertion, which
has doubtless been in fact believed by many people on many
occasions. Nevertheless, although not self-contradictory,
such an assertion is, I submit, always in fact false,
wherever and by whomsoever it may be uttered. Such an
assertion is like, for example, the assertion, 'It is
justifiable to deceive a trusting friend for the prospect
of financial gain' - which is always in fact false but
(unlike, for example, 'It is justifiable to violate a
binding obligation') does not embody a formal contradiction in terms. When we say, therefore, that the
educand's participation in an educational process must
be witting and voluntary, or that he must be in some
measure actively involved in what is happening to him, we
are stating propositions which need to be justified on
their own account, and ultimately this can only be done by
drawing on our fundamental ethical perceptions and the
ethical principles based upon them.

This whole analysis of education is, I think, in
harmony with most of the ways in which we ordinarily
employ the term, although it must be acknowledged that the
English word 'education' is employed in such a capricious
variety of ways that no useful analysis could hope to
remain faithful to all of them. However, the foregoing
analysis permits us, for instance, to continue to speak of
someone being 'badly educated'; while it can never,
strictly speaking, be bad to be educated (since education
is by definition the development of those intrinsically
good qualities constitutive of personhood), we can of
course accept the expression, 'badly educated', in the
same sense as we accept an expression like 'badly
repaired', as implying that a largely unsuccessful attempt
has been made to do something obviously worthwhile. Similarly, there is no reason why we should not continue to
speak of 'educational systems' - that of Nazi Germany, for
instance - which foster undesirable qualities in people;
strictly speaking, of course, such a system cannot be
considered an *educational* system, but if its adherents
sincerely believe the qualities fostered by their system
to be intrinsically desirable there is no reason why we
should not for convenience continue to refer to it as an
'educational system', provided it is clearly understood
that this is simply an elliptical expression for 'what its
adherents *believe* to be an educational system'. In what
sense, however, are we to understand someone who states
that in his opinion all education is worthless or even
downright bad? This is, on the face of it, a self-
contradictory statement. The speaker cannot really be
of the opinion that it is downright bad to foster desira-

ble qualities in people. Possibly we should understand him to be saying that education always conflicts with some other thing deemed to be still more desirable than the development of persons (social stability, perhaps, or individual happiness) - surely a highly implausible assertion in every respect. More probably, he might be expressing his distrustful rejection of some of the specific substantive goals at which education distinctively aims - the fostering of rationality, for example. Now, anyone who denied that rationality was intrinsically worth fostering would be asserting a proposition which, although in our view always in fact false, would nevertheless be a perfectly meaningful proposition. But he would not be denying the value of education: what he would be denying would be the specific thesis that in developing men's powers of rationality we were really and truly developing them as persons.

Any attempt to state the correct literal meaning of the term 'education' should not be unduly influenced by the fact that the term can be used metaphorically, or in an elliptical sense; far less should it be influenced by the fact that some people confuse the meaning of the term with some of its principal applications, while others scarcely trouble to use it in any consistent sense at all. To a critic who claims, however, that we have not in fact stated the correct literal meaning of the term and that he understands something quite different by 'education', the only possible reply is, I think, that the concept we have outlined is self-consistent, very widely acknowledged, and in keeping with our ordinary literal use of the term when we are not trying to conscript it for some object of special pleading. Whatever we choose to make of it, we do have the concept of a possible human activity aimed at helping people to become fuller, more significant persons and employing in this task only means which respect the dignities implicit in personhood. Of all the services we can try to perform for our fellow men, and they for us, this surely is the most fundamental. For this reason we justly demand that it be recognized by the terms we use, and thus that it be explicitly distinguished from other activities aimed at altering men in other ways or changing their conditions of life, however it may outwardly resemble these. In distinguishing it by the name 'education', we are according it this recognition by the use of a word which - as virtually everyone acknowledges, in whatever way they construe the term - does at least emphatically convey the sense of an activity rightly felt to be of the deepest importance and deserving of the highest esteem.

———————————

It was stated earlier that 'the concept of "adult
education" is wholly and exclusively the concept of an
educational enterprise.' (7) We have now seen something
of what is involved in the concept of an educational
enterprise properly so called. The question we must
therefore finally consider is this. When the term 'education' figures in the phrase 'adult education', is it
really being used in its correct literal meaning? Or is
it being used in some reduced or extended sense to connote
something which, despite close logical kinship with normal
educational activities, perhaps attempts rather less or
significantly more than these do, or perhaps at any rate
pursues (alongside strictly educational objectives) a
variety of other objectives not normally thought of as
'educational' in character?

There would be some justification for maintaining that
the education of adults cannot literally mean the project
of developing them as persons. It might be thought that
there must eventually come a time when we are bound to say
that a person's development is at last complete, and that
we do in effect say this when we bring a young person's
formal education to an official close, at the end of his
schooling. Indeed it might be thought that to describe
someone as an adult is by this very token to acknowledge
that his personal development is essentially complete, for
after all have we not ourselves declared that the state of
adulthood represents 'an end-stage of a process of
development'? (8) Our account of adulthood as an ethical
status resting on the presumption of various moral and
personal qualities (those indicative of 'maturity') also
suggests, it might be thought, that an adult is someone
who already manifests the central dignities of personhood
and to whom the notion of education is therefore strictly
impertinent. In any case, since adults are free agents
who in the limited time available to them for educational
pursuits will normally put aside their other favoured
occupations only if and when it pleases them to do so, and
only for as long as they please to do so, how can any educational agency possibly accept responsibility for their
all-round and consistent development as persons, or
pretend to discharge this responsibility if accepted?
Perhaps there is significance in the fact that some
providing bodies apparently prefer to describe themselves
as providing 'leisure-time activities', or even 'hobby
classes', with obvious diffidence about using so ambitious
a term as 'education'.

These misgivings are not entirely without foundation.
There obviously are special difficulties in the way of
providing education for adults, and if some of the agen-

cies responsible for this provision find it depressingly
difficult to carry out their educational responsibilities
it is understandable (though not particularly creditable)
that they should enthusiastically lay claim to responsibilities more easily discharged - perhaps providing
facilities for the devotees of this or that hobby, or
perhaps promoting a kind of random social welfare work
undisturbed by more exacting educational aspirations.
Nevertheless, whatever the practical difficulties, the
concept of 'adult education' involves no theoretical
impossibility, even when an absolutely literal construction is placed on the term 'education'. If adulthood
represents 'an end-stage of a process of development',
this simply means that adulthood is a status which 'can
never itself be revoked', (9) not that those who enjoy
this status are somehow no longer able to develop as
persons; the status of adulthood is indeed based on the
presumption of various personal qualities and capacities,
but these are of course only the minimum qualities stipulated for bare admission to the status of adulthood, and
in ascribing the status of adulthood to someone we only
presume him to have these qualities in some minimum
degree. The concept of a 'person', however, is an open-
ended concept. It is conscious selves who evolve as
persons, and as a conscious self a man is always capable
of becoming conscious of himself over and against his
present circumstances, behaviour, and identity; as a
conscious self, he is always capable of surpassing his
present level of personal existence, of transcending
himself. We can never say of a man that he has exhausted
all his potentialities as a person, or that he has fully
and finally realized in himself a perfect completeness of
personal being. Thus we can never say that a man's education is complete. Whereas we can say, for example, that
a man is now 'completely cured' or 'completely reformed'
(since the implicit reference is always to some specific
and limited physical ailment or moral defect - or at most,
some set of ailments or defects), it would be absurd to
say that a man was now 'completely educated', since a
man's capacities for personal development are understood
to be far-flung and in principle unlimited. This is
why, although education is by definition efficacious, (10)
it can never be completely efficacious: some degree of
personal development there must be, if a process is to
count as educational, but there necessarily remain
unachieved possibilities of further development, so long
as men are finite and their situation less than wholly
perfect. Whether the development of a particular individual can in practice be further advanced is, of course,

always an empirical question; but there can never be any
theoretical impossibility in the notion that further
advance can be made. There can thus be no theoretical
difficulty in considering any adult a fit subject for
education, and to this extent it would seem to follow
that the concept of 'adult education' in its full literal
sense is a perfectly viable one.

However, there are bound to be many important differences between the education of adults and the education of
children. While they are both educational enterprises in
the full sense of the term, we should expect them to
assert different priorities, enshrine themselves in
different institutional forms, and favour characteristically different styles of teaching and learning. We
should expect the education of adults to evince important
distinguishing features, based not only on the relevant
empirical differences between adults and children (their
higher degree of intellectual development, their wider
experience of life, and their greater physical strength
and dexterity, for instance) but also on the difference
between what it is appropriate to do with children and
what it is appropriate to do with adults. Consider, for
example, the notion of 'self-education'. As an empirical
fact, an adult is more likely than a child to be successful in devising and carrying out a programme for
educating himself without benefit of direct teaching or
qualified supervision and guidance, and a group of adults
educating one another without an official teacher would be
more likely to make advances than would a similar group of
children. But in any case, quite apart from empirical
probabilities of relative success or failure, it is
clearly more *appropriate* that adults should be entrusted
with a greater degree of responsibility for the shape of
their own education, since it is on the presumption of
precisely such attributes as responsibility and independence of judgment that their status as adults rests.
Logically, the notion of 'self-education' is perfectly
self-consistent, whether applied to adults or children,
since the concept of 'education' as 'the development of
persons in their personhood' does not logically entail
that the development of a person shall be the work of
another; nevertheless, the notion of self-education
properly applies to the case of adults in greater degree
than it does to the case of children. Of course it is a
matter of degree. Of course I am not suggesting that
adults ought to educate themselves (merely that it is more
appropriate to expect adults to do so than to expect
children to do so). And of course 'self-education' is
only one example of an educational genre offering dis-

tinctive intimations and demanding fresh emphases when
viewed within the perspective of the education of adults.
But as we re-examine the central normative issues of
education from within this perspective, we shall find,
I think, many examples of educational situations which
assume new forms and disclose latent motifs when we
reflect on how we may best relate them to the special
claims and aptitudes of the adult as an educand.

Most writings on adult education acknowledge, indeed
heavily emphasize, the differences in content and style
between the education of adults and the education of
children. They depict for us a striking array of educational activities which are designed to contribute to
the development of the individual, and therefore to the
quality of social life, in a large number of highly
characteristic ways. The following passage from the
Russell Report, for example, is entirely typical: (11)

> An integrated education system will involve postponing
> to adult stages of life certain educational experiences
> that are appropriate to the needs of maturity. In-
> cluded among these will be second and third chances for
> those whose first choice has led to a dead end; oppor-
> tunities for updating in the many fields where
> knowledge is continuously developing; opportunities
> for trying out one's ability to study in a new field
> before committing oneself to it; activities related
> to specifically adult responsibilities like parenthood
> and citizenship; and studies involving value judgments
> that require maturity of experience for their compre-
> hension. The need here, in terms of the educational
> system, is for a planned quaternary stage of education,
> identifiably *adult*.

And the Report goes on to describe many other ways in
which adult education can allegedly make a distinctive
contribution, giving as prominent examples 'remedial
education, or the completion of the school's unfinished
tasks', 'balancing education, that is, filling in the gaps
left by the inevitable specialization of schools and
colleges', and 'role education ... through which the
individual's role can be more responsibly discharged in
society, in industry, in voluntary service or in public
work of any kind'. (12) Now, when we come to review the
scattered assortment of functions, some relatively
straightforward, others highly complex, which are typically ascribed to adult education, we shall clearly want to
know on what general principles they are arrived at and
how in theory they are related to one another. In particular, perhaps, we shall want to know how such kinds of
adult education as 'role education', with its manifest

vocational uses, are related to our paradigmatic concept
of education as the development of persons and thus to
our concept of the enlargement of awareness as an undertaking of value in its own right, apart from all utilitarian considerations. In the light of everything that
has gone before, it is, I think, to contemplation of this
last question, with its many implications for the individual and society, that we ought in the first place to
turn.

2 Liberal adult education and its modes

The concept of 'adult education', we have seen, is the
concept of a purposive activity directed to the fuller
development of adults as persons in their personhood by
the taking of measures which are proper for this purpose.
The development of a person, it has been claimed, consists
essentially in the enlargement of his awareness, the
building up of his experience and knowledge in accordance
with various requirements of breadth and balance; and the
values implicit in this goal, it has been suggested,
demand that an educational activity be marked by the
qualities of wittingness, voluntariness, conscious
control, interpersonal encounter, and active participation
by the educand.

Now, in everyday usage the term 'education' and the
phrase 'adult education' are frequently prefixed by what
seem to be qualifying epithets, which at first glance
might appear to distinguish different species of education, as 'red' and 'yellow' distinguish different
species of colour. Thus we speak of 'liberal education',
'technical education', 'role education' and 'vocational
education', and it might seem natural to suppose that
these were all related to 'education' as species to genus.
We might further suppose that in speaking of 'a classical
education' or 'a medical education' we were speaking of
distinct sub-species of liberal and vocational education,
and that 'the education of engineers' or 'the education of
magistrates', for example, each represented a sub-species
of technical and role education. It is far from clear,
however, that the relations of these concepts to one
another, and of all of them to the master concept of
'education', are best expressed in terms of the genus-
species model, and indeed in one important case at least
this model would deeply falsify and seriously mislead.
The case in question is that of liberal education. By

analysing the concept of a liberal education we shall, I
think, be put in the way of clarifying the relations
between liberal adult education, role education, and the
vocational education of adults, and thus of establishing
how all of these are related to the concept of education
as this has hitherto been defined.

What, then, are we saying when we say that someone has
received, or is receiving, a 'liberal' education? In the
most general terms, of course, we are saying that his
education is one worthy of a free man, and therefore that
it is anchored in his personal freedom as a central value
guiding and underwriting whatever specific content it may
be given and whatever procedures it may be carried on by.
As P.H.Hirst reminds us:

> The Greeks attained the concept of an education that
> was 'liberal' not simply because it was the education
> of free men rather than slaves, but also because they
> saw it as freeing the mind to function according to its
> true nature, freeing reason from error and illusion and
> freeing man's conduct from wrong. And ever since Greek
> times this idea of education has had its place.

It has often been modified, extended, misinterpreted, and
opposed. 'Yet at crucial points in the history of education the concept has constantly reappeared.' (1) If the
free man in the required sense is taken to be one whose
choices are subject to no external constraints, whose
conduct is grounded in his own free assent, it follows
that he is a man who is liberated from the need to perform
tasks of a purely instrumental kind and who can therefore
attend singlemindedly to such things as are worth pursuing
for their own sakes. He is a man who, clearly seeing what
is truly good, is free to pursue it for its intrinsic
worth alone, and in so doing finds and fulfils himself as
a person. A liberal education will be an education *for*
free men, and it will be an education *of* free men. A
liberal education postulates men who are free to become
everything that it is intrinsically good for a man to be,
and a liberal education is one which in fact leads men to
become everything that it is intrinsically good for a man
to be.

If this is at bottom what we mean by a liberal education, however, it is evident that the concept of
'liberal education' is to all intents and purposes identical with the concept of 'education' as this has so far
been unfolded. Like 'liberal education', all education
properly so called treats men as independent centres of
value whose growth as persons is a matter of objective
significance in its own right; like 'liberal education',
all education frees men to enjoy a greater fullness of

personal being, to manifest in themselves a higher quality
of life, as something intrinsically and not merely instrumentally desirable. And (as Hirst points out (2)) liberal
education has traditionally been thought to consist in the
development of mind, the enlargement of knowledge and
understanding, the gaining - through deeper insight and
awareness - of a wider and surer grasp of reality. But
it is precisely this enhancement of awareness, this attainment of richer perspectives of experience and
knowledge, in which, we have claimed, that development of
persons which is the defining purpose of all education
also essentially consists. The two concepts, it would
seem, are indistinguishable, and the essential commitments
through which they are realized appear to coincide
exactly. If a man is being educated, then, he is
receiving a liberal education; and if he is not receiving
a liberal education, he is not being educated.

There is nothing remarkable about this conclusion. In
fact, it is very much in keeping with the ways in which we
ordinarily use the terms 'education' and 'liberal'. When,
for example, a course of technical study for electrical
engineers is broadened to include some treatment of, say,
the social history of engineering and the aesthetics of
industrial design, we are accustomed to say either that
the course has now acquired a 'greater educational value'
or, equally, that it has been made 'more liberal'.
Liberal education is not a species of education: it *is*
education. When we speak of a liberal education, the word
'liberal' is not a qualifying epithet adding some new
dimension to the term 'education' or deleting some characteristic element from the standard meaning of the term.
The word 'liberal' does not *qualify* the meaning of 'education', but rather *confirms and emphasizes* everything
that we intend to express by 'education'. In characterizing certain educational activities as 'liberal', we are
proclaiming that they *really are educational* activities,
we are certifying and reinforcing the claim that the
activities in question are intended to develop the
educands as persons by building up their stature as
conscious selves in ways which are appropriate to this
purpose. There are many such words which, when prefixed
to some substantively meaningful term, fulfil their sole
function in confirming and emphasizing the claims made by
the substantive term. To speak of true friendship, a
genuine antique, a pure coincidence, a good likeness, a
real stroke of luck or a veritable disaster is to certify
and reaffirm that these things are exactly what they
purport to be. Words like 'true' and 'real', of course,
are virtually unrestricted in the range of substantive

terms to which they may appropriately be prefixed, whereas
the word 'liberal' functions as a purely reaffirmative
epithet in the case of certain educational terms only.
But words like 'sterling', 'literal', and 'rigorous',
which are often employed with purely reaffirmative force
(as when we speak of someone's sterling honesty, of the
literal truth, and of a rigorous proof, for example), are
also restricted in their application to certain spheres of
discourse only - to the spheres of probity, descriptive
utterance, and reasoning or inquiry in the three instances
given. What 'literal' and 'rigorous', thus employed, have
in common with 'liberal', when prefixed to 'education', is
that in virtue of their original and independent meanings
they anticipate essential elements in the meanings of the
terms to which, in their reaffirmative usages, they are
prefixed. Their reaffirmative force derives from the fact
that the compound expressions which they help to form are
partly or wholly - in the case of 'liberal education',
wholly - pleonastic.

When we say that someone is receiving a liberal education, then, we are affirming that he is being really
and truly *educated*. It is often desirable, in education
as in other spheres, to emphasize that something really
is what it purports to be, since the common experience
may be of the second best, the makeshift version, the
tolerable substitute or even the clever counterfeit. We
should expect that reaffirmative locutions would be most
conspicuously used when it was felt to be desirable that
the real thing should be distinguished from surrogates
which closely resembled it. The question we must ask,
therefore, is this. With what is 'liberal education'
being contrasted, and for what specific reasons do we
judge it desirable that the contrast should be proclaimed?

Traditionally, liberal education has been chiefly
contrasted with studies which are vocational in character.
This contrast has perhaps been more marked in the domain
of adult education than in any other educational domain,
and indeed, as John Lowe regretfully notes, in England the
expression 'adult education' (or, we may equally say,
'liberal adult education') 'commonly refers only to *non-
vocational* education voluntarily undertaken by people over
eighteen'. (3) Many people who are deeply involved in
vocational studies would want to deny, however, that the
contrast commonly drawn between liberal and vocational
studies was grounded in any ultimately valid educational
distinction. They would want to claim that the kinds of
teaching and learning done in a vocational course of study
may be completely liberal in spirit, and that, judged by
the degree to which they enlarge and deepen students'

understanding, knowledge, and experience, vocational courses may be and often are *educational* in the full sense of the word. Already in the '1919 Report', (4) to which nevertheless Lowe attributes much of the responsibility for what he considers to be the deplorably narrow interpretation given to the term 'adult education', the presumption that there is a fundamental distinction between liberal and vocational adult education is strongly contested: (5)

> Nor is it possible to draw a rigid division between education which is professional or technical and education which - to use the conventional antithesis - is liberal or humane. The most severely technical of subjects is capable of being treated in a humanistic spirit so as to give a broad and liberalising significance to the work for which it is a preparation; and if a humanistic education is successful it ought to make the student more competent to deal with all the problems which confront him, including those of his own profession.

The issue here is obviously of fundamental importance. If in fact a clear distinction can and ought to be drawn between liberal and vocational adult education; if liberal adult education is essentially concerned with the development of persons, while vocational education is essentially concerned with preparation for work; and if preparation for work forms no part of personal development, nor personal development of preparation for work; then the concepts of 'liberal adult education' and 'vocational adult education' will in fact be mutually exclusive. It would not follow that they were logically incompatible, inasmuch as it would still be possible for an adult to be given *both* a liberal education *and* a vocational education. But he could not be given a liberal education *through* being given a vocational education. And since by a liberal education we mean an education which is really and truly educational, we should have to conclude that an adult whose education was wholly vocational had not really been educated at all.

This might seem a very high-handed conclusion. And yet that *some* processes of teaching and learning, at least, must be excluded from the category of 'education' is agreed on all hands. No one would claim that teaching an adult to wiggle his ears, or learning all the entries in the telephone directory by heart, counted as an educational activity, far less as a process of liberal education. Even Lowe, who favours an extremely broad interpretation of 'adult education', is evidently not inclined to embrace the activities of driving schools or the parade-ground

activities of drill-sergeants within the category of adult
education. It is not in the least high-handed or pre-
sumptuous to exclude from the category of educational
activities some activity which manifestly does not meet
the requirements of an educational activity, and perhaps
makes no attempt to meet them. The only question which
needs to be considered is: does a vocational course, or
does it not, in fact meet these requirements?

If the chief requirement of an educational activity,
and therefore of any process of liberal education, is that
it should seek to develop in the educand those intrinsically desirable qualities and capacities which are constitutive of personhood, then it must, I think, be acknowledged that the great majority of vocational courses
are very far from being exercises in liberal education and
cannot therefore, strictly speaking, be counted as
educational activities at all. Knowing how to instal a
certain make of refrigerator or how to maximize the use
of floor space in a supermarket, understanding the complexities of recent company tax legislation or the range
of engine faults to which a new type of civil aircraft is
liable - few would consider that these skills and capacities were worth having for their own sakes, or that simply
by acquiring them a man became a fuller, more complete
human being, more intensely alive as a person. Most of
the jobs men find themselves doing - driving buses,
removing tonsils, checking accounts - have a value which,
however high, is of a purely instrumental kind. We should
all prefer to live in a world in which most of the jobs
now consuming our time and energy were no longer necessary. When we can safely shed our work on to machines, we
nearly always do so. When we are asked to devote a
portion of our lives to overhauling television sets,
mining coal, or managing an office, we expect to receive
compensation in the form of pay or status. Far from
considering that these occupations add to the quality of
life of those who engage in them, we are only too well
aware that the time spent in these occupations reduces the
quality of life for those who have to engage in them. Far
from promoting our growth as whole persons, the paid work
which most of us do is only too liable to narrow us as
persons, to constrict our range of sensibilities, to cause
our manifold aptitudes and affinities to shrink and in
some cases to atrophy. A course which fits men for work
may very well unfit men for life.

None of this implies, to be sure, that the provision of
a given vocational course is always bound to be objectively less desirable than the provision of any given liberal
course. The world in which we actually live is one in

which it is perennially necessary that we should spend a
considerable portion of our time performing tasks which
we would not choose to do as things worth doing for their
own sakes, but which we nevertheless willingly do because
the alternative would be to go without many commodities
and services which we value very highly. The value of a
vocational course is judged by the degree to which it
develops skilled and efficient workmen capable of
producing some of the large number of things we consider
to be worth having, and by the degree to which these
things really are worth having. The instrumental value
of some vocational courses may be very great indeed,
perhaps ultimately much greater than the value of many
liberal courses, even although the latter are judged by
the degree to which they promote the all-round development
of persons as an end in itself. It is the overall value
of the course which we need to judge - its intrinsic
value, if any, but also the value of all those other
things to which it may be a means. And so the provision
of a vocational course which would be a means to creating
a more beautiful physical environment for thousands of
city-dwellers could very properly be judged to be more
worthwhile than the provision of, say, a course of liberal
study which marginally contributed to the further education of a handful of already well-educated people. What
we cannot properly do, however, is to set aside or obscure
the fundamental difference in character of the two types
of course. The one treats its students, no doubt justifiably and with their willing consent, as means to the
ultimate production of valuable goods and services. The
other regards its students exclusively in the light of
their status as conscious selves whose personal development or increased fullness of being is rightly held to be
an end in itself.

The fact that many people would probably claim that
they keenly enjoyed their work, and even that they felt
deeply fulfilled by it, by no means invalidates our
assertion that preparation for work is in most cases
preparation for activities of instrumental value only
(however high their instrumental value). We know that
in reality many people who profess to enjoy their work
are deriving their perfectly genuine enjoyment, not from
the range of specific tasks involved in their work as such
or from the knowledge and skills intrinsic to it, but from
the extrinsic rewards - chiefly pay, status, and prospects
- which act as powerful incentives, or from contingent
features of their work-situation, from the matrix of
agreeable experiences within which the performance of
their specific job takes place - the exercise of influence

or authority, the companionship of colleagues, the
pleasures of travel, even the pleasures of simply being
in the fresh air. But the aim of a vocational course is
not to enhance the worker's appreciation of his work's
extrinsic rewards or its concomitant satisfactions: it
is to enhance his performance of the tasks intrinsic to
the work itself. Where the tasks inherent in the work
itself bring faculties into play which a man might
reasonably want to exercise for their own sakes, or where
his work involves forms of knowledge and understanding
which are worth cultivating in their own right, then
indeed we can say that a man's preparation for work is at
the same time part of his development as a person (with
some qualifications, which we must shortly discuss). (6)
Here we ought to note, however, that a man may very well
feel deeply fulfilled in performing the tasks intrinsic
to his work, although these tasks do not in fact involve
the exercise of any faculties worth exercising or the
cultivation of any knowledge really worth cultivating.
A sense of fulfilment is no guarantee that the experiences
giving fulfilment are not trivial, inane, or even vicious.
A man who derived intense satisfaction from his repeated
performance of some inherently trivial task - continually
tying up parcels, for example, or checking the tightness
of screws on one metal container after another - would by
no means be in an enviable condition: in this one respect
at least, his condition would be pitiable. Of a vocational course which induced men to find their fulfilment in
such tasks we should be bound to say, therefore, not only
that it was not liberal, but that it was positively
illiberal in a very high degree.

   This is in no way to suggest that vocational courses
ought to foster a sense of active dissatisfaction in
workers who are being prepared to carry out tasks which
in themselves offer little or no scope for the exercise
of faculties worth exercising for their own sakes. There
are many different kinds of satisfaction, and a vocational
course may, for example, promote in its members a much
sharper awareness of the instrumental value of the work
for which they are being fitted, its distinctive usefulness to the community, and in so doing may create fertile
sources of well-grounded satisfaction in the contemplation
of services rendered to others. With M.V.C.Jeffreys, we
can say of vocational education that 'at its best it is
the consecration of service, ... possessing the added
urgency of meaning that comes from direct reference to
social utility'. (7) And when we *can* say this, no doubt
we can speak with some show of propriety of vocational
'education', since a course which develops in a man a

sense of service is unquestionably developing him in his
social being, his being-for-others, and in that measure is
unquestionably contributing to his development as a fuller
and more complete person.

It is surely very seldom, however, that we can correctly go on to say of a vocational course that it is 'as
generous and philosophical as the apostles of the liberal
tradition could wish'. (8) The essential characteristic
of a vocational course is that it aims to produce men who
will function more effectively in the job for which they
are being prepared. Vocational courses aim, not at the
development of persons as persons, but at the preparation
of *functionaries*. There may not be - perhaps never is -
any conscious intention of shrinking a man into his
function, of identifying him absolutely and exclusively
with his prospective tasks as foreman, sales manager, or
safety officer. Nevertheless, so long as a vocational
course remains strictly vocational in intention, it makes
no attempt to develop more than one single element in a
man's being, and that, moreover, one which is commonly of
little or no intrinsic value. As we shall see, a
vocational course can often be modified and extended in
ways which make it 'more liberal'. But in so far as it
remains strictly vocational in character, it clearly falls
very far short of anything that can be called a liberal
education.

The same must surely be said of those courses which the
Russell Report collectively describes as forms of 'role
education'. Included in this category, we are told, are
courses for magistrates, policemen, doctors, clergy,
social workers, trade unionists, local government officers
and councillors, training and personnel officers, and no
doubt many other members of occupational groups and
voluntary workers. (9) The principles on which this
motley collection is assembled are not made clear, for
they are plainly not just 'groups whose common element
is their role in society'. (10) No mention is made of
courses for craftsmen or technicians, although interior
decorators and heating engineers have a 'role in society'
no less than personnel officers or local councillors.
Presumably it is felt that the 'role' of a magistrate or
a social worker has a wider significance, in human terms,
than that of a car salesman or a cost accountant, and
calls for a correspondingly higher order of personal and
social awareness. Be that as it may, 'role education',
we are told, is specifically directed to 'providing the
background of knowledge ... through which the individual's
role can be more responsibly discharged', (11) and thus
it is abundantly evident (however 'role education' is

ultimately supposed to be distinguished from vocational
education) that like vocational education it is essentially concerned with the preparation of *functionaries*. The
activity of a magistrate, policeman, shop steward, or
local councillor is never an end in itself, for we should
all prefer to live in a world where the discharging of
these roles - treatment of offenders, prevention and
detection of crime, settlement of industrial disputes,
supervision of road maintenance and sewage disposal - was
happily no longer necessary. While in the actual world
they are vitally necessary, we thus can and should
recognize that their very high value is of an essentially
instrumental kind. In preparing someone to be a more
effective Medical Officer of Health, we should recognize
that 'the relevant background of knowledge and appropriate
intellectual skills' (12) with which we aim to provide him
are being selected, not for their intrinsic value (though
they may incidentally have this), but for their utility;
and we should recognize that in so far as we are preparing
him strictly for his specific role, we are not setting out
to develop him as an all-round person but are deliberately
focusing his development on one aspect of his life only.
Clearly, then, if a course has as its sole purpose the
equipping of a man to discharge some given role, the
Russell Report may well be entitled to ascribe to it the
highest degree of social usefulness and importance: but
it is not entitled to commend it to us as a course of
'liberal education'. (13)

Now, to say that vocational courses, and courses which
seek to prepare a man to fill some social role, do not
offer a liberal education to those who participate in
them, amounts to saying that the provision of such courses
is not really a form of *educational* provision properly so
called. Yet we do speak of 'vocational education' and of
'role education', and in so doing imply that these activities manifest at least some of the central features of a
bona fide attempt to educate people. It would indeed be
high-handed to declare that this widely-accepted usage
was simply erroneous, for we have a general duty to
respect the preferred locutions of ordinary language-users
unless on some given topic their language-habits can be
shown to secrete unresolvable contradictions. However, if
we accept that under certain conditions it is apt to
describe a vocational course as a course of vocational
'education', we need to be perfectly clear what these
conditions are supposed to be, and in what ways and to
what degree the fulfilling of these conditions is supposed
to confer upon a vocational course the status of an educational activity.

Thus vocational education is often distinguished from vocational *training,* and this is a distinction which can obviously be justified by appeal to a variety of relevant considerations. A man may be well trained as a waiter without having been encouraged to see his work in its wider perspective, in its relation to other kinds of hotel work and other service industries, and against the background of public health legislation or the provision of leisure facilities, for instance. A course of training does not require of the trainee an objective and critical attitude to the functions he will perform, or a grasp of the principles underlying them. The trainee is being taught to follow procedures already laid down, in order that he will efficiently perform a set of functions so defined as to limit strictly the degree of personal initiative involved in their performance. One might almost say that his training is successful in the degree to which he comes to be able to perform his functions mechanically and without reflection. In all of these ways, therefore, it is obviously possible for a course of preparation for hotel work to be much more than a course of training. The essential difference between courses of vocational training and courses which, in this respect at least, lay just claim to constitute 'vocational education' is that, whereas the former might be said to involve a deliberate restriction of the trainees' awareness (no doubt often justifiable, lest their native hue of resolution be sicklied over with the pale cast of thought), the latter deliberately foster in their students those qualities of judgment, discrimination, perceptiveness, and balance which promote the breadth of outlook and under-standing thought to be necessary for the more sophisti-cated functions they will be called upon to discharge.

However, a course of the latter kind would still be far from constituting a course of liberal education (that is, still far from being a form of truly *educational* pro-vision), if the enlargement of awareness which it promoted was kept strictly within the limits set by the specific function for which its students were being prepared. We might equip a man with a real grasp of the nature of hotel work, and we might foster in him the capacity to make intelligent and informed judgments in the sphere of hotel management, without going very far towards developing his capacity to interpret and judge his whole life-experience with the fidelity and discernment worthy of a sensitive and mature human person. In this case the phrase 'vocational education' would still not signify a species of education properly so called: it would be simply a term of convenience to distinguish vocational courses which, in respect of their development of knowledge and understanding, at least go beyond mere vocational training. Not until we can say of a vocational course that it fosters the development of a wide range of faculties which a man might reasonably want to exercise for their own sakes, and that it introduces the student to forms of knowledge which are worth cultivating in their own right, quite apart from their utilitarian relevance to the work for which he is being prepared, can we say that the course is engendering, and the student undergoing, something really very like a process of education in the correct meaning of the term.

Now, this may come about in either of two ways. The development of the mental qualities intrinsic to personhood, the general enhancement of awareness, may be a contingent *consequence* of the kind of curriculum which the student is required to follow in his vocational course. Or it may be the explicit *intention* of the course to develop him as an all-round person by building up the range of his insight and understanding, as a necessary and integral part of preparing him adequately for the functions he is being equipped to discharge. A course for sales managers, designed simply to create more effective sales managers and with no direct intention of benefiting its students in any other way, may nevertheless introduce a man to the methods and concepts of economics, sociology, psychology, mathematics, statistics, even social and economic history, and may include some teaching of a foreign language and a revitalization of his attitudes to his native language; and in doing all this, it may well go a long way towards shaping and extending his under-standing of himself, of others, and of the world, in the meaningful and systematic ways undoubtedly characteristic of a process of education. In such cases the student's overall development as an alert, perceptive, thinking person is an uncovenanted benefit accruing from a curriculum designed to satisfy altogether different requirements. In other cases, however, a vocational course may deliberately set out to foster the all-round personal development of its students as one of its distinctive and principal aims. There are some functions which can be satisfactorily discharged only by educated men and women, jobs like that of a personnel officer or 'roles' like that of the voluntary social worker which require of their incumbents a breadth of knowledge, a discipline of mind, a wide range of informed sensibilities, and a capacity to grasp essentials and make sound judgments in many different fields; and in these cases what we can reasonably call the further education of the student may well form a major part of his preparation to discharge the functions of his office.

Yet it would still be inappropriate to describe vocational courses of these last two kinds as courses of 'liberal education', granted that a course of liberal education must satisfy *all* the requirements of an educational activity properly so called. The concept of 'education', we have seen, (14) logically incorporates the concept of a distinctive purpose, the development of the educand as a person, to which any activity properly called 'educational' must therefore be explicitly directed; and so a vocational course not explicitly directed to this purpose, even when it in fact promotes the personal development of its students as a kind of welcome by-product or bonus, does not strictly conform to the requirements of an educational activity and for this reason can never be correctly described as a course of liberal education. Where a course (for personnel officers or voluntary social workers, perhaps) explicitly sets out to foster the all-round development of its students as an essential part of its general purpose, then indeed it comes much nearer to satisfying the requirements of an educational activity in their full strictness; but inasmuch as it undertakes the personal development of its students, not because breadth of understanding and informed sensibilities are intrinsically worth developing in every human being, but because these qualities will enable their possessor to discharge his specific functions more satisfactorily, such a course still fails to match up to the full requirements of an educational activity, since built into the concept of 'education' there is the requirement that the qualities constitutive of personhood be developed because they are *intrinsically* not just instrumentally desirable; (15) to develop greater fullness of personal being, not as an end in itself, but as a means to some extrinsic end, is to do the right deed for the wrong reason, and so not really to do the right deed in its fullest sense - the sense in which alone we can correctly employ the expression 'liberal education'.

We may not be entitled to describe such courses as courses of liberal education. But they may come so very near to satisfying all the requirements of a truly educational activity that we are surely entitled to refer to them as courses of 'vocational education' or 'role education', if only by way of distinguishing them from the many vocational courses which have little or no educational value and manifest few if any educational aspirations. We may, if we are purists, consider phrases like 'vocational education' and 'role education' in the light

of courtesy titles, signifying that the activities named
are next of kin to truly educational activities. The
courtesy, however, becomes more apt, to the degree that a
course surpasses a mere course of training, to the degree
that it develops the understanding of the student in
intrinsically worthwhile ways, and to the degree that it
does all this intentionally and on principle. Indeed, in
the case of some courses preparing men to assume far-
reaching responsibilities requiring complex and sensitive
intellectual skills and extensive working knowledge in a
variety of different fields, to shrink from using the term
'education' would indicate a puritanism become discourte-
ous to the point of ineptitude.

The relations between the master concept of 'education'
and the concepts of 'liberal education', 'role education',
'vocational education', and 'vocational training' are
perhaps best expressed, not in terms of the genus-species
model, but in terms of the kinship ties holding within an
extended family. In these terms, to speak of liberal
education would be to refer to the pure-blooded members of
the original and main branch of the family, and in so
doing to distinguish these from the members of cadet
branches, from near cousins and cousins by marriage, and
from a large assortment of cousins many times removed who,
having prospered in trade, are only intermittently mindful
of their aristocratic connections. The narrower kinds of
vocational training, we must suppose, base their claims to
kinship on a few external resemblances rather than on any
real consanguinity. Vocational courses which, while
remaining purely vocational in purpose, are conducted in
ways which keep faith with the proprieties characteristic
of a truly educational activity - which are conducted in
the spirit of a free meeting between equals, in which
students are taken fully into the confidence of teachers
and willingly participate in learning processes designed
to elicit personal and not merely mechanical responses -
such vocational courses have, by this token, established
a definite degree of kinship with courses of liberal
education, with educational activities in the full meaning
of the term. While we can never categorically assert of a
vocational course, however broad its curriculum and
generous its spirit, that it is a course of liberal education, we can appropriately say of many vocational
courses that they have become 'more liberal' in the degree
that they observe the proprieties of a truly educational
activity, develop their students as self-aware, critical,
thinking persons, and do all this as a deliberate part of
preparing men and women to carry out functions calling for
distinctively personal qualities of a high order.

Perhaps two last points need to be made before we leave
this whole subject of vocational education and its relation to liberal education. First, we should take note
of the difference between vocational courses which have
considerable educational value because of the liberal
spirit in which they are conducted or because of the broad
and intellectually exacting character of a curriculum
nevertheless devised with exclusively vocational ends in
view, and vocational courses with a narrower and inherently less liberal curriculum which seek to acquire a greater
educational value by deliberately incorporating a special
element of liberal study as something additional to, and
different in kind from, the rest of the curriculum. In
the former case, students are being in some measure educated *through* their vocational studies; in the latter
case they are being educated *along with* their vocational
studies. Where a liberal element is in this way attached
or appended to a vocational course, as something essentially extraneous to it, what we really have is two
courses running parallel, possibly interlocking and
fructifying each other at various points, but ultimately
remaining two quite distinct kinds of course, with two
quite distinct kinds of objective. In such a case, then,
it would be deeply misleading to claim that here we had a
vocational course of undoubted educational value; what we
really have is a liberal course of undoubted educational
value, running side by side with a vocational course of
perhaps little or no serious educational value in its own
right.

Second and lastly, we should note that, just as a
vocational course may have the contingent consequence of
developing its students as persons, so a course of liberal
education may have the contingent consequence of preparing
its students for the world of work. It may do this in the
sense that it may impart knowledge of great intrinsic
value which also happens to have worldly and workaday
uses, and in the further sense that the personal qualities
which it sets out to develop for their own sakes may stand
the educand in good stead when he comes to face the
demands and responsibilities of his day-to-day employment.
'I call therefore a complete and generous education that
which fits a man to perform justly, skilfully and magnanimously all the offices both private and public of peace
and of war', says Milton, and we can readily agree that a
well-educated man is likely to carry out a wide variety of
functions more wisely and efficiently than an ignorant and
unthinking man. However, this is simply a contingent
fact, not a logical consequence of our concept of education, since whether a 'complete and generous education'

fits a man for some office partly depends on the nature of
the office. Perhaps it is the case that any office can be
performed 'justly and magnanimously' (and certainly there
is a conceptual connection between 'education' and the
development of men's moral qualities), but there are
offices which we should not necessarily expect an educated
man to perform 'skilfully'. Milton might have performed
the office of pander to Charles II with justice and
magnanimity, but we should have been very surprised if he
had done so with any notable degree of skill. Nevertheless, as a matter of empirical fact, the intellectual
skills developed by a liberal education do tend to be of
very high utility for many of the more responsible and
exacting occupations in a civilized society, and that this
is so in no way erodes the concept of a liberal education
or makes it less 'liberal', provided always that the
course of education in question remains directed to the
development of persons as its essential and overriding
purpose. The concept of a liberal education rules out
the deliberate pursuit of vocational proficiency. But
it by no means rules out the incidental achievement of
vocational proficiency, as an element in the overall
value of a liberal education that is no less real for
being unsought.

Because a liberal education sets out to quicken and build
up in the educand all those intrinsically desirable
qualities constitutive of personhood, omitting nothing of
value which can possibly be included, there is an essential unity, an essential convergence of purpose, about
the idea of liberal education, which is lacking from the
ideas of vocational education or role education. In its
attempt to kindle and enlarge the educand's awareness of
himself, of the world, and of others, a liberal education
has to satisfy the criteria of breadth and perspective,
and thus has to incorporate every form of knowledge, every
skill, in the degree to which it can contribute to the
formation of an educated man. A man may be adequately
prepared for his work as, say, a typographer, without
there being any intention of concurrently fitting him for
any other kind of work whatever, and if the course preparing him for this one specific vocation is sufficiently
searching we willingly grant that he has had a 'vocational
education'. But we do not grant that a man has had a
liberal education, however adequate a grounding he has
had in, say, mediaeval history, unless in the course of
his education there has been a deliberate attempt to give
him at least some grasp of various other kinds of intel-

lectual inquiry and some direct acquaintance with many
other areas of human experience. The manifold elements
which go to make up a liberal education have to be held
together, moreover, in ways which ensure that collectively
they form the kind of structured and meaningful whole
capable of nourishing and disciplining a man's all-round
development as a perceiving, thinking, judging being.

   This concept of a well educated person as someone who
has a wide and coherent grasp of many different forms of
knowledge and awareness would, I think, be vigorously
upheld by most advocates, past and present, of a liberal
education. But it has by no means been without its
critics. Thus Mary Warnock, in the course of portraying
what she considers to be 'the enriching nature of specialization', attacks the view that - as she somewhat
tendentiously puts it - 'it is absolutely essential for
everyone to know a bit about everything'. (16) However,
the only reasons given by Mrs Warnock for her rejection
of the concept of a broad general education are, first,
that 'one cannot learn in detail about all subjects' (and
therefore, she contends, the generalist will only ever get
a smattering or at best a sort of 'profile' of a subject);
and second, that a pupil who is granted no more than a
brief and limited 'Cook's tour' around some subject is
likely to become rapidly bored. (17) Clearly, these
assertions of Mrs Warnock express empirical generalizations about the probable achievements and attitudes of
educands, not logical truths or declarations of educational principle based on the values inherent in the idea of
an educated person. 'Broad' does not *mean* 'shallow', and
breadth is clearly not *logically* incompatible with depth.
Clearly, therefore, while they may be true of some
educands, under some conditions, these assertions may
well not be true of other educands, under different
conditions. And in fact it is fairly obvious that,
whatever degree of truth they may have in the school
situation, where children and adolescents have to be
vouchsafed some sort of an education (often against their
will) before their period of schooling is brought to its
unavoidable close, such generalizations have very much
less application to the education of adults, whose participation in educational pursuits is normally quite
voluntary (and indeed commonly enthusiastic) (18) and
whose educational careers need never be brought to a close
but ought rather to be thought of as continually advancing
and evolving throughout the whole course of their ongoing
lives. In the course of a whole lifetime, one might
reasonably suppose, any man or woman with the ability to
reach what Mrs Warnock would consider to be a high level

of achievement in some specialized branch of knowledge
would also be likely to have the ability to reach at least
a demonstrably worthwhile level of achievement (and
certainly to achieve much more than a 'smattering') in a
wide range of educationally central forms of knowledge and
experience. The proof of this is that many people in fact
do so.

But in any case the requirement that a person's education should be broad and balanced, not narrow and
lopsided, expresses a stipulation built into the very
concept of education understood as the development of
persons in and through the enlargement of their awareness.
We have seen that the values of breadth and perspective
are inseparable from any ideal of human development that
we should be prepared to dignify with the categories of
personhood. (19) And we may add here that, in the sense
in which an educator speaks of someone's 'all-round'
mental development, it is in fact tautological to say that
a man's mental development must be all-round. A man's
'all-round' mental development simply means his mental development in every worthwhile respect, and to some appropriate degree in each respect; and in speaking of his
mental *development* at all it is of course of precisely
this that we are speaking. To the extent that a man's development has been constricted or distorted, to that
extent we consider him to be as yet undeveloped. Of
course, when a man gains educational ground in some one
particular respect only, this still undoubtedly counts as
a 'gain' (provided it is not won at the cost of ground
lost elsewhere). Similarly, when an invalid registers
improvement in respect of his breathing or digestion only,
this still undoubtedly counts as an 'improvement' (provided it is not purchased at the cost of placing strain on
his heart, say). But it would only be if he were recover-
ing in respect of every important physical function, and
to some acceptable degree in respect of each function,
that we should normally be prepared to say that our
invalid was 'being restored to physical health and
strength'. We should not consider a Hercules on crutches
to be a picture of physical health and strength. Nor
should we consider a Nobel Prize-winning physicist to be
exactly a model of an educated person if his musical,
literary, and artistic taste and judgments turned out to
be uniformly crude and facile, if in social and political
matters he showed himself to be naive and ill-informed but
dogmatic, and if he boasted of his indifference to, and
ignorance of, all the great philosophical and religious
questions which have traditionally animated mankind.
There has to be at least some measure of *balance* in the
distribution of an educated person's knowledge, tastes,

and interests. This by no means entails that he has to
know 'a bit about everything', for as we shall see in
Chapter 3 an educated man needs to know a great deal more
about some things (the cognitively important and central)
than about others (the cognitively trivial or peripheral).
(20) 'Balanced' does not mean 'evenly spread', and a
properly balanced education is not only compatible with
but positively *requires* the establishment of careful
priorities and procedures of intelligent discrimination.
But it also - indeed primarily - requires us to pay due
attention to the demands of completeness and comprehensiveness and therefore to overall considerations of
cognitive scope and amplitude. It is a tautology to
assert that something is intrinsically worth studying only
to the degree that it has intrinsic cognitive value. But
it is also a tautology to assert that *everything* which has
intrinsic cognitive value is intrinsically worth studying.

Built into the concept of education as the development
of persons by the enlargement of their awareness there is,
then, the stipulation that a man's growth in knowledge and
understanding shall be properly balanced and therefore
sufficiently comprehensive in its reach and dimensions.
The idea of an absolute and exclusive specialist - a
biologist, say, who literally knew nothing about anything
but biology - would be the idea of someone who was
absolutely unable to communicate with anyone except his
fellow specialists. (21) And to the extent that a man
pursues studies which are specialist in the sense that
other educated people might and for the most part do quite
reasonably remain comparatively ignorant of them, to that
extent he is sealing himself off from possibilities of
meaningful communication with other educated men and
women. But surely educated people, of all people, ought
to be able to communicate effectively with one another.
Indeed, if we agree that the very concept of a 'person'
in its normative sense includes the ability to communicate
meaningfully with other persons, we will surely be bound
to consider studies which tend to make general public
dialogue still harder and less successful than it already
is as being (whatever their other merits) at least in this
respect incompatible with the development of persons as
persons and thus with the defining objective of all
education. (22)

It is of course above all when it is a question of the
studies appropriate to a *liberal* education that considerations of cognitive breadth and balance rightly come to
the foreground. Perhaps it will be as well to recall here
that when we speak of someone receiving a 'liberal'
education we are merely reaffirming, re-emphasizing, that

he really is being *educated* in the full undiluted sense
of the term. (23) However, mankind's zeal for education,
like its zeal for so many other things admitted to be
greatly worthwhile, is seldom wholehearted or unmixed.
If we find it necessary to speak of someone receiving a
'liberal' education, this is because so often the studies
in which people engage do not even set out to be real
exercises in *education*. We have by now identified several
quite distinct, deeply important, and all too common ways
in which a man's studies can fail to satisfy the requirements of a truly educational process, and our use
of the terms 'liberal' and 'illiberal' in any given
context will usually indicate which of these specific
defects or shortcomings we particularly have in mind.
Thus the knowledge which a man is engaged in acquiring,
the skills which he is engaged in mastering, may be more
or less devoid of intrinsic value. The knowledge or skill
which he is acquiring may have considerable instrumental
value but instrumental value only, as in many if not most
forms of vocational adult education and role education;
but as we shall see in Chapter 7 it is unfortunately too
often the case that the knowledge and skills acquired by
students in non-vocational adult education (consider
courses on contract bridge or cake icing, for example)
are also of scant if any educational value. (24) To
describe a course of adult education as 'liberal' may,
then, be to emphasize the intrinsic worthwhileness of the
subject studied. Or it may be to emphasize that the
course in question is being conducted, on the part of
teachers and taught, in an educationally appropriate
spirit of free and active partnership, since this is
another basic requirement of educational principle which
is in practice all too liable to be neglected. In Chapter
7 we shall examine some of the grounds for regarding adult
classes as being altogether more likely to keep faith with
the proprieties of a genuinely educational enterprise, and
thus to be more 'liberal' in spirit, than classes of
schoolchildren. (25) Or in describing a course of adult
education as 'liberal' we may be emphasizing the fact
that, unlike so many courses of further and higher education, it really is being offered as a contribution to
the balanced all-round mental development - to the
'education' properly so called - of those taking part in
it. In Chapter 7 we shall look at this aspect of liberal
adult education from the point of view of the recipient.
(26) Here, however, it will be convenient for us to take
at least a brief look at it from the point of view of the
agencies of provision.
    Now, when we examine the provision of liberal education

for adults, we find many very different modes of provision and, whatever our basis for distinguishing these different modes, if what we have said above has any validity we clearly need to be satisfied that any given mode of providing liberal adult education is capable of upholding the essential balance and unity, of maintaining the essential convergence of purpose, among the manifold elements of which a liberal adult education has to be made up. Of course, the different modes of provision we distinguish will depend on the taxonomy we employ. We may classify modes of provision on the basis of financial, administrative, social, or other considerations involving no direct reference to the distinctively educational characteristics of the provision. Or we may classify them on the basis of features intrinsic to the educational activities involved - the level of study, elementary or advanced, for example. But however we may choose to distinguish modes of provision, we must be absolutely clear that for them to count as modes of providing *liberal* adult education they have to evince a systematic and purposeful concern for the comprehensive and integrated development of the adult as a complete person. How a particular course, falling within a particular mode of provision, in practice sets out to accomplish this will obviously be to some extent a matter for specific and detailed contrivance. But unless it does in fact manifest a real concern for the *general* education of its students, over and beyond their mastery of a particular skill or branch of knowledge, we cannot correctly describe it as a course of 'liberal' adult education.

Modes of provision distinguished by reference to administrative, social, and other such extrinsic considerations do not seem to enshrine any special difficulties of educational principle with regard to meeting this requirement (though there may often be practical difficulties). We can distinguish, for instance, the provision of liberal adult education by means of full-time courses, chiefly in long-term residential colleges like Ruskin or Fircroft, from its provision by means of part-time courses, usually meeting weekly in the evenings, which in fact make up far and away the greatest part of existing provision. While the disparity between these two modes of provision reflects obvious economic and social facts, above all the fact that adult students usually have a living to earn and a family to support and so can only pursue full-time studies when rather exceptional opportunities are made available to them, there is plainly nothing in the concept of a liberal education to rule out in principle its pursuit by means of part-time study. The distinction between full-time and part-time study is in any case one of degree, since in literal fact even the most zealous 'full-time' student spends only part of his time in study. No doubt the conventional full-time student enjoys various circumstantial advantages, facilitating learning, which empirical research can properly identify and exploit; no doubt it would be idle to expect a man, in three years of part-time study, to make educational advances comparable to those he might have made if studying had been his main occupation over the same period; but having granted all this, we must acknowledge that there is nothing in principle to prevent the educational advances which the part-time student does make from displaying the characteristics of balance, breadth, diversity, and integration, which we have seen to be essential requirements if his studies are to be characterized as 'liberal adult education'.

Another administrative or organizational basis on which we can classify the provision of adult education is, as John Lowe suggests, 'the degree of involvement' of the providing agencies, (27) but from this point of view there might seem to be some modes of provision which do give rise to difficulties of educational principle. The agencies or sponsors of adult education range from bodies like local education authorities, universities, and the Workers' Educational Association, which exist exclusively or at least primarily for educational purposes, to bodies like the BBC, Women's Institutes, museums, musical societies, film clubs, and many other national and local organizations which may undertake activities of a broadly educational kind, although they exist primarily for quite different purposes. One difficulty, which Lowe points out, is 'to know where to set limits'. (28) We can scarcely include in 'the educational life of the nation', as the authors of the 1919 Report would have us do, 'the presentation of good plays' and 'the creative work of the craftsman', (29) without further qualification, unless we are willing to describe as an 'educational' activity any and every cultural, artistic, scientific, and technical activity, for whatever purpose undertaken. However, the Report goes on to say, 'By education we mean the deliberate efforts by which men and women attempt to satisfy their thirst for knowledge, to equip themselves for their responsibilities as citizens and members of society or to find opportunities for self-expression,' (30) and this surely touches the nub of the matter. From the standpoint of the individual seeker after education, any agency - library, art gallery, television series, even newspapers and periodicals - can be an agency of education, and

indeed of liberal education, provided that the individual
is making a deliberate effort to use its facilities for
the express purpose of building up a systematic range of
knowledge and disciplined habits of outlook by sustained
and methodical study. At least, in such a case, we can
say that the individual is engaged in *acquiring* a liberal
education, even if we cannot correctly say that the agency
in question is *providing* him with one. This last we
surely cannot correctly say unless it is part of the
express intention of the agency to contribute, in a
planned and systematic way, to the general mental development of those who avail themselves of its facilities. The
normal broadcasting done by the BBC and the independent
television companies, for example, includes a large number
of programmes addressed to topics of a scientific,
religious, social, historical, or artistic character,
which we do not regard as part of the educational provision of these bodies because each programme is broadcast
as a self-contained entity, or at most as part of a self-
contained series, and because the subject ('North Sea
Oil', 'China Today', 'The Art of the Aztecs', and so on)
is chosen for any of a variety of reasons - its supposed
popularity, news value, or topical relevance, perhaps -
which are at best only marginally connected with the all-
round mental development of whoever happen to be the
listeners or viewers. The overt adult education courses
provided by radio and television, on the other hand, are
deliberately aimed at serious students; they offer
planned opportunities to gain mastery of important skills
and bodies of knowledge by progressive study, sometimes
extending (as in the case of foreign language courses)
over a period of several years; they are often supported
by printed material, records, or educational kits; they
are often closely linked with courses being run concurrently by conventional adult education agencies, in
evening classes or residential centres; they are subject
to overall educational planning, in collaboration with
other providing bodies: and thus, deliberately setting
out to provide a broad and balanced range of courses
capable, if used intelligently, of promoting the continuing general development of a student's knowledge and
understanding, this mode of provision surely can be
correctly described as a mode of provision of liberal
adult education. Whether a mode of provision counts as a
mode of liberal adult education depends, then, not on the
degree to which the providing body is involved in educational work, but on the character of its involvement.
It is providing liberal adult education if in its provision it has continuous regard for the *general* education

of the student. It may do so, like the BBC, by offering
a more or less comprehensive curriculum. Or it may do so,
like some more specialized organizations (some natural-
ists' societies and musical societies, for example) by
offering a distinctive contribution which reflects the
special interests of the providing body but which is at
the same time consciously designed to figure as a possible
element *within* the general educational provision of the
community - and of course this implies that the general
educational state of the community is being taken
consciously into account when the providing body is
determining the character of such educational provision
as it intends to make.

In classifying modes of provision, however, it is
perhaps more appropriate to base our classification on the
distinctive educational characteristics of the provision,
rather than on its external administrative or organizational forms. Thus we can differentiate between the
provision of courses which aim to advance the personal
development of the student by straightforwardly carrying
on his general education from whatever point it has
reached, and the provision of courses which aim to correct
specific defects, or supply specific deficiencies, from
which the student's education to date has demonstrably
suffered and which need to be remedied by courses of study
designed for that specific purpose. To be sure, there is
a sense in which every man's education is deficient in
some degree. As we have already seen, (31) a man's
capacities for personal development are theoretically
unlimited and so we are never entitled to say that a man's
education is perfectly complete; we are finite beings,
and for each of us there must always necessarily remain
unachieved possibilities of further development, in the
light of which our present achievements, however high, are
bound to be considered as in a general sense deficient.
The mode of provision which straightforwardly aims to
carry on the general education of adults, as a continuing
enterprise with no fixed terminus or limit, let us call
'continuing lifelong education'. Clearly the general,
metaphysically unavoidable deficiency which it sets out
to alleviate is quite different from the specific, in
principle avoidable defects and deficiencies - illiteracy,
for example, or badly outdated scientific ideas - which
need to be remedied by specially designed courses with
highly particularized objectives. Let us call this quite
different mode of provision 'compensatory adult education'. Despite its highly particularized objectives,
compensatory adult education can surely count as a mode
of liberal adult education, or at least as a mode of pro-

vision through which liberal adult education may well be
provided. (There can also be compensatory technical and
vocational education, and no doubt compensatory education
of many other specialized kinds.) Whether a course of
compensatory education is at the same time a course of
liberal education will depend on whether it consciously
sets out to contribute to the all-round personal development of its students. This is manifestly the conscious
aim of those courses to which the Russell Report refers
as forms of 'balancing education', which we are told is
education directed to 'filling in the gaps left by the
inevitable specialization of schools and colleges'. (32)
Concepts like 'balancing', 'remedial', and 'compensatory',
in any case logically include a reference to some
imbalance which has to be redressed, some defect which has
to be remedied, some lack for which compensation has to be
made, and so of necessity allude to other phases of the
student's education in which this or that element has been
neglected. As a matter of logical necessity, then, a
course of compensatory education has to take cognizance of
at least *some* other phase or phases of the student's education. But a course of compensatory education may very
well be framed in the light of the student's educational
background *as a whole,* taking into account all those
specific, essentially avoidable defects and deficiencies
which will need to be rectified before he can be considered to have been given a good general education. And when
this is in fact so, we can correctly describe the course
in question as directed to the all-round development of
the student and therefore, in this respect, as undoubtedly
a course of liberal adult education.

Perhaps the most obvious way of distinguishing
different modes of educational provision for adults is
on the basis of differing levels of study. Courses of
study may make heavier or lighter demands on the student's
ability and existing knowledge; the concepts and skills
which the student has to master may be highly complex or
relatively simple; he may or may not have to acquire
ancillary skills and bodies of knowledge (statistics for
the higher reaches of economic theory, for example, but
not for its mere rudiments); the pace and rigour of his
course may be quite fierce or rather gentle; the scope of
his studies may be fairly ambitious or fairly modest: it
is by such criteria that we judge a course of study to be
at an 'advanced' or an 'elementary' level, or at some
intermediate level which we then designate more precisely
by some suitable term. However, there is nothing about
the concept of a 'level of study' which makes it theoretically impossible for a liberal education to be provided at

any level, down to the most elementary. It is sometimes
alleged that there are certain subjects - the example of
philosophy is often cited - which of their nature can only
be studied at a fairly advanced level, perhaps because
their simplest concepts are quite complex and their
lightest demands quite exacting, compared with those of
other subjects, or perhaps because - and here physics is
often cited - their key concepts and principal findings
are virtually unintelligible to anyone without a reasonably high degree of sophistication in some other branch of
knowledge, such as mathematics. Clearly if this were so,
an elementary education could not include these subjects
and therefore could not possibly aspire to true breadth
and perspective. But unless there is this kind of cognitive threshold (and I very much doubt whether there is, in
any educationally relevant sense, for reasons which will
be discussed when we come to examine the nature of the
curriculum in adult education), (33) it would seem that
there is no reason in principle why programmes of adult
education operating at even the most elementary levels of
study should not display all the characteristics of
breadth, diversity, balance, and perspective which we have
seen to be among the chief characteristics of a liberal
education. And in every other respect - the spirit in
which they are conducted and which governs the relations
between teachers and taught, for instance, and the degree
to which the various elements of which they are composed
fructify and illuminate one another and so make up a
meaningful and coherent whole - educational programmes of
the most elementary kinds may well satisfy the requirements which a mode of provision has to satisfy if it
is to count as a mode of liberal adult education. There
is no justification in educational principle, then, for
the assumption, long prevalent in English adult education,
that only the universities and the WEA are capable of
providing courses of liberal adult education and that
local education authorities should confine themselves to
providing classes in dressmaking, motor car maintenance,
and other such educationally peripheral activities, many
of which are rightly considered to have little if any
place in a liberal education. To some extent this separation of functions has been based on a distinction
between 'academic' and 'practical' studies, but there is
no doubt that this distinction has been confused with the
distinction between advanced and elementary, exacting and
less exacting studies, and that this in turn has been
confused with the distinction between liberal adult education and other kinds of adult education. While this
separation of functions as between the major types of

providing body is less rigidly observed than once it was,
it still has the unfortunate result of largely restricting
the provision of liberal adult education to its provision
in courses of a fairly exacting kind, and so of preventing
many less able students from pursuing a liberal education
of any kind. Adults tend to be faced with the choice of
studying ethics, for example, at university or near-
university level, or of not studying ethics at all. But
if there is no necessary connection between the intellectual level of a course of study and its character as
liberal education, to restrict the provision of liberal
education to the provision of higher liberal education is
as needless as it is unjust.

There are many other ways of classifying modes of
educational provision for adults, but those which we have
differentiated perhaps suffice to illustrate the singular
morphology of adult education. Unlike the education of
children and adolescents which goes on in schools and
colleges, the education of adults tends to be very much
a part-time activity for those who engage in it; they
may pursue their education with the help of an extremely
wide variety of national and local organizations, many of
which are involved in educational work only as an adjunct
to their primary concerns; much of the work of adult
education has always been and no doubt always will be in
a broad sense compensatory, remedying the defects and
making good the deficiencies in a man's earlier education
or enabling him to catch up with advances in knowledge
which have rendered parts of his earlier education
obsolete; and unlike other sectors of educational provision - primary, secondary, further, and higher - adult
education has to be ready to provide for every stage of
progress, every level of study, from work with educationally retarded adults at an academic level little different
from that of the junior school up to work which in some
cases is as advanced as that done by postgraduate students
at a university. Because adult education, in all these
ways, *looks* very different from more conventional forms of
educational provision, it is easy to mistake its complexity for diffuseness, its indispensable flexibility for an
inherent looseness or educational flabbiness, its hetero-
geneity for a lack of clear educational purpose. It must
be acknowledged that the vast miscellany of activities
which go to make up 'adult education' affords many havens
for the dilettante, the crank, and the compulsive attender
of courses; much that is styled 'adult education' is
little more than the provision of hobby facilities,
regular recreation evenings, or opportunities for social
intercourse in an agreeable and inexpensive milieu; and

much else is really a kind of social work or community
development decked out in the trappings of an educational
enterprise. Nevertheless, in and through many different
modes of provision, as we have seen, it is possible to
provide for grown men and women broad and balanced courses
of sustained and progressive study which can build up the
knowledge and understanding of their students in systematic and sensitive ways, extend and enrich their awareness
of themselves, their fellows, and their surroundings, and
so foster their all-round development as perceiving,
feeling, thinking beings; and to say this is to say that
it is possible to provide for adults something which
fulfils all the requirements of an educational activity
properly so called, something which in the full meaning of
the term can be correctly called adult *education*. But
this, as we have also seen, amounts to saying that the
education provided for adults can be a *liberal* education,
no less than the education provided for full-time pupils
and students in schools and colleges. The conditions
under which the adult pursues his education are very
different, and the practical difficulties which he has to
surmount are different in kind as well as sharper in
degree. We shall find that the education of the adult
calls for characteristically different procedures of
teaching and learning, and that in many ways his educational needs assert distinctive priorities and carry
distinctive implications for the life of the community.
In the end, however, when the reckonings are made, it is
by the same criteria that we must judge his achievement,
for in every essential respect it is the same enterprise
on which he is embarked and the same achievement to which
he aspires.

Educational objectives

Part II

The communication
of knowledge

As the concept of a special kind of purposive activity,
the concept of 'adult education' cannot be fully elucidated until we have established the exact nature of the
purposes which the concept logically enshrines. Now, we
have already argued that an educational activity is one
which fosters the highest development of individuals as
persons, and that the development of persons essentially
consists in the enlargement of *awareness*. A person, we
have claimed, is essentially a centre of awareness, a
being who perceives, feels, remembers, imagines, thinks,
judges, desires, and chooses, and who *is* in the measure
that he is intensely experiencing and aware of what is
going on around him and within him. To foster the
development of the adult as a person, then, to educate
him, is to extend the scope and enrich the quality of his
awareness, and when we deem an activity to be educational
in character, we do so by virtue of its pursuit and
achievement of this governing purpose. Our first task,
therefore, must be to establish more precisely what is
involved in 'the enlargement of awareness', for until we
have done this our claim that adult education consists
essentially in the enlargement of the adult's awareness
may well strike the reader as somewhat vague and insub-
stantial, and indeed in some ways as rather implausible.

The term 'awareness' is here being used as synonymous
with 'consciousness'. Providing a synonym, however, is
very far from providing a definition, and in fact I should
want to claim that no definition of 'consciousness' or
'awareness' is strictly speaking possible. Purported
definitions, it will be found, are always incomplete, or
they are simply the provision of synonyms, themselves
indefinable, or they are definitions of something which
is manifestly something quite other than consciousness,
something which is intimately bound up with consciousness

perhaps (such as brain-activity), but which is nevertheless logically distinct from it and ought not to be
confused with it. Whether or not consciousness or
awareness can be strictly defined, however, is of little
importance for our present purposes. What is quite
certain is that, definable or not, we can assert many
true propositions *about* consciousness. Consciousness or
awareness, we can assert, is in the technical sense
'intentional', that is, of its nature it always reaches
out towards some object, it exists wholly as presence-to-
some-object *of* which it is the consciousness. While
consciousness is of course *distinct* from its objects,
transcending them in order to be present to them,
consciousness is nothing *apart* from its objects, for in
itself it is simply this perpetual pure activity of tran-
scendence and presence. We can speak of the 'objects' of
consciousness, then, but we must not speak of the
'contents' of consciousness. In contrast with the
opaqueness, the brute given-ness of its objects, my
awareness is sheer translucency or transparency: when I
see a house, the nature of my seeing is given wholly in
the nature of the house which I see. This must not be
taken to mean that my awareness is like a mirror which
passively records whatever objects happen to be placed
before it: on the contrary, to be aware is to be engaged
in an *activity* - of locating, discriminating, relating,
identifying, construing, and in many other ways attempting
to seize and make manifest the full character and meaning
of the objects to which in awareness I make myself
present.
    Consciousness or awareness engages itself with its
objects in various different modes - vision, hearing, and
the modes of sense-experience, feeling and emotion,
memory, imagination, conceptualization, inference,
judgment, and so on - but in any given conscious act (the
recognition of a house as one in which I spent a childhood
holiday, for example) we find that several different
faculties are brought into synthesis to form what is
always a single, indivisible operation of consciousness.
This unity of the single, instantaneous act of consciousness, punctually formed from the coalescence of faculties
widely different in kind, is reproduced in the unity of
the multiple, successive acts of consciousness, which
intermerge to form a single continuous identity across
time, the kind of identity to which we give the name of
'self'. Consciousness as we know it or can conceive of
it does not occur in discrete flashes, but is always
individualized, that is, bound tightly up within the
vital unity of a unique, ongoing self. And because each

conscious act is enfolded within the transversal unity of
a self, it is possible for consciousness to focus upon any
of its own acts, since the condition of self-consciousness
is that the act of reflection and the act reflected-on
should be bound within a common integument.

For our present purposes, the most important feature of
consciousness or awareness is that, while in all its
operations it aspires to a perfection of experience and
understanding, the degree to which it actually succeeds
in revealing and illuminating objective reality admits of
very wide variations. Every natural self is finite, and
the degree of its awareness fluctuates within wide limits.
One state of awareness may surpass or fall short of another, not only in the degree of its intensity, its vividness, but also in respect of its scope, the number and
variety of the objects which it encompasses, and its
perspicacity, the niceness of the distinctions and the
complexity of the relations which it grasps within the
objective manifold confronting it. We can grade our
states of awareness, and since all awareness is essentially intentional, directed to some object or objects, *of*
which it is the 'awareness', we are bound to evaluate
states of awareness by the *degree* to which they succeed
in revealing and illuminating the reality objectively
before them. Only to the degree that a state of awareness
succeeds in doing this can we say that there really *is*
'awareness' there at all; only to this degree can we say
that the awareness itself *exists*. And so in ascending the
scale of awareness we ascend a scale of being, from the
rudimentary, attenuated being of dim, barely felt organic
sensations, slumbrous and untaught, through the relative
clarity of informed sense-perception, up to the luminous
plenitude of being which asserts itself in those highly
developed, coherent, and comprehensive systems of
rationally grounded insight and belief to which we can
correctly assign the title of *knowledge*.

This scale of being which we ascend when we grow in
awareness is, we are claiming, the scale of *personal*
being. As we move from brute sentience to the rational
lucidity of objective knowledge, we develop as persons.
To this claim it might be objected, however, that the
concept of a 'person' is the concept of a being evincing
far more than the purely intellectual attainments suggested by the word 'knowledge'. It may be a necessary
condition of being a 'person' that someone should have
risen beyond the mental horizons of mere sensation, but
it is hardly a sufficient condition. A man with the most
subtle perceptions, the most disciplined intellect, the
most carefully assessed experience, might yet be brutal

or daemonic, might even be more like a machine or a thing
than a person in that normative sense of 'person' which
is crucial to education if this is to be defined as 'the
development of persons'. For someone to be a person in
the full evaluative sense of the term, it might be urged,
he not only needs to evince some degree of perceptiveness,
knowledge, and understanding: he also needs to base his
conduct on principled habits of responsible choice; the
attitudes which he displays towards others, to the world,
and to himself, should testify to scrupulous qualities of
sensitivity and concern; his motives should bear witness
to his freedom and dignity as an independent moral agent;
and he should show some degree of aptitude in certain
appropriate skills which are manifestly inseparable from
the idea of a person - certain social skills and skills of
communication, without which it would be impossible for
him to establish any kind of real relations with others,
but also at least some creative skills, for it is surely
part of being a person to take pride in fostering the
excellent and the benign.

The validity of all these observations must, I think,
be willingly allowed. We should not really be educating
someone, really developing him as a person, if all we
cultivated in him was a coldly accurate perceptiveness,
a powerful but completely detached understanding, and an
extensive range of knowledge to which, however, he himself
remained completely impassive and indifferent. To look at
the world with a glassy stare, even a stare which misses
nothing, is not to look at it with the eye of an educated
person. Indeed, knowledge which stays remote and unmoved
before the spectacle which it contemplates is typically
styled 'impersonal'. The notion of a 'person' does
include various appropriate habits, attitudes, motives,
and skills of active, outgoing kinds, all of which ought
to be pertinently *involved* with the many realities enfolded by a person's awareness.

However, this in no way annuls our contention that the
development of persons is essentially the enlargement of
awareness and that this culminates in increasingly richer
structures of knowledge and understanding. If certain
habits, attitudes, motives, and skills are indispensable
elements in our concept of a person, this is so only to
the degree that they are informed by a directing
awareness, sustaining and instructing them. The desirable
habits must be consciously formed and consciously
maintained, and they must be habits of conscious choice
and action, not of mechanical reaction or unthinking
routine, if they are to count as habits distinctive of,
and worthy of, a person. And the same is true of whatever

attitudes and motives are thought to be eminently characteristic of personhood. They must be more than simple
dispositions to behave in the appropriate ways, for
behavioural dispositions (however otherwise appropriate
they may be) can often be stereotyped and rigid, the
products of conditioning rather than clear conviction or
critical reflection, and where this is the case they lack
precisely those features which we look for in the attitudes and motives of someone to whom we are prepared to
ascribe the dignities of personhood. The tolerance or
the compassion which we look for in a person is not a
blind tolerance or a reflex compassion, but a tolerance
and compassion informed by experience, insight, knowledge,
and understanding - that is, informed by all the relevant
qualities of *awareness*.

This is no less evident when we consider the part
played in education by the acquisition of skills. The
value of a skill might seem to be essentially instrumental. The value of the sculptor's skill might seem to
reside entirely in the sculpture which results from it,
for undoubtedly it is the aesthetic features of the
resulting sculpture which confer upon the movements of
his hands their character as 'skilful' or 'clumsy'. If
beautiful sculptures could be produced by psychokinesis,
without bodily movements on the part of the sculptor,
there would be no good reason for a sculptor to keep on
going through the bodily movements, and presumably only
sentimentalists or Luddites would want to do so. Yet it
does not follow that the value of the sculpting resides
wholly in the sculpture, that its value is purely instrumental. The value of the *bodily movements* may be purely
instrumental, but the activity of sculpting is very much
more than the bodily movements comprised in it. To sculpt
is to understand the possibilities and limitations of a
certain kind of material, to see the potentialities of a
particular block of stone, to remember past errors and
imagine forthcoming pitfalls, to envisage qualities of
shade, line, and texture, to appreciate the demands of
form, scale, and balance, to discern an emerging shape
and perceive alternative routes to a desired outcome. It
is the awareness guiding the bodily movements, not the
bodily movements as such, which has intrinsic value, and
it is the quality of the sculptor's awareness which
determines the value of his skill from the standpoint of
education, that is, from the standpoint of his development
as a person. (The intrinsic value of the sculpture, of
course, does not figure as an *educational* value, since
education sets out to produce sculptors, not sculptures.)
Even if, owing to the niggardly endowment of a step-

motherly Nature - malformed hands, let us say - a man was
totally incapable of translating his rich aesthetic
perceptions into physical result, we should still say that
such a man was more highly developed as a person than
someone else who was perhaps able to produce fine
sculpture by a kind of blind instinct or happy knack but
who was utterly lacking in insight, sensitivity, and
imagination.

What is true of sculpting is true of other creative
skills, of the skills of communication and social skills,
and indeed of all skills which are correctly deemed to be
of educational value. The learning of skills has an
important place in the development of a person only in so
far as they enhance his awareness and so can lay claim to
be intrinsically worth learning, not merely worth learning
because of the desirable results to which they lead. If
cheap and portable instantaneous-translation machines were
made generally available, learning to speak French would
no longer be justifiable as an efficient means of communicating with French people; but in so far as learning
French gives a man an enhanced awareness of the unique
mental complexion of a deeply civilized people, their
thought-forms and the distinctive grain of their experience and outlook, which are peculiarly enshrined in their
language and ultimately inseparable from it, learning
French would remain *educationally* justifiable, as
something worth learning for its own sake, as one of the
things which go to make up a heightened percipience and a
more extensive understanding. Of course, in the case of
many skills (particularly skills of communication) it is
difficult if not impossible to dissociate a man's overt
performance from the awareness which guides his performance, since the bodily movements which constitute his
overt performance are shot through with the perceptions
and intentions guiding them and the whole complex process
forms a single ongoing continuum. And of course for many
skills the surest way of judging the quality of the
performer's awareness is by evaluating his overt performance. Nevertheless, in identifying the educational
reasons for learning some skill, we can and must distinguish between the physical transactions which constitute the overt performance of the skill and the guiding
awareness by which it has to be informed if it is to count
as the kind of performance which we can properly attribute
to the agency of a person; and when we make this distinction, we are, I think, bound to conclude that the
performer's awareness is the sole locus of whatever educational value we may correctly ascribe to his acquisition
of the skill in question.

We may return, then, to our original assertion. As the development of persons in their personhood, education is dedicated to the enlargement of awareness, since to develop as a person is to pass from the groping and twilight world of animal sensation, through increasingly lucid and coherent levels of experience, up to the fullness of rationally grounded insight and understanding which, in its many different varieties, we dignify by the name of 'knowledge'. This does not mean that education is exclusively concerned with developing detached intellectuals. While the communication of knowledge obviously involves, as one of its chief concerns, the development of men as intellectual beings, it is fallacious to suppose that the communication and acquisition of knowledge are exclusively operations of the intellect, and equally fallacious to suppose that the operations of the intellect are essentially passive, detached, and impersonal in character. As well as knowledge of the truth or falsehood of propositions, the knowledge *that* such-and-such is the case or is not the case, there is knowledge of what is appropriate in moral, social, aesthetic, and practical situations, the knowledge *how* to comport oneself in these situations. We speak as aptly of a man's *knowing* how to conduct himself in adversity, how to keep the children amused, how to play Brahms, or how to drive a car, as we do of his knowing that sound travels at 760 miles per hour or that Hector slew Patroclus. And we can pick out different degrees of moral, social, aesthetic, and practical judgment and sophistication, from doing something by instinct, merely sensing how to do it, through the kinds of skilled performance based on wide experience or strict training, up to the kind of highly accomplished performance which manifests a clear understanding of the standards inherent in some task and a sure grasp of the rules and criteria governing it - the kind of performance which leads us to say that a man 'really knows' how to perform the task in question. Moreover, it is a fallacy to suppose that even theoretical knowledge is entirely a matter of abstract and detached contemplation, if this is thought to rule out active qualities of engagement and concern. The most remote and impractical branches of knowledge - palaeontology or mediaeval history, for example - demand of their practitioners the liveliest and most ardent degrees of personal commitment, if they are to be pursued with the fidelity to truth, the passionate intellectual honesty, the burning respect for standards of inquiry, and the pertinacious singleness of purpose which are the marks of the pure scientist and the true scholar in whatever area of study he may be busied. Certainly,

the keenest joy of the scientist or scholar is derived
from contemplating the objects of his intellectual
activity. But, far from being an 'impersonal' state of
mind, the contemplative state of mind is fraught with the
most deeply personal of qualities - above all with the
quality of *caring,* in this case of caring intensely about
the meaning and integrity of the objects with which the
mind finds itself in touch. The instrumental attitude
towards things, forever seeking to alter, remove, or
replace them by other things, is the attitude of false
involvement and specious concern, for it is when we do
not really feel involved with something, when we do not
really care for it, that we feel moved to change it or
replace it by something else. The contemplative state of
mind has no wish to tamper with its objects, but for that
very reason it can justly claim to embody the more
authentic concern and the more deeply felt involvement.
In building up our knowledge, then, even (and perhaps
especially) when the knowledge is of the most purely
contemplative kind, we can claim to be refining and
cultivating the highest elements in our conscious life,
our life as conscious selves striving for a fuller and
more intense being *as* centres of awareness, as moving
centres of experience, thought, and understanding. And
when our explicit purpose lies in doing precisely this,
we can, I think, correctly say that the task on which we
are engaged is the development of persons in their
personhood: we can correctly say that the task on which
we are engaged is that of education.

While the communication of knowledge is right at the
centre of all education, and therefore of all adult education deserving of the name, this must not be taken to
mean that any and every extension of a man's knowledge is
educationally worth promoting. To be sure, every advance
in knowledge, however slight, is per se desirable; but
every advance in a man's knowledge has to be judged, not
per se, but in comparison with all the other advances in
knowledge which he might have made instead. When the
value of what a man learns from some course of study is
less than the value of what he might have learned from
some different course of study, we can obviously say that
his studies have been less educationally worthwhile than
they might have been; and when the value of what he
learns from a course of study is less than the value of
what he would have learned from the ordinary processes of
daily living in which he would otherwise have been
engaged, we can say decisively that his studies have not

been educationally worthwhile at all. Now, for the
acquisition of some piece of knowledge to count as
educationally worthwhile, the knowledge acquired has to
be worth acquiring for its own sake, as an end in itself,
not merely for its usefulness, its value as a means to
this or that extrinsic end. The question we must ask,
therefore, is this. On what relevant principles can we
determine the intrinsic value of a piece of knowledge, and
its comparative value in relation to other pieces of
knowledge? Or, in general, what kinds of knowledge are
intrinsically worth communicating and acquiring, and which
of these are of greatest intrinsic value and so educationally most worth promoting?

How we answer this question will partly depend on how
we set about distinguishing different 'kinds of knowledge'
and on the different kinds of knowledge which we in fact
distinguish. There are of course many ways in which we
can set about classifying and categorizing our knowledge,
but two ways in particular might be thought most likely
to yield systems of classification which will do justice
to the logical and epistemological character of our
knowledge as knowledge. We can distinguish one kind of
knowledge from another by reference to the different
procedures used in constructing a body of knowledge of
the one kind from those used in constructing a body of
knowledge of the other. Thus the procedures of inquiry
and validation used by the physical scientist (the formulation of inductively based hypotheses, let us say, and
their testing by controlled experiment) are quite different from those used by the historian (the scrutiny of
records, and the checking of one record against others,
for example). Or we can distinguish one kind of knowledge
from another by reference to their different *subject-
matters,* the essentially different bodies of fact of
which they constitute the knowledge. Thus the physical
sciences constitute our knowledge of the material
universe, our understanding of the unconscious behaviour
of material objects, while the mental and social sciences
(psychology, sociology, economics, and so on) constitute
our knowledge of a certain aspect of the mental universe,
namely our understanding of the motivated activities of
conscious selves.

A celebrated attempt by P.H.Hirst to identify the
various kinds of knowledge (1) in fact employs both of
these methods of classification, although Hirst somehow
manages to convey the impression that the distinguishing
features of what he calls a 'form of knowledge' are
essentially located in its procedures, its characteristic
styles of approach. Among the distinguishing features

which Hirst picks out is the group of central concepts
peculiar in character to a distinct kind of knowledge -
'for example, those of gravity, acceleration, hydrogen,
and photo-synthesis characteristic of the sciences;
number, integral and matrix in mathematics; God, sin and
predestination in religion; ought, good and wrong in
moral knowledge.' (2) Now, gravity and hydrogen are
clearly examples of *what* the physical sciences seek
knowledge of, not examples of intellectual instruments
with which the physical sciences proceed to seek
knowledge. (For what, then, would they be seeking
knowledge of?) If the *concepts* of 'gravity' and 'hydrogen' can be said to serve as instruments of the physical
sciences' modes of proceeding, to be part of their tool-
kit rather than part of their subject-matter, this is only
because they are concepts of objective realities, existing
prior to and quite independently of any scientific
proceedings, and constituting the indispensable subject-
matter without which there could not *be* any scientific
proceedings. Without entering into the difficult and
controversial question of the nature of concepts, we can
at least be sure that in distinguishing one kind of
knowledge from another by reference to their central and
characteristic concepts Hirst is ultimately trading on the
distinction between the different kinds of objective
reality to which the different kinds of knowledge characteristically direct their attention. And, since all
knowledge, to *be* 'knowledge', has to be directed to some
object or objects, *of* which it is the knowledge, this
might well seem to be by far the most relevant basis on
which to classify and distinguish different kinds of
knowledge one from another. The procedures used in constructing a body of knowledge, the intellectual instruments used (including the central concepts peculiar to
the body of knowledge, if these are to be regarded as
among the tools of inquiry, rather than the materials
inquired into), are in any case largely selected and
shaped by the kind of subject-matter into which inquiry
is being made. The nature of the physical universe
demands that it be investigated by the procedures distinctive of the physical sciences, rather than by the procedures distinctive of philosophy, for example. Moreover,
the procedures used in constructing a body of knowledge
are constantly subject to review and alteration, and
between one intellectual epoch and another may be changed
out of all recognition, although men continue to regard
themselves as engaged on essentially the same cognitive
pursuit. (Consider the history of astronomy, for
instance.) Indeed, in any one epoch men who have no
doubt that they are engaged on the same cognitive pursuit

may disagree violently about the procedures most apt for
opening up the body of fact to which their common inquiries are indisputably directed. (Since their in-
ception, this has been the case with most of the mental
and social sciences, and most notoriously with psychology.) It is by reference to the objects inquired into,
rather than the procedures of inquiry, that we rightly
tend to distinguish one kind of inquiry from another, one
kind of knowledge from other knowledge considered to be
quite different in kind.

When we say that one kind of knowledge is differentiated from another by the difference in their objects, this
of course does not mean that their objects have to be
numerically distinct entities, in the way that Westminster
Abbey and Lake Windermere are numerically distinct entities. A single entity - my copy of Renan's 'Les Apôtres',
say - can furnish materials for inquiry by the chemist,
interested in establishing the type of wood pulp used in
its manufacture, by the economist, interested in its
present market value, by the linguist, interested in
translating it, and by the historian and the theologian,
interested in its contents. To each of these the book
offers a different object of study, for each is interested
in the study of a different kind of reality, a different
dimension of the real, and as a particular existing thing
the book is a meeting-place of all these different dimensions of the real. Clearly, this is not the place in
which to attempt to render an account of the ultimate and
irreducible differences in virtue of which we consider one
kind of reality to be essentially different from another.
But that we do distinguish what we consider to be essentially different kinds of reality is surely indisputable. And it is also indisputable that these essentially
different kinds of reality solicit our cognitive attention, which we confer upon them, employing appropriately different kinds of procedures, to create bodies of
knowledge of essentially different kinds.

Thus the mathematician explores the world of numbers
and equations, the world of abstract quantity and quanti-
tative relations, while the physical scientist explores
the world of bodies and material processes, the changes
occurring in these and the conditions under which they
occur. The attention of the historian, dominated by the
reality of time, knowable only after it has flown, is
focused on the past and its patterns of emergence. The
human sciences (psychology, anthropology, sociology,
economics, political science) are concerned with men as
conscious agents, acting, reacting, and interacting with
their environment and with one another. The learning of

languages (native and foreign, ancient and modern) involves making contact with what might be called the
crystallized mind of one's own people or of other peoples,
the publicly accredited systems of signs disclosing the
world as-experienced-by the French, the English, the
Greeks, each with their characteristic mental stamp and
outlook upon the world, structuring their common experience according to shared traditions of emphasis and
interpretation. The pursuit of the arts, whether as
creator, performer, critic or amateur, involves encountering and responding to a unique family of values, expressed
through a wide variety of art-forms as diverse as pottery
and the ballet, painting and the novel, but nevertheless
constituting (together with natural beauties) one characteristic and instantly recognizable domain for the mind to
explore and enjoy, the domain of the aesthetic. Intimately related to this, yet crucially different from it, is
the domain of the ethical, the domain of moral values,
which we apprehend as claiming the ultimate authority over
our choices and conduct, particularly our conduct towards
other persons. Different again is that kind of reality -
the numinous, the mysterium tremendum et fascinans - to
which the religious experience of men is addressed and
which we try to grasp and expound in creeds and theolo-
gies. And different from all of these is the domain to
which the philosopher gives his attention, the domain of
logical relations, holding between concepts which
themselves belong to other dimensions of the real (physical, mental, aesthetic, ethical, and other concepts) but
which may be joined or disjoined only in obedience to
logical requirements of meaning, consistency, inconsistency, entailment, and so on, of which it is the proper
business of philosophy to give an account.

   For most purposes it is perhaps of little practical
importance whether we distinguish these essentially
different kinds of knowledge on the basis of the different
kinds of reality to which they seek access or on the basis
of their central and characteristic concepts. The same
distinctions will tend to arise whether we identify the
human sciences as concerned with the study of persons,
actions, cultures, and societies, for example, or as
involving the use of concepts like 'person', 'action',
'culture', and 'society'. However, if concepts are
regarded as essentially intellectual tools, *with which* we
seek knowledge, as being among the means rather than the
ends of inquiry, it will be natural to place them (as
Hirst does) alongside the distinctive techniques and
skills pertaining to a given kind of knowledge, that is,
to consider them as forming part of the procedures rather

than the subject-matter of that kind of knowledge. And
(since there is no other way of specifying the subject-
matter of knowledge, once concepts are assigned to the
category of procedures) the acquisition of knowledge will
in this case inevitably come to be identified with the
acquisition of expertise in procedures, expertise in
managing the tools of knowledge, perhaps even to the
extent of overlooking the objective realities which are
the raison d'être of intellectual expertise in the first
place. Thus scientific education may come to be identified with producing men who can think scientifically,
inquire scientifically, and test scientifically, rather
than with producing men who have an extensive knowledge
and a clear understanding of the fundamental processes of
the physical universe. No doubt a man's knowledge of the
nature of some objective reality may often be most
efficiently developed, as a matter of empirical fact in
the psychology of learning, by developing his knowledge
of the procedures which are used to advance knowledge of
the objective reality in question. And no doubt both
types of mental attainment are highly desirable. But
whereas knowledge of the workings of the physical universe
is something immensely worth acquiring for its own sake,
something of very great intrinsic value, it seems clear
that knowledge of scientific methods and techniques is
mainly worth acquiring for the sake of the substantive
cognitive results to which it leads, that it is mainly
of instrumental value and therefore, to that extent, not
of strictly *educational* value. To the extent that
knowledge of scientific or other procedures of inquiry
does have intrinsic value, and therefore educational
value, this is because the methods and techniques of
scientists, historians, artists, and others, and the
logical principles governing them, make up a field of
study (largely philosophical) which is of some interest
in its own right, all considerations of usefulness apart.
No one would claim, however, that in itself, and all
considerations of usefulness apart, a grasp of scientific
method was more desirable than a grasp of the fundamental
workings of the physical universe, or indeed anything like
as desirable, since we cannot study scientific method for
its own sake without realizing that it has not been
devised for its own sake but for the sake of man's understanding of objective physical reality, without realizing
that in cognitive status it is secondary to, because
derivative from, those fundamental processes of physical
reality which confer on scientific procedures their whole
character and meaning. While the horse of method may have
to precede the cart of knowledge chronologically, we

surely have no option but to recognize that in every other
respect - in logic, meaning, and intrinsic cognitive
value, and therefore in educational importance - this is
a case where it is the cart and its cargo that must always
have priority of esteem and the horse that must always
come very much second.

It must be admitted that by emphasizing the subject-
matter of knowledge rather than the procedures by which
knowledge is advanced we are flying in the face of much
recent thinking, in both philosophy and educational
theory. From Dewey to Popper, philosophers and educators
have in the last sixty years or so conspicuously tended to
give pride of place to the human and social dimensions of
knowledge, that is, to the part played by men and their
speculative or experimental initiatives in building up the
edifice of knowledge, which often seems to be viewed as if
it were indeed literally one immense human artefact, the
entire product, through and through, of human energy,
patience and ingenuity. The energetic, patient, and
ingenious humans in question are of course mainly the
professional men of knowledge, the scientists, historians,
philosophers, and scholars. We might call this widely
fashionable attitude to knowledge a 'subjectivism of the
professionals', and it is no less subjectivist for the
stress which it places on the notion of human inquiry as
a collaborative enterprise. There is a subjectivism of
the many as well as a subjectivism of the one, and both
distinguish themselves, or discredit themselves, by their
eagerness to ignore or belittle the absolutely central
logical role played by objective, extra-mental reality in
shaping and grounding those systems of human belief which
rightly claim the status of 'knowledge'. We need not and
do not deny that chemistry, zoology, and economic history
are what they are partly because of the creative activity
of chemists, zoologists, and economic historians, because
of the kinds of questions which they have asked, the kinds
of hypotheses which they have formulated, and the kinds of
conceptual framework which they have evolved. But to view
science and history as if they were pure artefacts of the
critical, speculative, schematizing, categorizing, inno-
vative and inventive praxis of scientists and historians
is to view them through the lens of a half-truth or
quarter-truth, which obscures and distorts a great deal
more than it clarifies and explains. A body of knowledge
is not a creation ex nihilo by a consortium of imaginative
methodologists. It is not a cobweb spun by the human mind
out of its own inner resources. No doubt there is a sense
in which 'chemistry', 'zoology', and 'economic history'
function as names for distinctive patterns or constel-

lations of formulae, propositions, conceptual schemes, hypotheses, techniques, conventions, rules, and traditions of inquiry: in this sense science is 'what scientists do' and history is 'what historians write' (and how they do or write it). But this kind of cognitive relativism obscures what is surely the logically central fact - namely that formulae, propositions, and concepts are themselves nothing but instruments which derive their whole meaning and significance from the objective realities which they are employed to express, communicate, and record (and to which ideally they ought to be, as it were, unresisting and 'transparent'), while hypotheses, techniques, rules, principles, and traditions of inquiry are devised and employed by us, not for their own sakes, not as some kind of self-justifying cultural exercise, but in order to open up and reveal actual objective features of *the world* by which we are surrounded and *into which* we are *making inquiry*.

When educational theorists are engaged in arguing that it is more important to initiate students into procedures of inquiry than into the subject-matters of inquiry, they almost invariably support their argument by such assertions as, 'It is important that people learn to find things out for themselves', or 'It is important that people learn to be critical of received ideas'. Now, no one in his senses would ever want to dispute these assertions. But we need to be clear that what even the most gifted student and indeed what even the most eminent professional scientist or scholar will ever be able to 'find out for himself', even when using the accredited techniques of his discipline with the utmost skill and success, can at best only ever be a minute proportion of what he needs to know if we are to be justified in thinking of him as someone possessing adequate knowledge of his chosen sphere. A distinguished ornithologist's knowledge of birds needs to be and always will be a great deal wider than, say, the knowledge of certain hitherto unsuspected patterns in the social behaviour of one or two rare species which he himself has over many years of patient effort been able to contribute to the common pool of ornithological knowledge. And in the case of the typical student in an adult education class on ornithology the disproportion between what is already known and available to him about birdlife and what he can possibly hope to find out for himself will obviously be much greater still. (3) Moreover, while people ought indeed to be 'critical of received ideas', it is far from clear that a man will be more likely to attain this indisputably desirable result if he is initiated into the procedures of

inquiry and validation characteristic of some form of
knowledge than if he steeps himself in the distinctive
facts and concerns, the distinctive transactions, causali-
ties, situations, relationships, patterns, and meanings
which make up the objective realities to which that form
of knowledge distinctively addresses itself. A really
wide, thorough, and discerning acquaintance with the
customs and behaviour of primitive peoples is, we might
feel, the best safeguard against swallowing whatever
fashionable dogmas may be current in this or that school
of cultural anthropology. And if, as is undeniably the
case, it is possible for someone to have a passive and
uncritical attitude to received ideas about the customs
and behaviour of primitives, it is no less undeniably
possible for someone to have a passive and uncritical
attitude to received ideas about methods of theory-
formation, observational techniques, conceptual
frameworks, and all the other methodological and second-
order questions which arise in connection with the procedures to be used in studying the customs and behaviour
of primitives.

We do not by any means deny that the kinds of procedural question which understandably claim much of the time
and energy of professional scientists and scholars ought
also to have a place in the higher education of the non-
professional adult student. The more advanced the
student, the more desirable it will be that he should be
made aware of the various ways in which, for example,
different strategies and styles of inquiry can select and
shape the body of ascertained fact which the inquirer will
ultimately bring back as his prize. The advanced student,
in particular, will need to spend much of his time amid
definitions, postulates, and principles of method, and he
will need to devote much of his energy to the reviewing of
aims, to the identifying and classifying of the most
urgent and relevant questions, and to the determining and
clarifying of his criteria of evidence and proof. However, we should plainly recognize what surely constitutes
by far the main reason for all this. We have already
acknowledged that procedural issues may be of some
interest in their own right. (4) But by far the *main*
reason for encouraging students to consider the procedural
issues generated by the subject they are exploring is that
if they do not do so their later explorations may be in
one way or another seriously hindered and disoriented - by
a confusion of aims, by a failure to recognize crucial
pieces of evidence, by the need to revise ill-judged
initial assumptions, and so on. It is therefore essentially a matter of making efficient preparations,

without which the *real* job may not get adequately done.
Acquainting oneself with different conceptions and
traditions of inquiry, reviewing the probable scope and
stages of the inquiry about to be embarked upon in the
light of earlier attempts, tightening up one's grasp of
the necessary methods and techniques to be used and one's
understanding of the characteristic snares and pitfalls
to be avoided - all this belongs essentially to the realm
of propaedeutics, to the *preparations* for the expedition
not to the expedition itself and its distinctive purpose
and rewards. (5)

In distinguishing one kind of knowledge from another,
then, it is to the nature of the subject-matter brought
under study, not to the nature of the procedures by means
of which it is brought under study, that we must above all
give our attention. Before we move on, it may be as well
to recapitulate the reasons which, I think, render this
conclusion inescapable. In the first place, all knowledge
- to *be* 'knowledge' - has to be directed to some object or
objects, *of* which it is the knowledge. Next, in terms of
cognitive point or worthwhileness it is and ought to be
the objects studied on which the interest of the student
focuses; chemical experiments are not mainly conducted to
improve the design of chemical experiments but to enlarge
our understanding of the properties of chemicals; a
deeper and wider knowledge of the subject-matter is the
raison d'être of the whole operation, and this amounts to
saying that it is primarily to our understanding of the
subject-matter that we attach intrinsic value, not to our
understanding of the logic of inquiry, which we value
primarily for its efficacy as a means. Next, the procedures of inquiry which we adopt are largely fixed and
governed by the nature of the subject-matter into which
we are inquiring, not vice versa; no doubt the procedures
which we adopt will in turn shape and limit the body of
fact which we will eventually succeed in wresting from
external reality, but that is not at all the same thing;
our cartography no doubt largely determines the kinds of
maps which we eventually succeed in making, but it is by
their fidelity to the actual mountains, rivers, roads, and
lakes of the region that our maps themselves have to be
judged, and clearly it is the objective success or failure
of our maps so judged which will ultimately determine the
kind of cartographical principles and techniques that we
find it sensible to employ. Next, the techniques and
strategies used to advance a particular form of knowledge
may radically alter without that form of knowledge in any
way ceasing to be that particular form of knowledge; the
study of history remains the study of history (that is, of

the past), whatever new methods historians may devise or
borrow from other disciplines (from sociology, for
example). And lastly, two scientists or two scholars who
do not for a moment doubt that they are both engaged in
the same cognitive pursuit may nevertheless disagree
violently about the best procedures for opening up and
grasping the particular body of distinctive fact which it
is their common and agreed purpose to explore and
understand.

On whatever basis we try to differentiate our knowledge
into essentially different kinds, we shall do well to
treat our conclusions with a high degree of reserve. The
undertaking is too vast, the ambiguities and dilemmas too
plentiful, and the pitfalls too deep, to permit much
confidence in any results reached, since what is ultimately required is nothing less than a complete topography of
human knowledge. It has been suggested above that nine
fundamentally different kinds of knowledge may be identified: namely the kinds of knowledge distinctive of
mathematics, the physical sciences, history, the human
sciences, languages, the arts, morals, religion, and
philosophy. A case could obviously be made, however, for
counting the life sciences as essentially different in
kind from both the physical sciences and the human
sciences as we have distinguished them; or for treating
the aesthetic and the ethical domains as essentially
kindred and grouping them together to make a single realm
of values, which would then form the subject-matter of a
general axiology. And on whatever basis we eventually
demarcate the different forms of knowledge, it would be
mistaken to view them as existing in chaste isolation from
one another, since in fact none of them could exist at all
without the collaboration and support of most if not all
of the others. The physical sciences rely on mathematics,
the human sciences use historical knowledge, the understanding of human history postulates a grasp of moral
values, and so on, although of course the ancillary forms
of knowledge used in building up a body of knowledge of
some given kind remain subservient to the central aim of
the kind of knowledge in question - its aim, that is to
say, of opening up to our understanding that particular
dimension of the real on which cognitive focus is directed.

When we have demarcated a form of knowledge, we may go
on to subdivide it into its various constituent branches,
each with its own character and identity. However, while
this internal subdivision of a form of knowledge is bound
to reflect the objective nature of that domain of reality
with which the form of knowledge is essentially concerned,

we must not assume that the basis of subdivision is the
same for each form of knowledge, or, for that matter, that
there is only one valid basis of subdivision within any
given form of knowledge. Within the physical sciences,
physics (concerned with the properties and interaction of
matter and energy in general) and chemistry (concerned
with the properties and interaction of particular
substances) seem to be differentiated on the basis of
logical and ontological priority: there could be a
material universe without there being any hydrogen or
sulphur, but not vice versa - or, to use the language of
concepts, such concepts as 'hydrogen' or 'sulphur' logically presuppose the concepts of 'matter' and 'energy',
but not vice versa. But this is manifestly not the basis
on which, within the arts, we differentiate music from the
novel and poetry from the ballet, or, within languages, we
differentiate Latin from Greek and English from French.
And within the general domain of religious knowledge, for
example, several completely different types of subdivision
may be invoked, each on a different logical basis, but all
of them perfectly valid and equally natural; although the
sense in which the study of Buddhism and the study of
Christianity are branches of religious knowledge is quite
different from the sense in which dogmatic theology,
soteriology, and hermeneutics are branches of religious
knowledge, there is no doubt that in either sense the
branches instanced represent natural cognitive unities
giving access to some of the key structures shaping the
religious domain.

Now, in constructing a curriculum for adult education,
designed to enlarge the student's awareness and put him
in more meaningful touch with reality by building up in
him rich and coherent bodies of worthwhile knowledge, on
what principles can we decide which items of knowledge
ought to be included and which kinds of knowledge ought to
be assigned priority? We can hardly concur in the blithe
insouciance of the Russell Report, when it declares that
'no academic subject or social or creative activity is
superior to another', (6) since this proposition, if taken
literally, would entail the abandonment, not only of
rational curriculum construction, but of education itself.
For education to be able to *foster* personal development,
that is, deliberately develop a person to a greater degree
than he would otherwise attain if left to the fortuitous
ministrations of ordinary life, there must obviously be
some experiences which are more conducive to this end than
others. A man cannot set out to educate others, or to
educate himself, without trying to determine, at least
tentatively and in general terms, what kinds of knowledge
are most worth communicating and most worth acquiring.

In determining the value of a specific *item* of knowledge, we undoubtedly need to know the place occupied by this item in the wider body of knowledge to which it belongs. A historical event, for example, is more meaningful, more significant, the more it points to, explains, and illuminates other historical events which collectively form an articulate pattern of emergence, and our knowledge of such a nodal event is, ceteris paribus, more valuable than would be our knowledge of some relatively isolated and peripheral historical episode. Of course, there are some items of knowledge which might well be thought to have very great cognitive importance, even when taken completely on their own. To know that one is mortal, or that the universe is the handiwork of an Intelligent Being - setting all practical implications aside, merely to learn that these things were so would be to acquire pieces of knowledge of the first importance, even if the information contained in them were to be no further amplified. We may accept that the vast cognitive importance of these propositions is mainly attributable to their momentous implications for the rest of our beliefs, whilst nevertheless recognizing that such propositions could not have these momentous implications unless they themselves embodied substantive claims about the nature of things which were of great moment in their own right. Moreover, a network of propositions, tied together by relations of one kind or another, could scarcely have overall cognitive importance unless at least some of its constituent propositions had at least some degree of cognitive importance in their own separate right. (Purely formal structures, like algebra, might seem to be the exception; it is the *relations* between 'a+b' and '$a^2+2ab+b^2$' which are important; but of course in such cases the propositions which really make up the body of knowledge are propositions *about* types of relation, and at least some of *these* must have cognitive importance in their own right, if an infinite regress is to be avoided.) Thus, in assessing the educational value of some item of knowledge we have to assess both the significance of this particular item for the wider body of knowledge to which it belongs and its value, if any, as a specific piece of knowledge in its own right.

Without endorsing some of the more dramatic claims made by absolute idealists and others who have pronounced the whole of knowledge to be one single 'seamless unity', we can certainly acknowledge that the extent and intimacy of the connections between some specific item of knowledge and the rest of our knowledge constitute by far the most forcible evidence of its cognitive importance. An item of knowledge, to *be* an 'item of knowledge', has to be at least a minimum unit of intelligibility, and so we must not allege that reference to its enveloping matrix of knowledge is needed for it to be literally understood; but certainly, for it to be fully evaluated, its full implications need to be traced and they in turn evaluated. To trace and evaluate its full implications may in practice be a most difficult task, and will normally call for specialist knowledge, often of more than one kind. However, since this dimension of assessment raises few if any difficulties of general principle, for present purposes we can, I think, simply note the crucial part which it plays and pass on to the second, and more contentious, dimension of assessment. How do we assess the cognitive value of a piece of knowledge in its own right, viewed quite separately from any other knowledge with which it may be connected?

The answer to this question is, I suggest, that the cognitive value or intrinsic importance of a piece of knowledge, thus viewed, depends primarily on the importance of its subject-matter. This is so, whether it is a specific item of knowledge, a whole body of knowledge, or indeed a distinct form of knowledge which is being evaluated. It is not the effort, ingenuity, sophistication, or complexity of technique expended in acquiring the knowledge that determines its value (though they may afford excellent clues), since the value of these is mainly determined by the harvest of knowledge which they serve to reap: the value of the procedures used is determined by the results gained, *not* vice versa. It is the objects *of* which knowledge has been acquired to which we must look for its value as knowledge, since its whole character as 'knowledge' is to look to these objects, to unveil and illuminate them.

The cognitive value of any given object in its own separate right is a product of two quite distinct factors, which need to be independently assessed but which combine to confer on the object whatever degree of cognitive value it possesses in its own right. First, there is what we may call the cognitive richness of the object; and second, there is its objective worth as part of the furniture of reality. The cognitive richness of an object, the sum of knowable content which it offers to the knowing mind, depends partly on the magnitude of the object, its scope, scale, or extensiveness, but also on its degree of internal complexity, on the multiplicity, density, and diversity of relations, structures, and configurations which it enfolds. The work of so prolific a philosophical writer as Rudolf Eucken, for example, is

both immense in bulk and encyclopaedic in the range of
topics to which it is addressed, but beside the comparatively slender writings of a Spinoza, with their narrower
compass of topics but much more intricately wrought
texture of closely packed argument and analysis, the philosophy of Eucken presents a conspicuously slighter and
poorer object for our attention. Clearly, a valid
judgment of the cognitive richness of some object of
knowledge can best be made by those most closely acquainted with that object and with other objects of a
similar kind. However, cognitive richness alone does not
determine the true cognitive value of an object of
knowledge. Our judgment of its cognitive richness has to
be modified by our judgment of its objective worth as part
of the furniture of reality, as something of which we can
correctly say that, viewed quite on its own and apart from
all consequences, its existence is in this or that degree
objectively desirable, objectively good. Thus a painting
by a Van Gogh or a Matisse, in its stark simplicity and
austerity of tone and draughtsmanship, may lack the
cognitive abundance offered by the work of some quite
commonplace artist of the late Baroque, but will nevertheless be judged, on grounds of pure aesthetic merit, to be
a far more worthwhile object of contemplation by the
serious student of art. The systems of metaphysics and
theology constructed by even the most obscure mediaeval
Schoolmen may far surpass the mystical writings of Boehme
or Eckhart in their scope, sophistication, complexity, and
logical rigour, but theologians who accord the works of
the mystics great importance of course do so, not because
of their cognitive richness, but because they embody an
intensity and depth of religious experience which elevate
them to a high position among the things which lay serious
claim to our capacities for appreciation, insight, and
understanding. In assessing the cognitive value of an
object of knowledge, we cannot leave out of account the
place which it occupies in the hopes and fears, the
appreciation, concern, and esteem of mature and reasonable
men, in short, its status as something commanding the
direct moral interest of mankind. (7)

  However, when we have determined the cognitive value of
a particular *object* of knowledge, considered quite separately and on its own, we have not yet fully determined
the value which should be assigned to our *knowledge of*
that object, so considered. Although the intrinsic value
of a specific piece of knowledge depends primarily on the
cognitive value of the specific object known, it depends
also on the scope and quality of such knowledge of it as
we have come to possess. An object may be eminently worth

knowing, but in fact our knowledge of it may be scanty or
unreliable. We know comparatively little about the
psychology of genius, for example, and what we do know we
cannot claim to know with much certainty, nor can we state
it with any very high degree of precision; and thus, when
we compare the intrinsic value of our knowledge in this
field with the intrinsic value of our knowledge of the
psychology of rats, we may well judge the latter to be the
greater, although the cognitive value of the subject-
matter is so very much slighter. An object may be cognitively rich, may offer us a great deal of knowable
content, but we may in fact have succeeded in learning
very little about it, and that little may be highly speculative and unsystematic. The result in this case will be
a body of knowledge with an instrinsic value, and
therefore an educational value, very much less than it
might have had (and might at some future time come to
have). In estimating the educational value of some piece
of knowledge, we have to estimate not only the cognitive
value of the object known, but also the degree to which we
can really be said to *know* it.

We have now identified four elements which together
make up the intrinsic value of any piece of knowledge, and
which therefore need to be assessed and compared when we
are judging the claims of a piece of knowledge to be
incorporated within a curriculum of adult education. For
educational purposes, we may conclude, the questions that
need to be answered are these. What is the intrinsic
worth of the object of which we possess knowledge, what
is its true status in the scheme of things? How cognitively rich is it? How much do we in fact know about it?
And what are the implications of this knowledge for the
rest of our knowledge, how extensively and closely is it
bound up with the other knowledge we possess?

We can and must, of course, ask these same questions
about the forms of knowledge or fundamentally different
and primordial kinds of knowledge which we earlier distinguished, as well as about particular items or bodies
of knowledge. And when we do so, we surely find that in
respect of the supreme worth and cognitive richness of
their distinctive objects, the scope and quality of the
knowledge which they enshrine, and their profuse and vital
implications for all our other knowledge, the great forms
of knowledge must be considered to enjoy an absolute pre-
eminence over all other systems and constellations of
human knowledge. Through the great forms of knowledge we
are given access to reality in its most fundamental
dimensions, we come to see something of its ground-plan,
the master structures and principles of its workings, its

key properties and their interrelations, and so ultimately
our whole experience becomes charged with meaning at its
deepest and most pervasive levels. We find that specialized bodies of knowledge, however rich, owe what richness
they have to the light shed by our understanding of the
forms of knowledge by which they are shaped and governed,
and that every advance we make in our understanding of one
of the forms of knowledge has a far-reaching, seismic
significance for our grasp of the many specialized bodies
of knowledge which depend on it. Our grasp of such
discrete social phenomena as homelessness or racial
discrimination, for example, may be transfigured by a
sudden access of understanding of such fundamental and
general social realities as community or alienation, and
for such reasons alone we should consider a thorough
grounding in the fundamental categories, general principles, and perennial questions of the social sciences to
be of far greater educational value than even the most
intensive studies of concrete but circumscribed and cognitively subaltern social issues and problems.

It is along these same four axes of evaluation,
moreover, that we may seek to determine the educational
value of the different forms of knowledge relatively to
one another. Clearly, to carry out this difficult and
contentious task in any detail would be a vast undertaking, calling for a far closer study of the forms of
knowledge and their distinctive objects than is remotely
possible here. Clearly, too, any education that deserves
to be called liberal will initiate the student into *all*
of the basic forms of knowledge. However, we must here
at least take note of the main ways in which our discussion so far might suggest the lines along which any
assessment of the relative educational importance of the
different forms of knowledge might be conducted, for in
constructing any comprehensive curriculum we have in
practice to decide what degree of priority should be
assigned to each of the distinct disciplines of which we
intend that it shall be composed.

If we were to consider solely the objective worth of
the different kinds of reality to which the different
forms of knowledge address themselves, we should, I think,
be bound to give primacy to moral and religious knowledge,
and whatever the exact position we assigned to philosophy,
the arts, languages, the human sciences, and human
history, these would all surely enjoy some measure of
priority over natural history, the physical sciences, and
mathematics. The good and the right, and all the moral
principles and ideals which hang upon these; the idea of
divinity, its attributes, purposes, and demands: these

lay just claim to being the highest objects to which we
can give our attention. The realm of rational excellence,
of logical standards and the canons of mental probity;
and the realm of aesthetic excellence, of the gracious,
the elegant, the beautiful: these might well be thought
to claim almost as high a place. The nature and destiny
of finite mind, expressing itself, acting, interacting,
and developing from age to age, manifestly come next: in
objective worth, as part of the furniture of reality, the
spheres of man, his language, society, and history
manifestly take precedence over the spheres of physical
nature and abstract quantity.

When we considered the cognitive richness of the
different kinds of reality opened up by the different
forms of knowledge, however, the picture might well shift
significantly. The various studies of *mind* in its several
aspects - including now our interpretations of the divine
and our involvement with the creative arts, as well as the
study of languages, the mental and social sciences, and
human history - would, I think, claim priority in respect
of cognitive richness both over the study of physical
science and mathematics on the one hand and over the study
of moral values, logical relations, and natural beauties
on the other. Whether the mind is that of God or man, it
is the essence of mind to hold up to its own consciousness, and point to, the objects *of* which it is the
consciousness: it is the essence of mind to reach out and
grasp objective reality. The study of physical nature is
simply the study of physical nature. But the study of
human society, for example, is more than the study of men
in society, men-encountering-one-another, since it inevitably also embraces the study of men-encountering-nature,
not only through their economies and technologies but also
through human *knowledge,* men reaching out to grasp nature
in the act of consciousness, and through human *imagination,* men transfiguring nature in symbol and image.
Knowledge and imagination are cognitively richer than the
things known and imagined, because knowledge and imagination necessarily refer *beyond* themselves, *to* the things
known and imagined. It is the *intentionality* of the
mental which inevitably makes it cognitively richer than
things physical. And it is the intentionality of the
mental which also makes it cognitively richer than the
objects of moral and philosophical inquiry. Rich as is
the sphere of moral values, for example, the sphere of
men-encountering-values is richer still, containing as
it does the almost limitless possibilities open to free
conscious beings who must choose their own attitudes and
frame their separate lives *in face of* the good and the
right.

Thus far, judged by the intrinsic worth and cognitive richness of their distinctive objects, it might seem that the kind of knowledge of greatest educational value was religious knowledge and that the kinds of knowledge of least educational value were the physical sciences and mathematics. This position would surely be reversed, however, when we went on to take into account the scope and quality of our scientific and mathematical knowledge, in particular the degree to which scientists and mathematicians have succeeded in creating complex and rigorously organized systems of precisely formulated truths, all of which have been subjected to, and have withstood, the most searching empirical or logical tests. Beside the well-grounded hypotheses and theorems of the physical scientist and the mathematician, the assertions of the theologian, the judgments of the moralist, and the insights of the artist are conspicuously lacking in the kind of cognitive authority which is rooted in clear and generally accepted procedures of validation. No doubt many of our historical beliefs, and our beliefs about human and animal behaviour, can lay just claim to a high degree of cognitive authority. But no one, I think, would seriously claim that even the most sophisticated bodies of knowledge constructed by historians, psychologists, and sociologists come anywhere near to rivalling our scientific and mathematical knowledge in formal perfection of structure, in quality of confirmation, or in what might be called the degree of cognitive mastery that they wield over their subject-matter.

Finally, when we tried to take into account the significance of each of the forms of knowledge for the rest of our knowledge - the degree to which a fundamental discovery in mathematics, for example, may have implications which reverberate throughout the whole of our knowledge, compared with an equally fundamental discovery in, say, natural history or psychology - then our estimate of the comparative educational value of the different forms of knowledge might well change again. Concerned as it is with the nature of knowledge itself, with the logical conditions of knowledge and the criteria of demarcation between one kind of knowledge and another, and with such all-pervading concepts as 'truth', 'reality', 'meaning', and so on, a strong case could be made for considering philosophy to be, of all the forms of knowledge, the one with the most far-reaching implications for human knowledge in general.

To make out such a case, however, would obviously be an enormous undertaking, and in fact the formidable difficulties in the way of estimating the overall cognitive impact

of any one form of knowledge should serve to remind us
again how very arduous and complex would be the whole
enterprise of assessing the comparative educational value
of the different forms of knowledge over and against one
another. In trying to assess the comparative educational
value of philosophy, history, and mathematics, for
example, we should be trying to do much more than simply
assess the degree to which philosophy, history, and mathematics could each contribute to the attaining of some
specific and limited purpose or set of purposes. To speak
of 'the educational value' of a body of knowledge (of
whatever form) is to speak of its total intrinsic value,
the total value attributable to it purely in its character
as knowledge, and thus in trying to assess the relative
educational value of philosophy, history, and mathematics
we should be trying to do nothing less than determine the
total value attaching to each of these as forms of human
intellectual achievement. Because human knowledge
advances so unevenly, a comparison of the total intellectual achievement represented by each of the various
forms of knowledge that was substantially correct at one
period might well stand in need of radical revision at a
later period. (Think of the relative levels of achievement that would have had to be credited to theology,
philosophy, history, astronomy, and chemistry in the year
1650, for example, and think of the very different relative levels of achievement that would have had to be
credited to them by the year 1950.) To try to determine
the inherent cognitive value, and therefore the true educational value, of each of the various forms of knowledge
at any given period would of course be an immense task,
and to try to establish a definite hierarchy of cognitive
value and therefore of educational importance among them
would, moreover, be immensely controversial. Before so
difficult and delicate a task could even be attempted, it
would obviously be necessary to conduct a much more
thorough examination of the nature of knowledge and the
distinctive claims of each of its basic forms than can
possibly be undertaken here. Clearly, the most that we
can with any confidence profess to do here is to identify
the main axes of evaluation along which any assessment of
the relative educational value of the different forms of
knowledge ought to proceed, and this, perhaps, we can now
claim in some measure to have done.· Whatever the degree
of priority which ought to be assigned to moral and
religious knowledge, philosophy, the arts, language
studies, the human sciences, history, the physical
sciences, and mathematics in the curriculum, we can at
least be sure that *some* degree of initiation into each

of the basic forms of knowledge is a sine qua non of any
education which can properly be called liberal. No doubt
the emphasis placed on any given one of the forms of
knowledge will reflect the bent and aptitudes of the
student, and the character and resources of the providing
institution, as well as the educational priorities
inherent in the nature of knowledge itself. It is to the
nature of knowledge itself, however, that we must look
when we come to *evaluate* what the student has achieved,
and it is above all in his understanding of the great and
central forms of human knowledge that the hallmarks of his
achievement are to be found.

We have now seen, in outline, the answer which ought to be
given to the question put earlier in this chapter: 'In
constructing a curriculum for adult education, designed to
enlarge the student's awareness and put him in more
meaningful touch with reality by building up in him rich
and coherent bodies of worthwhile knowledge, on what
principles can we decide which items of knowledge ought to
be included and which kinds of knowledge ought to be
assigned priority?' (8) It is the cognitive value of any
piece of knowledge, that is, its intrinsic value *as*
knowledge, which determines its educational value. It is
not in its value as a means to economic advancement,
either of the individual or of society as a whole, nor in
its value as a means to the resolving of social problems,
however grave or momentous, but in its intrinsic value as
knowledge, as part of the fabric of the knowing mind, part
of the very fabric of personhood, to develop which is the
defining purpose of education, that the educational value
of any piece of knowledge consists. We have seen that the
intrinsic value of knowledge, judged purely *as* knowledge,
is measured by the degree to which it discloses reality
and by the value of the reality which it discloses. So
judged, the knowledge which is of by far the greatest educational value is our knowledge of reality in its most
fundamental and pervasive dimensions, our knowledge of
those ultimate and utterly distinctive domains of reality
- constituted and differentiated by such unique and irreducible categories as mind, matter, quantity, value, time,
and so on - which give rise to those primordial and
schematizing kinds of knowledge which are the vehicles or
forms of all the knowledge we possess or can aspire to
possess. A well-constructed curriculum for adult education, then, will be one based on the great forms of
knowledge in the sense that the knowledge which it above
all seeks to communicate will be our knowledge of those

fundamental and architectonic features of reality which
are determining or constitutive of the whole of our experience. This does not of course mean that specialized
branches of knowledge, or particular bodies of knowledge,
the study of relatively concrete and specific phenomena,
will be neglected. In the nature of things, they hardly
could be. How could a man study physical science without
studying astronomy, biochemistry, or some other branch of
physical science? How could he study history, without
studying the history of England, the history of railways,
or some other body of historical knowledge? But it does
mean that, in incorporating this or that branch, body, or
item of knowledge within a curriculum of liberal adult
education, the educator will above all have a mind to its
value as a paradigm example or application of one or more
of the basic forms of knowledge, exhibiting or illus-
trating some key category, process, or principle essential
to the full understanding of our experience as a whole.

However, particular items or bodies of knowledge also
have a value of their own, quite apart from any value they
may have as paradigms of the forms of knowledge, and this,
too, must be taken into account in framing a curriculum of
liberal adult education. The study of this painting or
that novel may teach us comparatively little about the
nature of painting or of the novel, their characteristic
demands and achievements, perhaps because the work in
question belongs to some disfavoured genre or perhaps
because its creator was an innovator whose innovations
were much admired but seldom emulated; and yet the
artistic excellence and cognitive richness of the work
may be so great, in its own separate right, that room must
be made for it in the curriculum even at the expense of
more representative and cognitively fertile items.
Because the political theory of anarchism is of immense
interest in its own right it deserves to be included in
any course of social and political education, although -
cut off as it necessarily is from many of the central
questions by which Western political thinkers have been
typically exercised - it has comparatively little to teach
the student about social and political thought as a whole.
Our interest in the great continents which cover the map
of knowledge, which are its most outstanding features and
shape its contours, should not blind us to the lesser, but
no less real, merits of the many scattered territories, of
many different shapes and sizes, including the peninsulas
and islands - some in the centre of the map, some at its
outer margins - which go to make up the known world and
which rightly claim the direct interest, albeit in rightly
varying degrees, of the zealous explorer and the faithful
cartographer.

We may, then, be interested in Gnosticism or the Scottish clan system purely for their own sakes and not for what they tell us about religious experience or social institutions in general. Indeed, we could hardly be interested in religious experience or social institutions in general unless we were interested in things like Gnosticism and the Scottish clan system purely for their own sakes. It is a sufficient justification for studying the history of one's village that one's village has a history worth studying. Nevertheless, having granted this, we must recognize, first, that one cannot even begin to study the history of one's village without drawing on concepts, patterns of historical meaning, and facts which would be unintelligible without a much wider historical grasp; and second, that as an educational exercise studying the history of one's village becomes immensely *more* valuable, the more it enables one to understand the histories of other men's villages, other countries, and other civilizations, by putting one in touch with the basic processes of history and the basic principles of historical understanding, that is, by developing one's grasp of history in general as a fundamental and dis-tinctive form of human knowledge.

There has been nothing in our analysis so far to suggest any essential differences between a curriculum for adult education and a curriculum designed for the edu-cation of children or adolescents. We have, of course, been concerned purely with the kinds of knowledge which ought to figure in a liberal education, and obviously the cognitive requirements of role education and vocational adult education will be of a very different character, for obviously it will be the specific functional utility of a piece of knowledge, not its general intrinsic value, which will mainly determine its claims to be included in a curriculum for, say, management education or social work education. It goes without saying that the cognitive content of many courses of vocational adult education and role education will be radically different from anything to be found in the education of children and adolescents (even in further and higher education), simply because many of the adult courses (those for magistrates and for shop stewards, for example) are built around functions which only mature men and women are expected to discharge. But if we focus on liberal adult education - that is, adult *education* properly so called - there seems to be no reason for supposing that what is of educational value for the adult will be essentially different from what is of educational value for the child or the adolescent. Natu-rally, differences in intelligence, experience, and

previous education may affect what *can* be taught, in ways
which may differentiate adults from children (but which
may also differentiate some adults from other adults and
some children from other children). No doubt, as a matter
of empirical fact in the psychology of learning, it may
turn out to be easier or more difficult for the average
adult to master this skill or that body of fact. But the
normative principles by which, we have seen, the cognitive
content of a liberal education ought to be evaluated are
normative principles which apply equally to adults and to
children. However different the means we may have to take
to attain our ends, and whatever variations there may be
in the degree to which our ends can in practice be
attained, the educational ends remain essentially the same
in kind, at least in so far as the communication and
acquisition of knowledge are concerned. And so the
liberal education of adults will resemble the liberal
education of children in being based on the fundamental
forms of knowledge, in the sense that a liberal education
will seek above all to develop in the adult, as in the
child, a deeper understanding of those ultimate structures
of reality - nature, mind, the past, and so on - by which
his whole life-experience is shaped and governed. If at
the age of fifteen it is intrinsically good that the boy
should be aware of the nature of the physical processes
at play around him, at the age of fifty it remains intrinsically good that the man should understand something
of the workings of the physical world in which he lives.

Yet, while the education of adults will thus be like
the education of children in aiming first and foremost at
mastery of the great forms of knowledge, within this
essential identity of cognitive purpose we should expect
to find many characteristic examples of knowledge which we
should deem to be specially appropriate to the condition
of adulthood and significantly less appropriate, or in
some cases quite inappropriate, to the condition of
childhood. That is to say, there will be items of
knowledge or even bodies of knowledge which are characteristically 'adult' and which we judge to be so, not because
they are specially easy for adults or difficult for
children to grasp (though this may in fact be the case),
nor because of some special degree of intrinsic cognitive
value (which will not necessarily be any higher or lower
than that of other pieces of knowledge claiming a place in
the curriculum), but because of their distinctive perti-
nence to adulthood as an ethical and existential status.
Some studies may be specially appropriate to adulthood on
the negative ground that they are, in some degree or
other, inappropriate to childhood or adolescence. It

might be possible, but would I think be inappropriate, for
twelve-year-olds to study, say, the theory of the Oedipus
complex, or the phenomenology of decadence as presented in
some of the stories of Thomas Mann. Of course, when we
say that some piece of knowledge is 'inappropriate' to
childhood we do not mean that the child's knowledge of the
truth or truths in question is *intrinsically bad,* for as
part of the very fabric of one's being as a person any
knowledge one acquires, at any age and in any circumstances, is bound to be good, considered purely in itself
and apart from all consequences. What we mean is that it
will lead to *bad consequences,* perhaps by leading to a
serious blurring of judgment, or by distorting the child's
emotional development, or by damaging the interests of the
child in some other way; and in the case of the child -
unlike that of the adult, whose status as a fully developed moral agent entitles him to be entrusted with dis-
turbing and potentially damaging pieces of knowledge - we
recognize that this constitutes a good reason for withholding the knowledge from him.

Other studies may be judged to be specially appropriate
to adulthood on grounds more positively and directly
connected with the status of adulthood itself. If, for
example, it is more appropriate for a man of forty than
for a boy of fourteen to reflect on the nature of freedom
and responsibility as presented in Sartre's 'The Flies',
to examine marriage as a social institution and a vehicle
of deep personal relationships, or to study the Marxist
theory of the worker's alienation from his work, this is
not only or mainly because the man is more likely to have
a wider, richer, and more direct experience of life and
so is more likely to grasp what is at stake; it is above
all because the man, as we saw in Chapter 1, (9) is
rightly expected to evince all the attributes and competencies which we hold to be distinctive of maturity, and
because these distinctively adult attributes and competencies, if they are to be truly alive and wakeful, need
to be animated and informed by clear knowledge of the
kinds of moral and social circumstances which characteristically demand them. The moral qualities of prudence,
self-control, tolerance, objectivity, and so on, in
presumption of which we consider someone to be an adult;
personal qualities such as insight and balanced concern,
the capacity to enter imaginatively into the situation and
needs of another and to interpret one's own experiences
honestly and critically, the willingness to face obligations and shoulder responsibilities, all of which we
consider to be typical of mental and emotional maturity:
moral and personal qualities like these need to be put in

conscious touch with the kinds of reality to which it is
their nature to reach out, that is, they need to be
clothed in at least some minimum awareness of those
objective features of the world which solicit them and
give them their significance. A sense of civic duty, for
instance, to be meaningful and real, has to be informed
and shaped by at least some knowledge and understanding
of the social issues which it is the citizen's duty to
share in resolving, for we should not consider someone to
be a responsible citizen whom we knew to be avoidably
ignorant of the very matters for which he was supposed to
carry a share of the responsibility.

   As well as studies calling for abilities, knowledge,
and experience which the average adult is more likely than
the average child to possess, there are, then, studies
which are 'adult' in a more fundamental sense. There are
studies which demand a place in the education of adults
because it would be ethically inappropriate to give them
a place in the education of children, and there are
studies which are demanded by the nature of adulthood
itself, studies which give meaning, substance, and direction to those moral and personal attributes and competencies in presumption of which we accord someone the
status of an 'adult'. Of course, these distinctively
adult studies will form only part of any well balanced
curriculum of liberal adult education: they will tend to
build up around specific moral, social, and psychological
questions, and the forms of knowledge on which they will
mainly draw will be moral, historical, philosophical, and
religious knowledge, the human sciences, and literature,
rather than the other arts, languages, mathematics, or the
physical sciences. And of the basic forms of knowledge
themselves, there is surely none which can be regarded,
qua form of knowledge, as belonging peculiarly and exclusively to the education of adults. When, in Book VII
of the 'Republic', Plato advocates that the study of
'dialectic' be reserved for mature men and women of thirty
and over, he is far from suggesting (as some would have us
believe) that ethics and philosophy should not be taught
to the young, certainly if by ethics and philosophy we
understand those fundamental forms of human knowledge
which put us in touch with moral values and standards of
logical reasoning. All that he is in fact saying is that
young people are seldom mature enough to study ethics and
philosophy in the spirit of high seriousness required for
the most searching and sophisticated investigations into
the ultimate intellectual foundations of these forms of
knowledge. A liberal education, whether for adults,
children, or adolescents, is one based on *all* the forms

of knowledge, although no doubt at varying levels. In the
case of adults, there will be certain special topics or
even whole areas of particular concern which will be
studied for the first time or which will be studied with
special care and intensity. But in forming part of a
liberal education for adults these specially adult studies
will be subject to the overall cognitive purpose of a
liberal education, and this amounts to saying that in the
end, like all special studies undertaken for whatever
reason, they must serve, honour, and obey the general
requirements of cognitive balance, coherence, and comprehensiveness.

Of course, if it were the case that, of their nature,
certain forms of knowledge could only be studied at a
fairly advanced level, perhaps because they postulated a
mastery of quite complex and difficult procedures, a
mastery of quite subtle and delicate tools of inquiry, or
perhaps because they could only be approached by way of
arduous and exacting propaedeutic studies, then as we saw
in Chapter 2 (10) it would not be possible to provide a
truly balanced and comprehensive education for those
students who, for one reason or another, were unable to
reach the minimum level of study required. If a basic
grasp of philosophy could not be imparted to men and women
incapable of mastering certain key procedures, or if even
an elementary understanding of physical science could not
be imparted to anyone incapable of attaining a high degree
of competence in mathematics, then many adults (and indeed
many children and adolescents) would be simply incapable
of acquiring a liberal education.

This fear, however, can now be seen to rest on a
confusion. While a liberal education certainly demands
some degree of immersion in all the central forms of human
knowledge, 'immersion in a form of knowledge' does not
mean 'immersion in the procedures used in advancing
knowledge of that form'. Even if it did, we ought not to
assume that only the fairly sophisticated procedures used
by professional scientists and scholars can be correctly
counted as 'procedures for advancing knowledge' and that
therefore the cruder procedures used by primitives,
children, and untutored common sense do not count as
cognitive procedures at all. But in any case we have
seen that the basic forms of knowledge have to be defined,
not in terms of their procedures, their distinctive
methods and techniques, but in terms of their distinctive
objects, in terms of the ultimate and irreducible kinds of
reality to which they address themselves. Now, every
conscious being is *already in touch with* each of these
ultimate and fundamentally distinct kinds of reality.

However dimly and gropingly, every conscious being is
aware of reality as presenting itself to him in these
ultimate and fundamentally distinct forms. (This is of
course a conceptual truth, not an empirical truth in
genetic psychology; we consider these kinds of reality
to be the ultimate and fundamentally distinct kinds of
reality partly *because* they are facets or dimensions of
the real with which all consciousness seems to make
contact.) From the first glimmerings of our existence as
conscious beings we are aware of quantity, of the greater
and the less; of the external world pressing itself upon
our attention; of the passage of time, and the disap-
pearance of our experiences into the past; of our actual
or potential being-with-others, the occurrence or possibility of interaction with others, and the occurrence or
possibility of intercommunication; we are aware from the
start of things which delight and repel our senses, the
beautiful and the ugly; of responses which are fitting
or unfitting, right or wrong; of thought-processes which
are clear or confused, and which lead to truth or error;
and religious believers at least would claim that, through
the sense of creaturely dependence, we have from the start
an embryonic awareness of the divine. Thus we cannot say
of an adult who is unable to cope with the study of, say,
philosophy or physical science at some given level of
sophistication, however seemingly low, that he is simply
incapable of studying philosophy or physical science at
all, as distinct forms of knowledge. There is no 'minimum
level' of sophistication, no absolute cognitive threshold,
below which the study of some fundamental division of
reality ceases to be a study of that fundamental division
of reality. In coming to distinguish between uttering
that which is 'true' and uttering that which is 'false',
and in coming to accept that he must not state one thing
at one moment and at the next moment state something which
implies the very opposite, the youngest child is already
operating within the domain of logical concepts and
relations; in simply coming to see that the higher he
throws a ball into the air the longer he must wait for it
to return to him, a mentally retarded child or adult is
already engaged in exploring the domain of physical
nature, its properties and its characteristic regulari-
ties. We can, of course, artificially build into the
definition of 'history', 'physical science', 'philosophy',
and so on, the requirement that these studies should
proceed at or above some stipulated level, but while this
may be a desirable and convenient move for some purposes
such a stipulative definition clearly cannot be used to
settle our present issue without committing a circularity

in reasoning. There is no cognitive threshold - and it
is hard to see what meaning could be attached to the
assertion that there was one - below which the study of
the past ceases to be the study of the past, the study of
a person's physical environment ceases to be the study of
his physical environment, or the study of logical relations ceases to be the study of logical relations.
There is no minimum level of study, below which the
cultivation of a form of knowledge ceases to be the
cultivation of that form of knowledge. We may not care
to dignify the student's states of awareness by conferring
on them the title of 'knowledge' in the more restricted
and intellectually stringent sense - to dignify his
studies of physical nature by conferring on them the title
of physical 'science', for example - until they have attained some stipulated level of sophistication: but
whether we do so or not in no way affects the central
educational issue, for the fact remains that if what he
is doing involves a deliberate reaching-out in consciousness to reality in all its fundamental and pervasive forms
we can undoubtedly say of him that he is at work enlarging
his awareness, and moreover that he is doing so in those
broad and balanced ways which we rightly dignify with the
title of 'educational'. And in such a case we can
undoubtedly say of him that, however humbly and haltingly,
he is working at acquiring a liberal education.

The advancement of reason 4

As the development of persons in their personhood, we have
claimed, education essentially sets out to build up the
educand's being as a conscious self by deepening and
extending his awareness of reality in all its fundamental
forms. To grow in awareness, we have emphasized, is to
enter into closer touch with reality, to encounter and
become present to what is real and to dis-cover its objective properties, structures, and meanings. In putting
the matter like this, however, we may perhaps have run the
risk of giving a somewhat unbalanced picture. If we describe a man's growth in awareness entirely in terms of
the richer patterns of reality to which he becomes
present, entirely in terms of the increasing range,
complexity, and worth of the *objects* of his awareness,
this may do justice to the 'intentionality' of our
awareness, its character as pointing-to and yielding-
itself-up-to what lies outside and beyond itself, but it
may run the risk of doing less than justice to the native
agency of the awareness which does the pointing and the
yielding, its character as a unique force surging up and
initiating the manifold dis-coverings of the objective
reality to which it makes itself present. There is a
subjective as well as an objective pole to the
consciousness-object axis. Certainly, the enlargement of
our awareness is wholly asserted in the greater scope and
significance of the objects which our awareness opens up
and illuminates. When I see a house, the extent and
limits of my seeing are wholly defined by whatever actual
features of the house my seeing discloses. Nevertheless,
while there is no seeing apart from the objects seen, my
seeing is always *distinct from* the objects seen, and
stands in need of distinct characterization. And in
general, my awareness - as an activity distinct from the
objects to which it is directed - can be, ought to be, and

in fact commonly is characterized in terms altogether
different from those we use in characterizing the objects
of awareness (except, of course, when these objects are
themselves acts or states of awareness, my own or another's). My awareness of this house is a seeing of its
shuttered windows, a noticing of its dilapidated condition, a remembering of its late owner, a deploring of
its standing empty: my awareness is simultaneously or
successively all of these and many other activities which
combine to initiate the appearance of this house as an
object of my awareness. To exercise one's powers of
awareness (one's 'mental powers' in the widest sense,
one's distinctive powers as a conscious being) is to
exercise one's powers of sensing, focusing, discriminating, judging, interpreting, imagining, anticipating,
recalling, evaluating, admiring, loving, and a thousand
other distinctive powers of perception, thought, and
feeling which can only be exercised in relation to the
objects that solicit them, but which can nevertheless be
distinguished from these and assessed as realities in
their own right.

We can say of education, then, as the enlargement of
awareness, either that it assists the educand to make
contact with wider and more meaningful regions of the
objective world beyond his consciousness, or, equally,
that it transforms his consciousness itself, stretching,
sharpening, and refining it, and making it at once more
generous and more penetrating in all its operations -
since both of these assertions in the end amount to the
same thing. A liberal education, we can therefore say,
will be one which sets out to vitalize and transform a
man's consciousness in all its basic modes, to extend and
intensify his powers of perception, thought, and feeling,
and to make of him a being who sees and hears, conceives,
fancies, remembers, connects, distinguishes, conjectures,
infers, appreciates, delights, and sympathizes more
abundantly and more intelligently than ever before. A
liberal education, we can say, will set out to vitalize
and transform a man's consciousness at a thousand points
and in a thousand ways.

However, there is one major form of a man's mental
development which is generally recognized to be of crucial
importance for his education as a whole and which
therefore deserves to be singled out for special discussion in any analysis of the main objectives of adult
education. This is the educand's development as a
rational being, his development as a being whose actions,
motives, attitudes, thoughts, and feelings can with
increasing justice be described as *reasonable*. The edu-

cation of an adult of course starts from the presumption
that he is in some minimum sense 'rational'. And in determining the measure of its success we are bound to ask,
as a necessary if not a sufficient requirement: to what
extent can this man, as a result of his education, be
correctly described as a more reasonable human being?
Of a man whose studies had made him into a more reasonable
human being, even if he remained a comparatively ignorant
man, and perhaps still lacking in taste and still without
most of the skills we consider central to a developed
mind, of such a man we should nevertheless be prepared to
say that he had undoubtedly received some education,
albeit sadly incomplete. But of a man whose studies left
him not one jot more reasonable than he was before, even
if he had acquired considerable knowledge, taste, and
skill, we should be inclined to think that something vital
was missing, and we might well be doubtful about the
quality and reality of the knowledge, taste, and skill
which he appeared to have acquired. Because reasonableness is such a fundamental and pervasive mental attribute
or set of attributes, because indeed it is inseparable
from our very concept of a 'person', a man who showed no
sign of being in any way more reasonable than he was
before might well cause us to doubt whether he had really
been educated at all: we should be inclined to feel that,
whatever the extent of his studies, they had not really
touched him as a person.

If reasonableness is such a fundamental and pervasive
element in our concept of a person, this is partly because
of the very high value we attach to reasonableness
(witness the immense commendatory force of the words
'reason', 'reasonable', 'rational'), but also because the
concept of reasonableness itself is extremely diffuse and
therefore liable to permeate very many of our other
concepts, shaping them in very many different ways. This
diffuseness is reflected in the many different senses
given to such terms as 'reason', 'reasonableness', and
'rationality' by philosophers, moralists, psychologists,
and ordinary language users. Thus to many people the word
'reasonable' expresses significantly more than the word
'rational': whereas they would call a man 'rational'
provided merely that he satisfied some norm of emotional
balance and mental coherence and was essentially in touch
with reality, they would be prepared to call him 'reasonable' only if he showed himself to possess a certain range
of moral and social qualities - for example, a willingness
to compromise, to heed the claims of others, and to
acknowledge when he was in the wrong. To some people the
words 'reason' and 'rationality' both signify a frame of

mind which they would describe as detached, impersonal, and unemotional. Others conceive of reason and rationality as excluding certain types of emotion only, perhaps the more turbulent emotions, like terror and ecstasy, or perhaps what they would consider to be negative and destructive emotions, like jealousy and anger. Others again use the words 'reasonable' and 'unreasonable' as comprehensive terms of moral commendation and reprobation, in fact almost as synonyms for 'right' and 'wrong' or 'just' and 'unjust'.

It would be mistaken, then, to proceed as if there were a single, fixed, and agreed understanding of what was meant by the terms 'reason', 'reasonableness', and 'rationality', their cognates and derivatives. And so in what follows I shall not be particularly concerned with whether my employment of these terms is in accordance with this or that general or specialized usage. There are, I shall claim, various mental attributes which as a matter of objective fact are closely linked with one another and with the concept of personhood, and whatever collective name we decide to give to these attributes they are, I shall submit, crucially bound up with the central purpose of education as this has so far been outlined and analysed. They are, I think, the attributes most commonly adduced when we call a man 'reasonable' or 'rational', but be that as it may. The word 'reasonable', it seems to me, best expresses them when they are regarded as ideal attainments to which we should aspire, although perhaps the word 'rational' is more appropriate when what we have in mind is the least degree of their attainment compatible with a man's enjoyment of what we might call a basic minimum of mental health.

What, then, are these attributes which, taken together, constitute reasonableness or rationality in a human being and which need to be fostered by any education worthy of the name? They comprise, in the first place, I suggest, a distinctive group of moral and personal qualities, a distinctive constellation of desirable character traits, in short, a distinctive range of *virtues*. And in the second place they comprise a certain range of cognitive capacities, certain types of competence in thinking and judgment, certain *logical skills* which are integral to the business of any functioning mind.

A reasonable man is a man who exhibits a number of characteristic virtues. He tries to be objective, balanced, and impartial in all his judgments. He is willing to listen to other people, to heed their criticisms, to tolerate the expression of opinions sharply different from his own, and to make strenuous and imagi-

native efforts to understand the views of others on
subjects which lie outside the scope of his own direct
experience. In practical matters he is prepared to find
against himself, and he gives the legitimate claims and
interests of others equal weighting with his own. He
prizes intellectual honesty, is resolved to base his
conduct on what he finds to be true after patient and
systematic inquiry, and tries in all his thinking and
discourse to observe the highest standards of accuracy,
meaningfulness, and relevance. He seeks, not to evade
or varnish reality, but to face it clear-sightedly and
calmly. Because he desires to know and understand what
he has to do with, he is always ready to question, to
examine assumptions, to look for a reason or an explanation, and where necessary to look for a justification.
And of course he is ready to give an explanation or justification of his own beliefs or conduct, when asked by
others to do so.

However, a man would surely not count as reasonable
unless he also showed himself able to achieve for these
virtuous dispositions some kind of effective expression
in practice. For example, it is not enough for him to
want sincerely to be accurate, meaningful, and relevant,
since if in fact his thinking and discourse were habitually inaccurate and full of incoherencies, and if he were in
practice chronically unable to stick to the point, we
should hardly be inclined to pick him out as an example of
a reasonable man, in those respects at least. A reasonable man must be capable of deploying various basic cognitive skills of an essentially logical kind. However much
or little he may have succeeded in learning about some
subject, he ought to be capable of thinking clearly,
consistently, and methodically about what he has learned.
He should be able to spot inconsistencies, to spot
fallacies in reasoning and to avoid fallacies in his own
reasoning. He should be capable of evaluating an
argument. Given sufficient knowledge of the subject in
hand, he should be capable of identifying the assumptions
underlying statements made on that subject, and of tracing
their logical consequences. He should be capable of
drawing appropriate distinctions, of connecting things
which are really connected, and assimilating things which
are really similar. He should be capable of going to the
heart of a matter, disentangling what is trivial or peripheral from what is important and central. He may not
be closely acquainted with the special techniques in
contemporary use within particular branches of knowledge
(he need not be closely acquainted with the techniques of
radio-astronomers, for example, or with the dating tech-

niques favoured by contemporary archaeologists), but he
should have a firm sense of what counts as *evidence* for
a judgment, in all of the main forms of human knowledge,
and he should at least have some grasp of the main difficulties in the way of collecting evidence and of the main
criteria to be employed in assessing it, in different
areas of experience: he should be neither too lax nor too
exacting in his view of what constitutes good grounds for
this or that theoretical or practical judgment. Intimately allied with all these types of competence there must be
a competence in his use of *language*. A reasonable man
need not be eloquent, but in his utterances he should
demonstrate his ability to use whatever linguistic resources are at his disposal with efficiency, restraint,
and responsibility.

Someone who possessed, in adequate degree, most of the
virtues and the basic cognitive skills which have just
been described would, I suggest, be rightly thought of as
a reasonable man at least in that sense of 'reasonable'
which is crucially bound up with the central purpose of
education as the development of persons by the enlargement
and transformation of their awareness. The two sets of
qualities are inextricably connected, not only by the
obvious connection between a general attitude of will
and the mental competence which renders that attitude
of will effectual in practice. Both the virtues and the
basic cognitive skills are interwoven when a man actively
grasps what it is to have a *reason* for believing or doing
something - that is, a good reason, one which will justify
his belief or proposed course of action - since a reasonable man not only has to be able to recognize a good reason
when he sees one, but also has to value it for what it is,
namely a guide for his thinking and acting. Both sets of
qualities are opposed to any form of arbitrariness, in
judgment or in conduct: they combine to promote a just,
well-grounded, comprehensive, and unbiased outlook on the
world and on human affairs, and hence they foster a mode
of life based on public and attested facts and on established principles and impartial laws, which do not
twist or slither to accommodate some particular incli-
nation or to avoid some incidental inconvenience at the
expense of a balanced overall view. This is essentially
because both the virtues and the basic cognitive skills
which go to make up human reasonableness are geared to the
discovery and proclamation of what is true, of what is
actually the case: they both foster a mode of life based
on knowledge not on illusion, on a clear awareness of
reality not on a flight from or evasion of reality. And
so they both work in favour of a form of human life in

which the motives of actions and the grounds of belief are
open to free scrutiny and criticism by any interested
party, not shielded and shut against independent examination by the narrow strategies of moral and intellectual
arrogance, prejudice, or insecurity. Of course, to say
that the virtues and the types of competence which make a
man 'reasonable' are inextricably connected in these ways
is not to report a contingent psychological fact. Rather,
it is to point out some of the ways in which our concepts
of these virtues link up with our concepts of these types
of cognitive competence: it is to point out conceptual
connections. The concepts of 'objectivity' and of
'assessing evidence', for example, converge and meet in
the concept of 'knowledge'. To 'know' something is to
believe what is true, and the objective attitude is one
governed by the intention of believing only what is true;
but to 'know' something is also to have good grounds for
one's true belief, and in assessing evidence a man is by
definition engaged in distinguishing well-grounded from
ill-grounded beliefs. Thus, because each logically
alludes to the concept of 'knowledge', we find that the
concepts of 'objectivity' and of 'assessing evidence' are
logically interlocking, and in fact that they are connected by the closest relations of logical entailment.
As a matter of logic, a man could not be objective on some
issue and yet make no attempt to assess the evidence
carefully; and conversely, if he were assessing the
evidence carefully, it would follow logically that he was
manifesting objectivity in this respect at least.

However, it is not only the concepts of 'objectivity'
and of 'assessing evidence' which are logically linked by
their common dependence on the concept of 'knowledge'.
All the qualities which we think of as constituting human
reasonableness are picked out by us because they are
ultimately bound up, in one way or another, with what we
conceive to be the nature of knowledge. If all these
various qualities - both the character traits and the
basic cognitive skills - form a distinctive network or
recognizable family of qualities, this is because to give
a full account of each and any of them would require us at
some stage to appeal to the concept of what it is to *know*
something. None of the qualities which go to make a man
reasonable entails that its possessor be specially versed
in any of the different forms of knowledge (with the
exception, as we shall see, of moral knowledge and the
knowledge of logic, at least in so far as these are postulated by the reasonable man's virtues and cognitive
skills), far less that he be conversant with this or that
branch of knowledge or this or that specific item of

knowledge. We recognize some men to be deeply reasonable
whom we also recognize to be comparatively ignorant men.
But each of these qualities does entail that its possessor
be in essential accord with the *idea* of knowledge as such
- that he uphold the general principle that the truth
should be known and acted on whatever it may happen to be,
in the case of the virtues of reason, and that he grasp
the essential conditions which all knowledge and inquiry
must satisfy whatever the subject known or inquired into
if they are to *be* genuine 'knowledge' and 'inquiry', in
the case of the skills of reason. Valuing and understanding what it really is to 'know' something (in
contrast with mere belief, conjecture, or dogma), the
reasonable man is the man who, in a diversity of ways,
has an active concern for, and a working grasp of, the
idea of knowledge in general as an idea which can be and
ought to be prized and understood in and for itself.

We have already seen (in the previous chapter) why education, as the development of persons, involves cultivating in the educand increasingly wider perspectives of
knowledge and understanding. To grow as a person is to
grow in awareness, and the enlargement of awareness above
all proceeds by building up in the educand those articulate, comprehensive, and well-grounded structures of
insight and belief which we dignify by the name of
knowledge. We have seen why, in educating someone, we
are committed to deepening his knowledge of reality in all
its cardinal forms, through the absolutely basic and
schematizing kinds of knowledge or 'forms of knowledge',
and we have seen why some kinds of knowledge are of
greater educational worth and importance than others. The
questions we must now ask are these: what special and
distinctive reasons are there for fostering the development of *reasonableness* in the educand, that is, for
fostering in him an active concern for, and a working
grasp of, the *idea* of knowledge as such, as distinct from
merely equipping him in the chief forms of knowledge and
acquainting him with various specific branches and items
of knowledge? and in what ways, if any, is the development of reasonableness a matter of peculiar moment for
the education of the adult?

Now, when we sit down to try to answer these questions,
it is no doubt natural for us to think first of the
immense benefits ensuing to the human race in general, and
to any given society, as a result of the existence of
large numbers of reasonable men and women. It seems
highly probable that where there exists, for example, a
widespread understanding of the nature of inquiry, the
requirements of proof, and the uses and abuses of

language, and where there exists a substantial body of
goodwill towards intellectual standards, reasoned argument, and the free exchange of ideas, the result will be
to create a mental climate in which the frontiers of human
knowledge will be pushed forward, a mental climate in
which scientific research, philosophical investigations,
moral and theological reflection, historical inquiry, and
perhaps also serious artistic and cultural experiment and
innovation will tend to flourish and bear fruit. Moreover, it seems highly probable that the existence of large
numbers of reasonable men and women in a society will be a
powerful factor working in favour of better social conditions and more enlightened forms of social life: a body
of reasonable men and women will tend to act as a leaven
in society, pointing out abuses and stimulating desirable
reforms, identifying problems and creating the kind of
atmosphere in which solutions can be found and acted upon,
and in general befriending and strengthening all those
forces in society which are likely to bring about a
raising of the quality of life.

There can be no denying that considerations like these
constitute a massive justification of human reasonableness. A reasonable society is likely to be a more
advanced society, intellectually and culturally, and it
is likely to be a more wisely ordered society, an altogether better society to live in. (I forbear to mention
the increased material benefits which a society of reasonable people is likely to enjoy.) However, from the educational point of view this type of justification is
surely unsatisfactory. To point to the massive *instrumental* value of reason, the wealth of intellectual,
cultural, and social benefits which tend to *result from*
the hegemony of reason, is to justify it by reference to
things distinct from and ulterior to reason itself. It is
to suggest that the value of reason really lies in these
other things, and since the connection between reason and
these other things is a causal and therefore contingent
connection, it remains logically possible that these other
things might be brought to pass by some different means,
without the instrumentality of reason and perhaps by more
economical or reliable means - in which case the diffusion
of reasonableness would cease to be justifiable, unless
some alternative justification could be produced. Now,
the concept of an 'educational' activity is the concept of
an activity directed to building up in a person those
intrinsically desirable qualities which are constitutive
of his personhood, and thus, while a given human quality
or set of qualities - the qualities of reasonableness, for
example - may as a matter of contingent fact produce all

kinds of desirable consequences, unless these qualities
can be shown to have some kind of value in their own right
as an inherent part of the ideal of personhood they cannot
as a matter of logic be considered to be proper *educational* objectives.   It is not the purpose of education, qua
education, to develop in people any and every quality
which happens to be culturally, socially, politically, or
economically useful, and indeed to take so latitudinarian
a view would be to rob education of any distinctive
purpose whatever - or rather it would amount to a refusal
to take cognizance of that activity which distinctively
sets out to develop persons in their personhood, as its
intrinsic purpose, and to which we traditionally annex the
name 'education'.   If the development of reasonableness is
to be justified as an *educational* objective, then, we have
to find its justification in the nature of reasonableness
itself. (1)

One of the ways in which we might attempt to show that
reasonableness had a value in its own right, that it had
a value which was inseparable from the nature of reasonableness itself, is by employing what has been called (with
explicit reference to Kant) a 'transcendental' form of
argument.   Briefly, this form of argument professes to
show that a given principle, claim, or belief is necessarily valid, justifiable, or true because the very act
of questioning the principle, claim, or belief logically
presupposes its validity, justification, or truth.   In
recent years this form of argument has been much discussed
as a result of the use to which it has been put by
R.S.Peters in his attempts to show why certain types of
activity justifiably claim inclusion in the educational
curriculum.   However, in its special application to the
skills of reason, the argument is of considerable antiqui-
ty.   It appears in Epictetus: (2)

When one of the company said to him, 'Convince me that
logic is necessary': Would you have me demonstrate it
to you? says he. - 'Yes.' Then I must use a demon-
strative form of argument. - 'Granted.' And how will
you know then whether I argue sophistically? On this,
the man being silent: You see, says he, that even by
your own confession, logic is very necessary; since,
without its assistance, you cannot learn so much as
whether it be necessary or not.

The trouble with this type of argument, which is logically coercive as far as it goes, is that it does not take
us nearly far enough: it falls very far short of proving
everything that we need to have proved.   In the first
place, while it does show that there is a kind of inconsistency involved in asking such *questions* as 'Why should

I be logical?' or 'What reason is there to be reasonable?', which explicitly ask for a reasonable answer, the
argument fails to show that there is any inconsistency
involved in making such *statements* as 'I shall not attempt
to be logical' or 'I do not intend to be reasonable', at
least where these are offered as bare, undefended
statements which themselves make no claim to be in any way
'logical' or 'reasonable'. In the second place, while
this type of argument shows that a grasp of logic is
necessary to grasp why logic is necessary, or that without
reason we cannot understand why we ought to be reasonable,
we are surely bound to insist that 'being logical' or
'being reasonable' involves far more than simply understanding why we should be logical or reasonable. A man
might well see in the abstract why he should be reasonable
without coming anywhere near to being what we should
consider a reasonable man in the full sense of the word,
since 'reasonableness' is the concept of a range of
qualities which may be instantiated in many varying
degrees and since we only begin to distinguish a man as
'reasonable' when he instantiates several of these qualities in a fairly high degree. If to the question, 'Why
should we be reasonable?', we are given the answer, 'You
need to be reasonable in order to understand why you
should be reasonable', we are being given an answer which
is viciously equivocal. The 'reasonableness' for which we
seek a justification is the full-blown reasonableness of
the reasonable man, but the 'reasonableness' which we need
in order to understand this justification is no more than
a minimal ability to follow one simple argument - which
might well be followed without difficulty by many people
whom we know to be extremely unreasonable people.

It is not really very surprising that empirical arguments, which seek to demonstrate the intellectual,
cultural, or social utility of reasonableness, and purely
formal arguments, which try to show that reasonableness is
somehow logically inescapable, should both fail to
establish the high intrinsic value of reasonableness as an
attribute of persons (and therefore its high importance as
an object of educational endeavour). The most that the
first kind of argument can hope to establish is that
reasonableness is useful. The most that the second kind
of argument can hope to establish is that reasonableness
is reasonable. It actually fails to establish this, in
the sense required, but in any case, even if we willingly
grant that 'reasonableness is reasonable' in the full-
blown sense required, this logically queer, quasi-tauto-
logical statement takes us no nearer to establishing the
intrinsic value of reasonableness. There is no contra-

diction involved in asserting that something is reasonable
whilst denying that it has any intrinsic value. We may
willingly grant that it is reasonable for a man to be
reasonable, then, but we still have to establish the
educational justification for helping a man to be what we
agree it is 'reasonable' for him to be. Since the
question with which we are concerned is a question about
intrinsic values, it needs to be answered, not by tracing
the cultural and social consequences of reasonableness,
nor by exploring the logical implications of the concept,
but by reflecting attentively on those features of human
reasonableness which we find, on inspection, to solicit
our regard and which we judge to be inseparable from the
ideal of personhood.

Now, we have seen that the distinguishing feature of
all those qualities which together form what we think of
as human reasonableness is their involvement with the idea
of knowledge in general as something which can and ought
to be prized in and for itself. And it is precisely this
feature of reasonableness, I suggest, which gives it its
high claim on our regard. Nearly everyone feels that
there is something noble in a willingness to accept the
truth, whatever it may be. Nearly everyone feels that
there is something ignoble and contemptible in a refusal
to look the truth in the face. Nearly everyone feels that
lucidity is better than illusion and knowledge better than
ignorance. To be deeply committed to knowledge, fully
understanding what is entailed by this commitment; to
submit oneself to be guided solely by what one believes
on good grounds to be true, exposing and repudiating error
and fallacy even when to do so is contrary to one's
interests and inclinations: such qualities confer on
their possessor that distinctive moral standing to which
Kant applied the name 'dignity' and which we feel to be
the rightful due of those qualities which raise a man
above the demands and blandishments of what is merely
private, local, transitory, and particular. There is no
formal argument which could convince the cynic that
reasonableness was a fit object of such regard. But
neither is there any formal argument which could convince
a man who doubted that sugar was sweet. The fact is that
the vast majority of men and women do find sugar to be
sweet, whether they like it or not, and they do find that
the spectacle of reasonableness commands from them what
Kant called 'respect', even if - from frailty or self-
interest - they shun it or are angered by it, as Anytus
was angered by Socrates. If men and women in general did
not find themselves in this way impelled, almost irre-
sistibly, to acknowledge the deep moral authority radi-

ated, as it were, by the spectacle of reasonableness, it is hard to see why the words 'reasonable' and 'unreasonable' in our language (and their equivalents in every other civilized language) should have the immense laudatory and pejorative force which they indisputably do have. In any case, whatever degree of reliance we place on this direct apprehension of the inherent dignity of reasonableness (and the depth and universality of our feelings in this matter surely encourage us to place considerable reliance on it), the test of immediate awareness is ultimately the only test we have for our conviction that something has intrinsic value - just as it is ultimately the only test which the cynic has for *his* claim that it is without intrinsic value. And certainly, if we are right in believing, as we nearly all do, that the development of reasonableness must be a primary and central objective of education, it is our feeling that reasonableness has this special and inherent dignity, making it worthy of our respect for its own sake apart from all utilitarian considerations, which gives us our first and principal warrant for holding this belief.

Perhaps it might be well to emphasize here that what we have called 'the skills of reason' (the ability to think clearly and consistently, to draw appropriate distinctions, to see when and why one thing follows from another, and so on) do not exist as a distinct set of faculties which can operate well or ill in their own separate spheres without necessarily affecting the rest of our mental life. In this respect clarity of thought, for example, is not like keenness of sight or hearing. While the loss of sight or hearing necessarily restricts the scope of a man's awareness, it does not necessarily impair those forms of awareness which remain to him. However, the logical skills which form an essential part of reasonableness permeate the whole of our conscious awareness above the level of mere sensation. They are integral to the life of man as a 'thinking being' in the wide Cartesian sense, that is, his life as a being who, as well as registering mere sensations, actively perceives, remembers, imagines, conceives, judges, deliberates, and chooses. Someone who had no notion of consistency, or who was totally unable to draw relevant distinctions, for example, would be quite incapable of recognizing, identifying, comparing, contrasting, estimating, locating, expecting, explaining, appraising, or performing the thousand and one types of mental act which make up the life of a thinking being - not because he suffered from some contingent psychological deficiency, but because the very concepts of these types of mental activity postulate

an adherence to the key procedural and logical principles
in question. All thinking has to be 'logical' in the
sense that it has to observe such logical principles as
the principle of contradiction, simply because to violate
these principles is to negate one's attempt to think; we
cannot both 'remember' that a is b, and that a is not b,
simply because the second act of remembering is a ne-
gation, a literal voiding or cancelling-out, of the first
act of remembering. 'Illogical thinking' is not a kind of
thinking, any more than tottering is a kind of balancing:
to the extent that one is tottering one is simply failing
to maintain one's balance, and to the extent that one is
'thinking illogically' one is simply failing to think.
Similarly, incoherent discourse is not a kind of discourse: it is a failure to assert, describe, suggest,
avow, put a question, give an answer, or in some other
way use language for the purpose of discourse. It is only
in so far as a man has a clear and consistent statement to
make, that he can be correctly said to have an idea at all
or to have anything to state at all.

Unreasonableness, then, can be quite literally identified with *mindlessness,* and the refusal or inability to
use language clearly and consistently can be quite
literally identified with *speechlessness*. Perhaps this is
why those writers and movements which are commonly and
correctly regarded as hostile to the values of reason -
Nietzsche, D.H.Lawrence, fascists, neo-Marxist radicals -
are seldom to be found explicitly condemning reasonableness and explicitly advocating unreasonableness, since
they naturally have no wish to avow and explicitly take on
the public character of mindless, mumbling subhumans or
growling apes. Instead they are typically to be found
attacking attitudes of mind or forms of behaviour which no
truly reasonable person would ever want to defend. (It is
of course another question whether the individuals and
institutions attacked really do exemplify these attitudes
of mind or practise these forms of behaviour.) Thus
irrationalist writers and movements are to be found
attacking the coldness and sterility of 'narrowly intellectual' attitudes; they condemn the lack of backbone,
the evasiveness, the moral cowardice and emotional lassi-
tude of individuals or institutions which they see as
fussily scrupulous or pointlessly tolerant; they pour out
their contempt on the shallow conjuring-tricks of effete
logicians producing needlessly multiplied distinctions,
and on the empty pretensions of 'mere cleverness'. The
values which such irrationalists defend - courage, sponta-
neity, firmness, passion - are real values, and the vices
which they anathematize are real vices. But the values

are in no way incompatible with reasonableness (only with
a stilted and shrunken caricature of reasonableness, which
truly reasonable people would be the first to condemn),
and while the vices may indeed be characteristic of a
certain type of inept and garrulous pedant it is gro-
tesquely false to put forward a picture of hair-splitting
ineptitude as the portrait of a reasonable person: like
James I a man can be a learned and clever fool, and in
describing him as the wisest fool in Christendom Henry IV
was clearly not putting forward his fellow monarch as the
example and paradigm of a reasonable prince or a reasonable man. It will, I think, be found that irrationalists
seldom mount a direct assault on the authentic and distinctive virtues and skills of reason which we have been
depicting and that the moral weaknesses and follies which
they do assail are characteristic, not of reasonable
people, but of the entirely different (and no doubt
depressingly common) type of person who greatly prefers
the superficial resemblances and outward trappings of
reason to the harder and more exacting reality. And this
is so, I suggest, because at some sunken level of their
awareness, at least, irrationalists in fact recognize that
to abdicate from reason in the widest sense is ultimately
to resign any claim to validity in respect of all those
quite lengthy and involved processes of thinking and
communication in which, it seems, they themselves nearly
always want very much to engage. (3)

The connection between practising the skills of reason,
or observing basic procedural and logical principles, on
the one hand, and successful thinking and discourse on the
other, is not a causal or extrinsic connection. Being
logical is not a means or instrument, of which thinking is
the subsequent result, but rather an essential feature of
all thinking, without which it would not *be* 'thinking'.
The coherence of a piece of discourse is not an optional
quality stamped upon it from outside in order to change it
somewhat for the better, but an essential feature which
all discourse must manifest if it is really to *be*
'discourse'. And so, since a man's capacities to think
and to engage in meaningful discourse constitute two of
his most important claims to the status of personhood, we
are entitled to conclude that his capacity to reason,
which is *logically* embedded in both of these, also constitutes a major element in his personhood. And from this we
are, I suggest, clearly entitled to conclude that, as an
essential feature of the development of persons, the development of reason must figure as a major objective of
any process which we can consider to be a process of
education.

Although a process only counts as a process of education if it involves the development in the educand of those characteristic virtues and logical skills which together make up human reasonableness, this does not mean that the only processes which count as processes of education are those which involve the explicit teaching of morality and logic as distinctive forms of knowledge or awareness. To be sure, moral education and the teaching of logic (or philosophy in general) are peculiarly concerned with the cultivation in the educand of such qualities as impartiality, objectivity, tolerance, and intellectual honesty, in the one case, and with the development of his capacity to think clearly and consistently, to evaluate arguments, and to make distinctions, in the other, since the cultivation of moral qualities and logical competence, respectively, is largely what differentiates moral education and philosophical education from education in the other main forms of knowledge and awareness. (4) We have already seen, however, that forms of knowledge do not exist in splendid isolation from one another. The teaching of history, for example, while peculiarly concerned to develop in the student an understanding of the past and its patterns of emergence, can, should, and typically does also set out to develop in him many of the moral qualities and logical skills which we count among the assets of reason - for example, by imparting to him a veneration for evidence and a knowledge of how to identify and evaluate evidence. Every teacher can and should be a teacher of reasonableness in and through the subject which he is teaching. He need not do this, and in most subjects is unlikely to do it, as a specific and separate exercise. The example of his own bearing and practice within his own subject will often convey much that would seem flat, abstract, and oversimplified if conveyed by means of formal instruction. In adult classes, the habit of free but purposive discussion, with tutor and students participating as equals on a footing of mutual respect, often serves as a midwife of reasonableness. Clearly, the question of precisely how and under what conditions the qualities of reasonableness may best be nurtured is largely a question of practical pedagogics, which it would be out of place to enter into here. The only question to which we can properly address ourselves here is the question of justification, the question of why the development of reasonableness rightly figures as a chief objective of education, and by now we have, I think, seen in broad outline the kind of answer that needs to be given to this question.

However, we have not yet seen the complete answer. We

have seen that a man's reasonableness is something which
has intrinsic worth, bestowing on its possessor a characteristic dignity of which we are directly aware when we
find it exacting our respect. We have seen that to
dispute the value of reasonableness would be to dispute
the value of *knowing*; it would be to dispute the superiority of knowledge over ignorance and error and the
superiority of lucidity over confusion. We have seen
that all our thinking and discourse, in so far as they
succeed in really *being* 'thinking' and 'discourse',
postulate a grasp of and an adherence to those key
procedural and logical principles which distinguish
rational sequences from irrational sequences, and that
the skills of reason are thus logically inseparable from
two vital elements in our concept of personhood. We have
seen that the words 'reasonable' and 'unreasonable' in our
language (and their equivalents in every other civilized
language) have an immense laudatory and pejorative force
which obviously reflects a deep and enduring moral con-
sensus; we have seen that hardly anyone - not even those
typically thought of as irrationalists - would willingly
avow himself to be 'unreasonable', since hardly anyone
would want to come forward in the public character of a
muddled and inept or deliberately equivocal and dishonest
speaker and thinker. But there is a further aspect of
reasonableness which we must now note - one of great
significance in the education of children but one which,
I think, makes the development of reason a matter of
special moment in the education of adults. This is the
relation between the concept of reasonableness and the
concept of *mental autonomy*. Reasonableness, as we have
defined it, is connected with the concept of mental
autonomy through the concept of 'thinking'. A mentally
autonomous person is a person who 'thinks for himself'.
But of course to say that someone is thinking for himself
is really to say no more than that he is thinking.
(Indeed, a man who thinks for himself is often simply
referred to as 'a thinking man'.) A man who relies for
his opinions on others whom he blindly trusts is a man who
makes no attempt to scan evidence, draw distinctions, make
comparisons, examine assumptions, trace implications - in
short, he is a man who makes no attempt to think, beyond
the minimum amount of thinking needed to understand the
opinions which he holds. When we say that a man is
mentally autonomous, then, or that he is a man of independent mind, a man who forms his own judgments, we are
obviously denying that he takes over unquestioningly
judgments which have been formed by other minds (whether
formed by the minds of some other specific individual or

individuals, or emanating from some species of institutionalized mind - dogma, tradition, or Heidegger's
'das Man'). But what we are saying of a *positive* character about him is that he *uses his reason*. The idea of
mental autonomy essentially has this strong positive
connotation, for we should not think of someone as autonomous if he were just mulish, heedless of other people's
arguments and experience, or given to forming arbitrary
and eccentric opinions. To be a man of independent
judgment, one has first to be a man of judgment. And to
be a man of judgment is ipso facto to be a man of independent judgment. It would be self-contradictory to
assert, for example, both that a man's opinions on some
issue were entirely attributable to his careful and
intelligent scrutiny of the evidence and also that they
were entirely attributable to pressures brought to bear
upon him by other people.

Now, while the fostering of mental autonomy is an
important objective in the education of children, it is
of special importance in the education of adults. In
deeming someone to be an 'adult', we are ascribing to him
various rights and responsibilities in virtue of certain
distinctive moral and personal qualities and capacities
which we presume him to have, namely those qualities and
capacities which we consider to be distinctive of 'maturity'. In Chapter 1 (5) we saw that, among other things, an
adult is someone who is entitled to participate in the
making of social decisions, to conduct his private affairs
according to his own lights, and to accept or ignore the
opinions of others as he himself thinks best; and we saw
that, among the various obligations peculiar to the adult,
he is morally obliged to take a full share in the tasks of
his society, including its active betterment, and he has a
duty to be mindful of his own deepest interests and to
accept responsibility for his own character and conduct as
a moral agent. In the case of a man who is unable to
think for himself, however, who has no grasp of what is
involved in making a rational decision or of how to evaluate for himself the opinions advanced by others, and who
therefore blindly concurs in whatever opinions happen to
be foisted upon him, we are surely bound to feel that the
rights and obligations intrinsic to his status of
adulthood are pretty much a dead letter: he formally
possesses these rights and is subject to these obligations, but in practice there is little or no likelihood
of his really exercising the former or really carrying out
the latter, since to exercise one's rights only as and
when others decree is not really to 'exercise one's
rights' at all and to carry out one's obligations only

because other people have so decided is not really to
'carry out one's obligations' at all. In Chapter 1 we
also saw that the status of adulthood, with its inherent
rights and responsibilities, is conferred upon a man
because in view of his age we presume him to have, among
various other moral and personal qualities and capacities,
the qualities of impartiality, objectivity, and balance,
at least in some minimum degree, and the ability to draw
on his experience with some measure of sense and skill.
But in the case of a man who is in fact unable to think
for himself, we are bound to feel that these claims to
adulthood rest on nothing more than a formal presumption
on our part, a purely formal genuflection to his age
without any real basis in his character or attainments to
lend it substance and conviction.

In the following two ways, then, the fostering of
mental autonomy - and therefore the development of reason,
as a necessary and sufficient condition of this - must be
acknowledged to have a special importance in connection
with the education of the adult. In the first place, it
gives substance and reality to the status we ascribe to
him. In developing a man's ability to think for himself,
we are developing his capacity to exercise those rights
and discharge those obligations which are inherent in his
status as an adult. In other words, we are equipping him
to take full and active *possession* of the status which he
has already been ascribed. And in the second place, the
development of a man's ability to think for himself forms
an essential part of any process designed to bring him
actually and authentically to *merit* the status of adult
which, on grounds of age alone, he has been presumed - but
only presumed - to merit. Unless suffering from some
grave mental handicap, a man of mature years is presumed
to be a mature man and thus to have a rightful claim to
be treated as an adult; and in fostering his mental
autonomy, his capacity for independent judgment, we are
trying to give substance and reality to this presumptive
claim. An adult is someone whom we already treat as
mature. In developing his capacity to think for himself,
we are trying to make it more likely that he will be in
fact mature.

In both these ways, the development of reason finds a
special and distinctive place in the education of adults.
The project of fostering mental autonomy is the project of
helping adults to be adult. And since a rational society
has to be composed of rational men and women, of adults
who are truly adult, we can say of the development of
reason through adult education that it is a vital ingredient in the building up of a rational society. While good

laws and free institutions are also necessary, they are
fragile safeguards unless operated by reasonable men and
women; and they will not survive unless honoured and
understood by reasonable men and women. This is not an
instrumental argument for the development of reason.
Reasonable men and women are not merely a *means* to a
rational society, but rather an essential part of the very
stuff of a rational society; and a rational society, like
the reasonable men and women who compose it, is something
to be prized in and for itself. No doubt the spread of
reasonableness, the existence of a rational society, will
generally be instrumental in procuring all kinds of
additional benefits for the members of the society in
question (scientific and cultural progress, for example,
or social and economic improvement). Nevertheless, when
we contemplate the intrinsic nature of a rational society
and contrast it with an irrational society, we are, I
think, bound to judge that the spread of reasonableness
throughout society is something which would deserve to be
welcomed for its own sake, even if it brought no other
benefits along with it. Now, the reasonableness of any
society depends on the reasonableness of its *adult*
members. A society whose citizens act and think unreason-
ably is an unreasonable society, even if the children in
its schools are models of reasonableness. Of course, the
development of reason in its children is a crucial part of
their education which a society must nourish if it hopes
that the next generation of its citizens will think and
act as reasonable men and women. However, human reasonableness is not a flame which, once kindled, continues to
burn brightly in all conditions. It can flicker and be
extinguished, since, as we have seen, a man's 'reasonableness' is made up of various cognitive skills (which can
atrophy from disuse) and various distinctive qualities of
character (which can be sapped by emotional failures or
adverse circumstances). The honest and open-minded
inquirer of twenty may become the bigot of fifty. If,
therefore, the will and capacity to reason are to be kept
alight among those in whom they have already been kindled,
and nursed into life among those in whom reasonableness
has hitherto been stifled; if, indeed, a general advancement of reason is to take place; then we should,
I think, expect to see many of the most significant gains
made, and many of the most serious losses checked, within
the domain of the education of adults. Not only is the
development of reason an integral part of all adult education worthy of the name. The continuing education of
adults, we must conclude, is an integral part of the
general advancement of reason.

The moral education of the adult 5

The development of reason, we have seen, involves the development in the educand of certain distinctive *moral* qualities, 'the virtues of reason'. In developing the educand as a reasonable being, then, it follows that we shall be to some extent contributing to his development as a moral being, for we shall be helping him to become at least a somewhat more tolerant, more honest, and more impartial person than he was before. If through education a man can be correctly said to have become a more reasonable person, we can correctly say of him that through education he has, at least to some extent, become a morally better person. Now, few if any teachers would dispute that an essential part of the education of children and adolescents consists in promoting their development as moral beings, in helping them to become morally better persons by helping them to become more charitable, considerate, and responsible as well as more tolerant, honest, and impartial. In this sense, 'moral education' is recognized to form an essential part of their general education. We suppose that it is possible for a teacher to help form the moral character of his pupils, and we believe it to be highly appropriate that he should do so. However, where the pupil is an adult - that is, someone whom we presume to be already a mature person, and whom we therefore consider to be entitled to all the freedom and independence of a full moral agent - can we still consider it appropriate that the development of his moral character should figure among the objectives of whatever education he may in later life be receiving? And in what sense, if any, is it possible for education to foster the moral development of grown men and women?

Clearly, the second of these questions is the one that needs to be answered first. We need to establish precisely what we mean by 'fostering a man's moral develop-

ment', that is, we need to know what this logically
includes and what it does not logically include, before
we can determine whether the moral development of the
educand can appropriately figure as one of the objectives
of adult education. We cannot attempt to justify the
moral development of the adult as an educational objective
until we have elucidated precisely what it is that stands
in need of such justification.

One widely held view, frequently advanced in connection
with the education of schoolchildren, is that fostering
someone's moral development must at least include, as a
major element, the fostering of his moral *autonomy*. Just
as a mentally autonomous person is a person of independent
judgment, someone who thinks for himself, whose thinking
is not done for him by others, so a morally autonomous
person is a person of independent moral judgment, someone
who makes his own moral choices, someone whose moral
choices are not made for him by others. In fact, moral
autonomy is merely a special case of mental autonomy. And
it is obvious that, just as there are grown men and women
who seldom think things out for themselves but more or
less blindly embrace the opinions of others on a variety
of subjects, there are also many adults who seldom stir
themselves to make a real moral choice but habitually take
over, without reflection, the moral attitudes and convictions of their associates, their peer-group, or their
society. The relevant question is that asked by
Kierkegaard: (1)

Do you relate yourself to yourself as an individual
with eternal responsibility? Or do you press yourself
into the crowd, where the one excuses himself with the
others, where at one moment there are, so to speak,
many, and where in the next moment, each time that
the talk touches upon responsibility, there is no one?
Do you judge like the crowd, in its capacity as a
crowd?

However, there is one possible source of confusion and
misunderstanding which perhaps needs to be cleared up at
the outset. Developing a man's capacity to choose for
himself does not mean bringing it about that in this or
that situation a man shall at least make some kind of a
choice who otherwise would not be making a choice of any
kind at all. The man who would be carried along with the
crowd at a political meeting, and who would always conform
to the choice of the crowd whether it chose to lynch the
speaker or to deck him with flowers, would nevertheless in
fact be making some kind of a choice; he could not,
indeed, be correctly described as 'choosing' to treat the
speaker in one way or the other, but he could be correctly

described as choosing a certain relationship - conformity
- to the crowd surrounding him. Consciousness, we have
seen, is essentially an active force, distinguishing,
connecting, selecting, focusing, ignoring, and in a
thousand other ways purposively relating itself to its
surroundings, and so to be conscious is already to be
engaging in an activity of choice, however crude and
unreflective. In the succinct formulation of Sartre:
'Choice and consciousness are one and the same thing.' (2)
To be conscious of going along with the crowd is to choose
to go along with the crowd. And so if, with Peters, we
think of moral education as helping a man to 'become a
chooser', (3) we must never forget that, strictly, a man
is always *already* a chooser. Developing a man's capacity
to choose for himself must not be thought of as a kind of
Godlike activity, whereby free moral agents are created
out of some inert and passive material which, to begin
with, was utterly without the faculty of choice. The development of moral autonomy does not mean conferring on
the educand a faculty which he previously lacked. Rather,
it involves helping him to employ his native capacity to
choose from among the available options with a greater
clarity of vision and with a surer judgment of what the
options facing him really are.

The paradigm case of the 'heteronomous' man is the man
who blindly accepts the decisions of others. But the man
who is apparently transfixed by some obsessive emotion,
such as adulation, hatred, or fear, and the man who is
chronically unable to settle on any consistent course of
action, who vacillates, reverses his decisions, or gives
up, would also be commonly considered as cases of men
whose moral autonomy (in a somewhat looser sense) was
gravely diminished, since moral self-government seems to
be equally ruled out whether it is other people or some
overmastering object by which one's choices are governed,
and to be no less surely ruled out when the individual
finds himself paralysed by indecision. In none of these
three cases, however, do we have a case of a man whose
capacity for choice is literally in abeyance. In each
case what we have is a man whose choices are dominated
by a single powerful factor or combination of factors (or
a conflict of factors) by which the realities of his
situation are overshadowed to such an extent that he is
no longer clearly aware of the many other material issues
which solicit his attention and concern. When we speak of
helping such men to become autonomous, we do not mean
performing some metaphysical operation on their wills.
We mean helping them to identify most if not all of the
morally relevant features of their situation, to apprehend

these at their proper worth, and thus to see their whole
situation in its true perspective. We mean helping them,
for example, to view the decisions of others at their true
value, as something which ought to influence one's own
attitudes up to a point but not beyond it, and in some
ways but not in others; helping them to appreciate the
respects in which, and the degree to which, some person,
object, or event is truly lovable, hateful, or fearful,
and to grasp why their habitual responses are misdirected
or excessive; helping them to evaluate the reasons which
tend to justify, fail to justify, or tend to disfavour a
contemplated course of action, and to judge when a pre-
ponderance of reasons counts as decisive in one direction
or the other. Of course, it is not the business of the
educator to try to resolve the educand's personal inse-
curities, obsessions, and doubts. But the business of
the educator does consist in developing the educand's
capacity to make choices which are based on a clear perception of all the relevant features of his situation, not
just certain features to the exclusion of others, and on a
balanced assessment of their comparative importance or
unimportance. The business of the educator consists in
developing the educand's capacity to make reasoned and
perceptive moral judgments. Needless to say, it is not
enough for a man merely to recognize in a detached and
abstract way that some feature of his situation has great
significance or little significance. He must really see
and feel that this is so, he must *perceive* this for
himself, if we are to say of him that his faculty of moral
judgment has been in some measure educated. This may be,
and no doubt is, an extremely difficult task to accomplish. Be that as it may, it is, I think, the task
which we set ourselves when we set out to foster the development of moral autonomy, whether in the child or in
the adult.

There is one very obvious requirement which needs to be
fulfilled if a man is to make reasoned and perceptive
moral judgments, or indeed moral judgments of any kind.
Since part of the concept of any action is that the agent
shall have some understanding of the nature of what he is
doing, a man cannot be correctly described as 'making a
moral judgment' (or even 'making a moral choice') unless
he has at least some understanding of *what it is* to make
a moral judgment (or moral choice), that is, unless he
has some understanding of the distinctive nature of those
judgments and choices we call 'moral'. From this elementary logical truth some philosophers - notably R.M.Hare
- have inferred that the development of moral autonomy, in
fact moral education as a whole, consists mainly or

entirely of developing the educand's understanding of the
formal characteristics of morality, moral judgments, and
moral situations. The characteristic features of bona
fide moral judgments, according to Hare, are that they
are 'prescriptive' and 'universalizable', and to impart
an understanding of these formal truths, apparently, is
to fulfil the necessary and sufficient requirements of
moral education: 'for if the form is really and clearly
understood, the content will look after itself'. (4) However, such extremely formalistic views of moral education
surely call for the following three comments. First,
since very large numbers of ordinary people who regularly
make genuine moral judgments would be quite unable to provide a formal definition of a 'moral judgment' if asked,
it is clear that a man need have no more than an intuitive, implicit grasp of what it is to make a moral
judgment in order to qualify as genuinely making one;
and indeed if he did not in some sense already have this
intuitive knowledge, he could not even begin to follow his
teacher's attempts to analyse the concept of a 'moral
judgment' and articulate its characteristic features.
Second, there is in fact very little connection between a
man's degree of understanding of the formal characteristics of moral judgments and the degree of moral autonomy
or of general moral virtue which we are inclined to attribute to him; moral heroes and saints are seldom moral
philosophers, and the degree of sophistication with which
a man can discuss the logical properties of moral concepts
is a somewhat unreliable index of his moral stature: and
of course in acknowledging that there is very little connection between the degree of development of a man's
purely formal understanding of the nature of morality and
his general degree of development as a moral being, we are
in effect acknowledging that the contribution which the
development of a purely formal understanding of morality
can make to a man's moral education is of necessity
strictly limited. Third, the capacity to make reasoned
and perceptive moral judgments surely depends above all
on a thorough and intimate acquaintance with the living
moral realities to which such judgments refer, that is,
on a thorough and intimate acquaintance with the actual
subject-matter of our moral judgments and moral choices,
with the manifold complex issues, principles, demands, and
options of which our concrete moral experience is actually
made up - and indeed to speak of 'moral percipience' at
all is surely to speak of our capacity to put ourselves in
conscious touch with the actual *content* of our moral
problems, with the rich variety of living and substantive
concerns which give rise to authentic moral situations.

Now, in the specific context of adult education
(whatever may be the case in the education of adolescents
and young children) we are clearly entitled to presume
that the educand already possesses at least a minimum,
implicit understanding of what it is to make a moral
choice or moral judgment. While any further development
of a man's understanding of the formal characteristics of
morality beyond this minimum level will of course make a
valuable contribution to his philosophical education, if
what we have said above is correct the further development
of such a purely formal understanding will not significantly advance - nor will its neglect seriously hinder -
his further development as a moral being. And so we may,
I think, validly conclude that any moral education which
will be appropriate to the specific condition of the adult
will consist above all in extending and deepening his
understanding of the actual *subject-matter* of our moral
choices, in sharpening his awareness of those ambiguous,
shifting, but objective and exigent values and validities
which supply the *content* of our moral judgments. To
recognize more clearly, for example, when an obligation is
binding and when it may rightfully be set aside, or under
what circumstances forbearance is called for and under
what circumstances it would be out of place; to judge
more accurately when and in what ways sympathy, gratitude,
or indignation, for example, may be demanded by some
situation, and to gauge more confidently the fit scope and
proper limits of such feelings; to understand more fully
the qualities which go to make up human merit and those
which we count as moral defects, and to perceive more
distinctly when and how such qualities manifest themselves
in one's own demeanour and that of others: it is in
coming to grasp the nature and interconnections of living
moral realities like these and the myriad others by which
our ordinary experience is permeated, with increasing
depth of insight and sureness of touch, that a grown man's
further growth as a moral being surely above all consists.
Obviously it is not possible here for us to draw
anything remotely resembling a detailed map of the massive
and complex firmament of values and validities by which
our entire moral outlook is shaped and by which our hourly
and daily choices and actions ought to be governed. But
it is desirable that we should at least make clear at this
stage what it is (in our opinion) that 'moral' choice and
action essentially *consist in,* in the hope of making it at
least to some extent clearer what it is (again in our
opinion) that moral experience and reasoning are experience *of* and reasoning *about*; for unless we do this the
notion of 'moral education', understood as the development

of someone's capacity to make reasoned and perceptive
moral judgments, will still be largely unanalysed in
respect of what is surely its most fundamental feature.
And so it is desirable that we should at this stage offer
at least some sort of general characterization, incomplete
though it obviously must be, of the distinctive kinds of
realities around which our moral concerns revolve and the
main kinds of cognitive relationship in which we stand
towards them.

Let us therefore begin by noting that the universe
contains a great many different kinds of things to which
we can correctly ascribe not only a great many different
empirical properties but also various types and degrees
of *value* (or disvalue). Thus the universe contains oak
trees, sunsets, cancer, symphonies, pleasure and pain,
knowledge and ignorance, broken promises, envy, courage,
tolerance, affection and a great many other kinds of thing
which we can correctly describe as green, blue, heavy,
light, sweet, sharp, rare, common, of short or long
duration, narrow or wide in scope, reliable, unreliable,
or as possessing or lacking some definite empirical
property or combination of properties out of the immense
variety of empirical properties which we know to exist;
and we can go on to say of these sunsets, symphonies,
broken promises, and so on, that they are in one or
another degree attractive, unattractive, delightful,
squalid, admirable, contemptible, magnificent, paltry,
desirable, honourable, right, undesirable, dishonourable,
wrong, or in some other way worthy or unworthy of our
approbation or worthy of our disapprobation. In other
words (to use the most general terms of approbation and
disapprobation that we have at our disposal) the universe
undoubtedly contains a great many kinds of things which
are in one way or another 'good' or 'bad' and which we
judge to be good or bad, not because of any consequences
they may have, but because we consider them to be *in
themselves* the kinds of thing the very existence or non-
existence of which in the universe is a matter rightly
soliciting our approbation or disapprobation in some way
and in some degree.

We can, I think, divide those things we deem intrinsically good into three large classes. First, there are
many essentially physical qualities which make their
appearance in very many different kinds of physical
objects, processes, and states of affairs and which
justify us in looking upon these, admiring them, and
pronouncing them to be good - for example, the aesthetic
qualities that we find in works of art like great
paintings and symphonies as well as in natural beauties

like venerable oak trees and glorious sunsets. Second,
there are various states of awareness - for example,
pleasure, insight, perception, understanding, the appreciation of beauty - in which we are in various ways aware of
important (but indeed not *necessarily* good or beautiful)
aspects of the world around us, for in the light of
everything that has been said in the course of this book
so far we are surely right to consider the existence and
dissemination of greater awareness as something of very
great value in its own right. Third, there are certain
forms of awareness of others - affection, concern, gratitude, tolerance, respect - which we rightly count among
the very highest and best of all the things we know of or
can conceive. We can also, I think, divide those kinds of
thing we deem intrinsically *bad* into three similar
classes. Thus there are the qualities distinguishing
those physical objects, processes, and states of affairs
of which we can say that, quite apart from any consequences they may have, it would be simply better if they
did not exist - the qualities which constitute things
coarse and vile in art as well as the unclean, the
chaotic, or the squalid in nature. There are various
states of painful, warped, or shrunken awareness (including sheer mental blindness or lack of awareness) which
we rightly consider to be not only lacking in goodness but
in themselves positively bad in one degree or another -
distress and misery in their many forms, for example, but
also admiration of and liking for the ugly or vile, and of
course ignorance, incomprehension, and illusion. Finally
there are certain forms of awareness of others, certain
attitudes of people to one another, which we rightly count
among the very worst things by which the world and human
life can be stained and disfigured - for example, such
attitudes as envy, deceitfulness, ingratitude, hatred,
rejection, and contempt, in all their many permutations
and degrees.
    When we assert that something is intrinsically good or
bad, this is an ascription of value which undoubtedly
needs to be sharply distinguished from any descriptions
we may in addition give of the empirical properties of
the thing in question. Ascriptions of value are certainly
not the same as descriptions of empirical fact. When we
have fully and accurately described the size, shape, age,
and colouring of the oak tree, we have not yet said
whether we consider it to be a thing of beauty. We can
describe the naturalist's detailed knowledge of the
ancient tree, and his feelings of reverence for it,
without as yet implying any kind of approval of the fact
that he has this knowledge and these feelings. And when

we have described the affection and respect with which the
naturalist is regarded by those who know him, we have not
yet in any way committed ourselves to the proposition that
attitudes of affection and respect towards learned and
devoted people are things of great intrinsic worth. However, having said all this, we need to recognize that in
an important sense values do *depend on* empirical facts.
For it is the empirically discoverable features of things
which *have* value (or disvalue). Affection, for example,
is an objective human attitude which we can directly
experience in ourselves and others and which can be
scientifically investigated by psychologists and sociologists, and it is *to* this objective empirical actuality
that we correctly ascribe a high degree of intrinsic
value. Values do not float about in a vacuum, waiting
for us to attach them to things. Values *inhere in* facts.
(Indeed this is really only another way of saying that
there are things which have 'intrinsic' value.) The
intrinsic goodness or badness of something is not a
quality affixed to it from without but rather a character
which that thing possesses, a dimension which we find in
it, simply by virtue of its being *that particular kind of
thing*. And thus our knowledge of the intrinsic goodness
or badness of things, while by no means the same as, is
nevertheless essentially inseparable from our specific
factual knowledge of these things. We cannot possibly
know that attitudes of affection and respect towards
learned and devoted people are things of great intrinsic
worth unless we know what these attitudes essentially *are,*
not just in their outward and visible expression but also
- and more especially - in their inward and spiritual
temper as specific forms of interpersonal sensibility.

In order to learn that something has some degree of
intrinsic value or disvalue, then, we must first of all
be presented with that thing. We do not need to encounter
it in our own immediate experience, in our own perambu-
lations around the world. Most of our knowledge is
knowledge by description rather than knowledge by acquaintance, and in many of our most important moral
judgments we may well have to concern ourselves with
things which lie quite outside the sphere of our own
direct experience. But unless we can at least imagine
with some measure of vividness and accuracy what it is
like, say, to be a keen athlete given the opportunity to
develop his growing physical powers to the full, or what
it is like for a young married woman to suffer sudden
bereavement, it is hard to see how we can even set out to
make responsible moral judgments in situations where the
fostering of such goods and the avoidance of such evils
figure prominently among the tangle of issues giving rise

to moral disagreements and conflicts. We cannot judge
the importance of something of which we are wholly
ignorant.

However, having acknowledged this, we need to keep
in mind that the presentations of sense-experience, the
deliverances of the intellect, and the enactments of the
imagination cannot *of themselves* reveal to us that the
things perceived, understood, or imagined are worthy of
our approbation (or disapprobation). For this to come
about, I suggest, our capacities of *feeling* need to be
involved. If nothing ever excited, dismayed, delighted,
disgusted, amused, angered, or in some other way stirred
and moved us, we would, I suggest, be totally without the
concepts of the intrinsic 'goodness' or 'badness' of
things. It is in the first instance our feelings which
stimulate us to view things as intrinsically good or
bad. No doubt, as evidence for the worthwhileness or
counterworthwhileness of things, our feelings are often
erratic and stumbling guides. As generations of philosophy tutors have pointed out to students of Chapter 4 of
Mill's 'Utilitarianism', from the fact that people desire
something it does not by any means *follow* that the thing
in question is desirable. However, what Mill in fact says
is not that our feelings and desires are infallible guides
to the desirability or undesirability of things, but
merely that in the end they are the only guides we have.
'The sole evidence it is possible to produce that anything
is desirable, is that people do actually desire it.' (5)
And with this assertion we can surely agree, provided that
we take it to mean (as it manifestly does) that our most
basic and irreducible value judgments, namely our
judgments of intrinsic value, ultimately need to be
grounded because ultimately they *can* only be grounded in
the distinctive feelings which we find this or that valued
or disvalued object directly arousing in us. It is the
disclosures of feeling that supply us with the indispensable raw materials, as it were, out of which the most
complex of our value judgments all ultimately need to be
woven. (6)

Of course, when a man has once been deeply moved by the
spectacle of unselfish love or stirred to revulsion by
some act of cynical treachery, on subsequent occasions he
is able to recognize these things for what they morally
are although the appropriate feelings may no longer be
aroused in him with anything like the same immediacy or
to anything like the same degree. Habit, memory,
judgment, knowledge of principles - these normally act
as the trusted ministers of our feelings, administering
our moral life on their behalf, and indeed it is clearly

very necessary that they should do so, since our capacities for sustained and intense feeling are of their nature
limited while the moral demands which life can make on us
observe no such given limits. Moreover, just as the
disclosures of our senses need to be compared and checked
against one another if sensory error is to be avoided, so
the disclosures of feeling frequently need to be submitted
to processes of scrutiny and adjustment if we are to avoid
making value judgments which will be seriously misguided.
Our initial visual impressions may need to be corrected in
the light of our whole relevant experience if we are to
see some remote or unfamiliar object in a true perspective; and similarly, if we are to see our own
conduct and that of others in its true moral perspective
we shall need to be willing to modify our immediate
responses of indignation, admiration, contempt, approval,
and so on, in the light of what we already know about the
various forms taken by injustice, courage, disloyalty,
self-sacrifice, or whatever specific cases of good or
evil it may be with which we believe ourselves to be
presented. Without the data provided by our feelings,
the moral intelligence would have nothing to get to work
on; but without the critical control exerted by our
intelligence, the moral feelings of mankind would be only
too likely to vacillate, flounder, and at last go
hopelessly astray.

    We may conclude, then, that the human mind does have
access - through feeling superintended by intelligence -
to what we may properly think of as the content or
subject-matter of morality, namely the many forms of
intrinsic value and disvalue which we find around us and
which we by our own choices and actions can in various
ways foster or impede. 'Moral experience' is our direct
awareness, our feeling perceptions, of the worthwhileness
or counterworthwhileness of things (although the things
themselves which *have* the worthwhileness or
counterworthwhileness need not be directly presented to
our senses but may instead be grasped by the operations
of the understanding or held up to view by the imagination). 'Moral reasoning', when it is not in fact a
species of empirical reasoning about moral issues (about
how such-and-such an evil can in practice be averted in
such-and-such circumstances, for example), is simply our
capacity to identify the intrinsic worthwhileness or
counterworthwhileness of things by drawing on our
knowledge of principles and moral generalities rather
than relying on the immediacy of our feeling responses -
on which indeed all these principles and generalities must
ultimately be based but which they in turn can neverthe-

less help to stabilize, harmonize, render more definite
and systematic, and in one way or another organize,
reinterpret, modify, adjust, and correct. 'Moral choices'
and 'moral actions' (whether morally good or morally bad)
are choices and actions which directly or indirectly have
some effect on the overall balance of good and evil in the
universe. (7) Finally, a 'morally good' man, or for that
matter a 'good' man tout court, is a man who by his
choices and actions to some extent helps to alter the
balance of good and evil in the universe in favour of the
good, perhaps by positively adding to the good in the
universe or perhaps by reducing the amount of evil. We
earlier claimed that by far the best we know of or can
conceive are certain forms of awareness of others - love,
loyalty, compassion, tolerance, respect, fairness of mind,
and the many other attitudes of one person to another that
form the very stuff out of which the richest and most
deeply worthwhile personal and social relationships are
made. But if this is so it follows that the production
by a man in his own heart of these supremely valuable
qualities and dispositions of temper *of itself* makes the
universe an immensely better place. While it is undeniably still better if these qualities of heart lead to all
kinds of good results, as they commonly do, it is scarcely
possible that they should ever lead to results which could
remotely equal in value these qualities of heart themselves. And while there are very many other intrinsically
good things which it is the part of a good man to produce
- namely, those belonging to the first two classes of
intrinsic goods which we earlier distinguished - it could
hardly be claimed that a man who tended or created objects
of great physical beauty, say, or a man who had developed
in himself a greater capacity for contentment and for
enjoying life without protest or complaint, was for these
reasons a morally better person, a better human being, or
indeed on the sole basis of this evidence anything like as
good a human being, as someone from whose character there
shone great love and generosity, say, or whose actions
bore witness to great candour and fairness of mind.

'Moral error' typically occurs, I suggest, not because
a man mistakenly considers something intrinsically bad to
be intrinsically good or vice versa, but rather because he
is prone to overestimate, or underestimate, the *degree* of
goodness or badness of the things with which he has to do.
In particular, we are all prone to attach too much weight
to the benefits which will accrue or the harm which will
follow to ourselves from some contemplated course of
action, and to attach too little weight to the harm which
will follow or the benefits which will accrue to others

from that course of action. No doubt this is because it
is so very much easier for a man to appreciate his own
relief at obtaining a seat in the lifeboat than for him
to appreciate the despair of his neighbour who is left to
sink or swim, since he can of course experience his own
joys and terrors directly whereas the joys and terrors
lived through by his neighbour will impinge upon his
consciousness only in the measure that his powers of clear
perception, of balanced understanding, and of prompt and
vivid imagination, are all fully and actively engaged and
intelligently and accurately directed. Be this as it may,
it is surely above all by coming to see things at their
true value relatively to one another, by establishing in
our own hearts a priority of motives which truly reflects
the actual moral priorities objectively beckoning and
addressing us from without, or in other words by learning
to find our way and move about the world of living moral
realities surrounding us with increasing sensitivity and
sureness of touch, that we can hope to make some significant advance as moral beings and thus in this highest
dimension of personhood help to build up our stature as
persons.

It is in this sense, then, that a man's moral education
must above all put him more closely in touch with the
actual *content* of the moral life, with the actual *stuff*
of our moral choices and moral decisions. To develop as
a moral being is to develop one's mastery of these
delicate and explosive areas of our experience, for
example by learning to discriminate cases and perceive
nuances, and this means being steeped in the many complex
moral realities - the many nicely differentiated forms of
worthwhileness and counterworthwhileness - which are
continually making their concrete demands upon us. However, everything we have been saying so far about the
content or subject-matter of moral education can still be
adequately expressed in terms of the development of 'moral
autonomy', as we earlier outlined this concept, provided
that the concept of moral autonomy is properly understood.
While a morally autonomous man is indeed a man who 'makes
his own moral choices', a man of 'independent moral
judgment', we saw that this way of putting the matter is
liable to misinterpretation. Every moral agent 'makes his
own moral choices', but a man who can be described as
exhibiting some degree of moral autonomy is (to that
degree) a man who makes moral choices which are reflective
and discerning. He is a man whose choices are based on
balanced and informed judgments. Moreover, to speak of a
man of 'independent judgment' - as we saw in the previous
chapter (8) - is really only to speak of a man of

judgment. A man who 'judges for himself' is in fact
simply a man who really *judges*. If it makes sense to
speak of developing the moral autonomy of an adult, then,
this is because it always makes sense to speak of developing a grown man's capacity to make moral judgments which
are at least more reasoned and perceptive than those he
has been in the habit of making in his life so far. And
the making of reasoned and perceptive moral judgments
depends above all on a thorough and intimate acquaintance
with the concrete realities of which our substantive moral
experience is compounded - those values or disvalues,
licences or prohibitions, which are enshrined in our
experience of honesty and dishonesty, fairness and un-
fairness, loyalty, gratitude, guilt, forgiveness, pride,
courage, sympathy, suffering, and so on.

Now, to say all this is in effect to acknowledge that
the business of moral education essentially consists in
developing the adult's capacity to make moral judgments
which contain *truth*. Indeed the concept of a 'reasoned
and perceptive' judgment, of any kind, necessarily alludes
to the concept of some truth or other, since it is by
virtue of the truths they characteristically yield that we
pick out certain mental processes and dignify them by the
names of 'reasoning' and 'perception'. If the moral
judgments we seek to foster are to be both reasoned and
perceptive, there can be no escaping the conclusion that
in moral education what we are doing is seeking to foster
judgments which - if the concepts of 'moral reasoning' and
'moral perceptiveness' are meaningful at all - will be
true to whatever objective moral realities a man may find
himself confronting. If, for instance, we want a man to
be able to work out for himself when some course of action
would disappoint another person's legitimate expectations,
this amounts to saying that we want him to be able to make
judgments about the legitimate expectations of others
which will in fact be true, which will, that is, correctly
seize the morally valid features of the expectations of
others and assign to these whatever degree and type of
validity they actually have.

Moreover, as we have already seen, to develop a man's
capacity to 'perceive' moral distinctions, moral attributes, and moral imperatives, means developing his capacity to feel their full moral force, to appreciate the
demands which they make upon him in their full intensity
as well as in their true nature, and so to be really moved
by the moral realities presented to him. Perhaps it is
possible for a man to feel that an action is wholly
unjust, to be truly moved by his perception of its
injustice, and still proceed to do that which he fully

knows to be unjust. I do not think that this is so, but
in any case I am not concerned to argue this difficult
question here. What we can certainly claim here, however,
is that a man who fully and clearly sees what is honest
and just and what is dishonest and unjust, and who is
stirred in his own being by what he sees, sincerely loving
what is honest and just and hating what is dishonest and
unjust (since this is what 'clearly seeing' these things
means), is by this token a man who has bodied forth in his
own heart distinctive and deeply admirable qualities and
dispositions which manifestly rank among the very best we
know of or can conceive. We can certainly claim that, in
these respects at least, the man whom we are considering
is a morally good man, and thus if such an outcome can be
in any sense induced by processes of education we can
correctly claim that moral education consists in helping
the educand to become, in some measure, a morally better
person.

In claiming that moral education consists in helping
the educand to become a morally better person by extending
and sharpening his awareness of objective moral realities,
we are still not in any way stating a further or additional aim of moral education, over and above its aim of
developing moral autonomy. From what has already been
said about the concept of 'developing moral autonomy' it
should be obvious that this concept, properly understood,
includes everything that we should wish to include within
the concept of 'enlarging moral awareness'. And whether
we describe the aim of moral education in terms of developing moral autonomy or of enlarging moral awareness,
it remains equally the case that in moral education we are
setting out to foster the development of morally better
persons. R.F.Dearden is able to observe that 'great
criminals are markedly autonomous men' (9) only because
he is using the term 'autonomy' to express a significantly
narrower concept than the concept of autonomy to which we
have been addressing ourselves here. Strictly speaking,
deeply immoral conduct can at most be said to satisfy the
negative conditions built into the concept of autonomy:
it proclaims the 'autos' but not the 'nomos'. The great
criminal may flaunt his defiance of the moral judgments
of his fellow men, but it is precisely because the moral
judgments which he makes are flawed, partial, insensitive,
and inconsistent that we describe him as a great criminal
and not as a great moral reformer. We acknowledge his
independence, but we do not acknowledge him as a judge.
He does not, indeed, allow himself to be guided by what
others see: nevertheless he is incapable of seeing moral
realities for himself. A deeply wicked man may manifest

moral autarky, but his conduct cannot be described as
manifesting moral *autonomy*.

To foster the educand's moral autonomy, then, is to
foster his development as a moral being by fostering his
capacity to reach true judgments concerning the moral
situations by which he may find himself confronted. The
moral judgments which he will make must be more than
abstract and theoretical deliverances, for if they did
not have the most intimate connection with his choices
and actions we should not be prepared to count them as
'*moral* judgments' to begin with. To the extent that a
man can be described as making true moral judgments, to
that extent he must really feel, and be stirred by, the
weight and intensity of the moral realities which make
their demands upon him. In these ways, it is literally
correct to say that the moral education of the adult sets
out to help the educand to become a morally better man or
woman. This does not, of course, mean that in undergoing
moral education a man's essential freedom of choice is in
any way put in abeyance, modified, or abridged, so that
his moral betterment can proceed regardless of his own
will in the matter. In the first place, no such
abridgment could ever be brought about if we are right
in ascribing to the educand an essential freedom of choice
which is both ingenerable and inalienable because inherent
in his nature as an individual human person; (10) moreover, as we saw in Chapter 1, (11) processes which seek to
alter a man's outlook or behaviour without regard to his
own will in the matter or without due respect for his
dignity as a free moral agent cannot even be counted as
processes of 'education' properly so called, far less as
processes of moral education, but are rather to be classi-
fied along with 'conditioning', 'propaganda', 'brainwashing' and other such processes which are admittedly non-
educational and may well be anti-educational in character;
and in any case, if it is part of the meaning of moral
goodness that it can only be displayed by a man exercising
his own free initiatives, there is a clear logical contradiction in the notion of constraining or coercing a man to
become a morally better person. (12) Thus no teacher can
cause a pupil to develop as a moral being. As L.A.Reid
puts it, 'The whole of the process of being educated
depends upon the free independent initiative of the self's
synthesizing activity', (13) and what is true of education
generally is particularly true of moral education. In the
Thomist phrase, the teacher is merely 'the external proximate agent'. When it was said at the beginning of Chapter
4 that a man's education 'transforms his consciousness
itself, stretching, sharpening, and refining it', (14)

this was by no means intended to suggest that the educator could produce a direct alteration in his pupil's consciousness by shaping it in the way that a potter shapes his clay. In moral education (as elsewhere) the most that the teacher can do is to place before the pupil, as clearly as he can, those features of a situation which he confidently expects will elicit appropriate responses from his pupil - in the case of moral education, such responses as admiration, approval, indignation, disgust, and so on - together with the matrix of relevant fact in which these distinctive features are embedded. Moral education consists, not in directly altering the pupil's consciousness in a causal sense but in clearing the path and opening up access to the realities of the moral life, so that the consciousness of the pupil can find its free way home to them. Moral education does not consist in instilling moral values, but simply in making them visible, in order that the pupil can then, if he chooses, reach out to grasp them.

But *how*, exactly, can moral education set out to open up and expound the many different kinds of moral values and render them more clearly visible to the educand? As Protagoras reminded the young Socrates, there are no specialist teachers of virtue. Moral values penetrate so deeply into every aspect of human life; justice and injustice, honesty and dishonesty, consideration and lack of consideration, benevolence and malice, can all announce themselves under so many different guises, in such a variety of circumstances, and are called forth by objects, situations, and events of so many different types; that it is scarcely to be wondered at that no systematic, comprehensive, and unmistakably validated body of moral knowledge exists, to be mastered and expounded by specialist teachers in the way that a specialist teacher can demonstrably master and properly expound the accredited systems of truths which make up, for example, our mathematical knowledge or our historical knowledge. I have not the slightest wish to deny that many important moral truths can be wisely imparted and even, in the clearest cases, proved to the satisfaction of reasonable people. But it would be idle to claim that they can be formed into a systematic body of knowledge comparable to history or mathematics. The attempts of moralists to formulate and systematize our moral convictions, where they are not hopelessly narrow and one-sided, invariably produce systems of so high a level of generality and abstraction that they fail, often dismally, to clarify and resolve the real moral issues which arise in complex living situations - and so, while indeed such general

systems may have great theoretical value, we can scarcely
represent them as bodies of moral knowledge, since moral
knowledge (to be *moral* knowledge) has at least to bite
deeply enough into the actualities of our specific moral
situations to be truly 'prescriptive' in these situations
(and thus to fulfil, in these situations, the central
function of any 'moral' judgment properly so called).
Moral truths - at any rate where they refer to a level of
life of adult complexity, that is, the normal level of
complexity on which human beings must lead their lives
and serious moral decisions must be taken - cannot, it
would seem, be systematically arrayed and imparted as a
single coherent body.

Moral education, then, cannot be undertaken as a
separate and distinct exercise, to be carried out by
competent specialists versed in the teaching of moral
autonomy or moral goodness. University extra-mural departments cannot offer special courses on how to become
a morally better man or woman. It is often said with
regard to schoolchildren that moral education has to be
a function of the whole curriculum. With regard to the
education of adults we can say that moral betterment has
to come, in all kinds of discrete, fragmentary, and
unannounced ways, from many different types of educational
experience, arising within the pursuit of widely different
activities and forms of knowledge. (For this reason alone
we should be entitled to consider a broad and balanced
provision to be a sine qua non of liberal adult education.) The personal example of the teacher is no doubt
of some importance, but it has nothing like the central
importance that it has in the moral education of children.
What is of paramount importance is that the educational
opportunities available to the adult should make it
possible for him to develop his insight into and grasp of
the many different elements which combine to create a
moral situation, so that he can then go on, by his own
efforts and in his own way, to use whatever knowledge and
understanding he has gained to build up a meaningful and
coherent moral basis on which to shape a personal way of
life for which he himself, after all, has to carry the
sole responsibility. The texts for any 'lessons on
Morals', says F.D.Maurice: (15)

> must be furnished by the topic in which we find that
> our pupils are taking the most direct interest,
> whatever that may be. We need care little what the
> occasion is, whether it seems an important or an
> insignificant one in our eyes. It cannot be insignifi-
> cant if it is stirring the hearts of any number of
> people, - if it is deeply stirring the hearts of even

the one or two we are conversing with. If they are
attaching an extravagant consequence to some trivial
point, we shall not make them think less of it, by
treating them or it with scorn. We can only dispossess
them of their exaggeration, by leading them from the
paltry subject-matter to the principle which lies
beneath it, and which really gives them their interest
in it. When they have come into the daylight of a
principle, they will perceive the relevant magnitude of
different objects which were distorted by the twilight
and morning mist.... Lessons on Morals, I think, will
be good for nothing if they are not illustrated from
Biography and History; nay, if biography and history
do not supply the substance of them.

We must never underestimate the importance of a wide
general knowledge of the objective world in the equipment
of a morally educated man. R.M.Hare himself points out
that 'to be able to discern and discover the effects of
our actions is something that the morally educated man has
to have learnt', since 'all our moral education will be
wasted if the products of it are so ignorant that they do
the most terrible things with the best of motives', (16)
and this is undoubtedly a highly relevant consideration.
But the chief, peculiar, and logically inescapable reason
for insisting that moral education has to take place in
and through the student's encounters with the objective
world of general human experience - not only in the
domains of biography and history, psychology and sociology, but also in the domain of physical nature and its
processes, together with the representation of these in
literature and art - is that ultimately moral judgments
have to be rooted in the perception that some actual or
possible state of affairs is intrinsically good or bad,
intrinsically worthy of being brought about or calling
out for us to avert it, and obviously we can only judge
that this is the case if we have some knowledge of the
things, events, processes, thoughts, and actions (all
themselves intrinsically good, bad, or indifferent) which
make up the state of affairs in question. Before we can
judge, for example, that deception, pain, and contempt are
in various degrees intrinsically bad, or that veracity,
pleasure, and affection are in various degrees intrinsically good, we need to know what these very different
kinds of things are, and we need to be able to recognize
them when they occur in different kinds of situation, in
combination with many other kinds of thing, if we hope to
be in a position to make true moral judgments amid the
changing complexities of life as it actually has to be
lived. It is quite useless merely to know in the abstract

that suffering is intrinsically bad, if we have totally
inadequate conceptions of the forms that suffering can
take and are unable to recognize cases of great suffering
when they are set before us. It is quite useless merely
to know in the abstract that affection between human
beings is something to be valued for its own sake, as an
end in itself, if we are totally incapable of determining
what kind and degree of value we ought to attach to, say,
a Christian's cheerful and unselfish love of his fellow
men in comparison with a lover's passionate devotion to
his beloved or a father's affection for his son, because
we lack direct experience of such emotions and have little
or no imaginative grasp of them. Our lack of experience
and understanding will incapacitate us for making genuine
moral judgments in those cases - the vast majority - where
what we are called upon to do is to choose from among a
whole field of competing possibilities which are perhaps
all obviously in general good or bad, but in crucially
different ways and in pertinently different degrees that
need to be wisely and knowledgeably weighed and balanced.
For the adult, at any rate, there is little difficulty in
grasping and assenting to moral principles in the
abstract. Moral doubts and problems arise because we
find it extremely difficult to identify the exact ways
in which a moral principle should be working itself out,
alongside other moral principles, within the concrete
actualities of a practical situation. If a man is to
become morally educated, then, the moral knowledge he
needs to acquire will have to be acquired in and through
his involvement with various other forms of knowledge
(history, the arts, language studies, and so on) which he
may well have elected to pursue for reasons apparently
unconnected with any desire on his part to foster his development as a moral being. (17)

Perhaps the kinds of knowledge which are of greatest
importance in a man's moral education are those which
increase his understanding of himself and give him greater
insight into the minds of others. Clearly the study of
psychology, and of the human sciences generally, can do
much to develop a man's self-understanding and his imaginative insight into the thoughts, feelings, and motives of
other people. But arguably it is through the study of
literature and drama, through a living encounter with the
characters and situations to be found in Racine and Ibsen,
Dostoevsky and George Eliot, that a man's grasp of the
complexities of human nature, and of the moral ambiguities
which haunt the human condition, can be quickened and
extended in the most penetrating and sensitive ways. And
among the most complex human phenomena, which literature,

drama, and the mental and social sciences can in their
different ways illuminate and bring home to him, are the
moral judgments made by other individuals in circumstances
which he himself faces, the moral codes to which the
members of other groups (including deviant groups) adhere
in this or that sphere of their experience, and the
different systems of morality on which whole societies
and civilizations, past and present, have tried or are
trying to base their institutions, their patterns of human
relationship, and their distinctive ways of life. A man's
discovery of new perspectives on old problems can play a
crucial part in his moral education, for the development
of a man's moral autonomy, the development of his capacity
to make true and discerning moral judgments, must in large
measure consist in his freeing himself from narrow prepos-
session and confining habit, from the dominion of the
repetitive and the inert, and in his coming to recognize
the many sides that there are to any moral issue and thus
to appreciate the range and the difficulty of the moral
choices by which he is faced.

Any detailed discussion of the sorts of ingredient
which might furnish the subject-matter of a worthwhile
moral education would itself entail the making of many
substantive moral judgments, and of course it would be
quite out of place to enter into such a discussion here.
The contribution which philosophical analysis can properly
make consists simply in setting out what is logically
involved in the notion of 'moral education', and this task
we have now, I think, carried out in its main essentials.
To contemplate the notion of advancing the moral education
of an adult is to contemplate the notion of his developing, through education, as a moral being and becoming in
some measure a morally better person. Because a moral
agent has to accept responsibility for his choices and
actions, it is appropriate to think of a man's moral development as the building up of his moral autonomy, so
long as this is understood in a broad and positive sense,
as the building up of his capacity to make reasoned and
perceptive moral judgments. This in turn, we have seen,
involves developing a man's knowledge and understanding
of the concrete realities of which our moral experience is
made up - the values and disvalues, the licences and
prohibitions, the manifold options, imperatives, temp-
tations, and ambiguities which distinguish the moral life,
as these assert themselves through an immense variety of
natural objects and events and human actions and reactions
which may converge and mingle to create distinctively
moral situations. Moral education, in short, is the
development of a man's moral awareness. Moral failure

so often results from a lack of direct experience combined
with a failure of *imagination* - for example, a failure to
grasp the plight of others in meaningfully vivid ways -
and thus a great part of moral education consists in
building up a man's capacity to think and feel himself
into situations which he may not yet himself have en-
countered at first hand. Indeed unless a man has been
brought really to *see* the moral realities by which he is
surrounded, and to be stirred in his being by what he
sees - unless, that is, he has developed into a man who
really *feels* the full force and urgency of the moral
demands upon him - we cannot as yet consider him to have
come anywhere near to attaining the status of a morally
educated man.

Two basic questions concerning the moral education of the
adult were put at the beginning of this chapter. We have
seen the answer to one of them. We have seen in what
sense it is possible for education to foster the moral
development of grown men and women. We must now turn to
the remaining question, which has fewer ramifications and
raises fewer issues of principle and on which, therefore,
much less needs to be said. Is it appropriate, we must
ask, is it desirable, that we should include a man's moral
development among the objectives of whatever education he
may be receiving as an adult? On what grounds can we be
justified in setting out to foster the moral development
of someone whom we deem to be already a mature human
being, enjoying the full status of an independent moral
agent?
     In general, of course, the activity of helping our
fellow men to develop morally needs little or no justification. Indeed it is a manifest duty, which we are bound
to perform whenever the opportunity presents itself
(although it is a duty so difficult to perform, and our
confidence that we can perform it successfully is very
often so faint, that we more commonly view it in its
negative aspect as the duty of at least not hindering the
moral development of other people). Admittedly there are
many activities which are manifestly justified, and even
duties, but which nevertheless cannot rightly be regarded
as educational activities. For an activity to be *educationally* justified, it must have as its aim the fuller
development of persons as persons, that is, it must be
specifically directed to building up in a man all those
intrinsically desirable qualities which we deem to be
constitutive of personhood. However, it has been one of
our principal claims throughout this chapter that the

qualities in the building up of which 'moral development'
chiefly consists - such qualities as love, compassion,
tolerance, considerateness, honesty, fairness of mind -
while they have great instrumental value and would be well
worth fostering in an individual for the benefits which
they confer on society at large, are aslo of the very
highest intrinsic value and are above all to be fostered
because moral goodness, in itself and apart from all
consequences, takes first place among all the things that
we rightly prize and admire for their own sakes. The
qualities which chiefly make up what we think of as 'moral
goodness' constitute by far the main source and ground of
a man's intrinsic worth as a person. And thus, given that
it is in some measure possible, the moral education of the
adult must surely present itself to us as something
supremely worth undertaking. (18)

While an 'adult' is someone who is already presumed to
possess a certain moral stature, we have seen that the
moral qualities he is presumed to possess are merely the
minimum qualities stipulated for bare admission to the
status of adulthood, and that in ascribing the status of
adulthood to someone we only presume him to have these
qualities in some minimum degree. (19) In any case,
however mature a man may be, as long as he is human there
will still be many moral lessons for him to learn and many
moral errors for him to correct. But in claiming that his
further growth as a moral being can (at least in part) be
accomplished by processes of education, are we not in some
danger of attributing to those who are responsible for his
education a kind of moral superiority over him which would
be not only invidious but also out of keeping with the
evident facts, since teachers of adults do not seem to be
conspicuously higher moral beings than the adults whom
they teach? We take for granted that the teacher of
children will be at a higher stage of moral development
than his pupils, with a greater breadth of insight and a
surer capacity for making moral discriminations, but we
by no means feel obliged to make any such assumptions
about the teacher of adults.

Such fears that a recognition of the moral development
of the student as one of the objectives of adult education
would result in ascribing to the teacher a quite un-
warranted moral superiority are, I think, utterly
groundless. In the first place, we must remember that
the teacher of adults, unlike the teacher of children, is
not placed in a position of general authority over his
students. His students, who may be forty, fifty, or sixty
years of age or even older, are in no sense his 'charges',
and it would be absurd to think of him as in loco parentis

towards them. It would be absurd to imagine that society
might have entrusted him with some kind of general superintendence over the moral development of men and women
whom he probably sees for only two or three hours a week,
for six months of the year, and who may well be members of
his class during one particular year only. And in the
second place, we must remember that the individual teacher
makes his appearance, not as a teacher of morality, but as
a teacher of history, literature, philosophy, sociology,
and so on. In teaching his subject, he may or may not
focus explicitly on its moral dimensions or on the relevance of this or that fact, concept, or generalization to
this or that moral issue. Whether he does so or not,
however, his subject itself will often present his
students with data for moral reflection: of itself it
will often create opportunities for the student to gain
fresh moral insights and will open up for him bodies of
meaningful experience that may clarify the ways in which
moral principles define themselves in concrete human
situations. If we feel obliged to think in terms of a
'moral teacher', we shall often have to say that it is
the individual student, studying perhaps history or literature under someone whose role is that of a specialist
teacher of these subjects, who is operating as his own
moral teacher. And certainly, the responsibility for
building up his personal moral character and for weaving
whatever knowledge and understanding he has gained into a
meaningful pattern of moral convictions on which to base
his life is a responsibility that must rest on the
shoulders of the student alone. Certainly, in the last
analysis the moral education of the adult has to be a form
of self-education.

Some critics might have misgivings about the notion of
moral education, even when viewed as a form of self-
education, on the grounds that the complexities of actual
living situations rendered the making of moral judgments
so very difficult and the validity of our purported moral
insights so very questionable that we were seldom if ever
entitled to claim that moral 'learning' had taken place.
They might object that to claim we had 'learned' moral
truths, in any educationally reputable sense akin to the
senses in which we undoubtedly learn scientific truths or
sociological truths, would be to deceive ourselves, and
perhaps also to impose on the credulity of others. However, while undeniably moral issues are very often complex
and difficult, objections such as these are surely based
on far too bleak an estimate of what moral inquiry and
moral reasoning can achieve. Admittedly our moral
judgments are nearly always tinged with doubt, but so are

many of our scientific and our sociological judgments.
Cognitive certainty - I do not mean logical certainty, of
the kind attainable in pure mathematics, for example, but
rather the degree of confidence we are entitled to repose
in our beliefs, given the evidence or reasons for them
that we have in fact managed to assemble at any given
point of our inquiries - *is* very much a matter of degree,
and although we can claim a much higher degree of cognitive certainty on behalf of our scientific or sociological
beliefs, we are surely entitled to claim *some* measure of
certainty on behalf of some of our moral beliefs at any
rate. Even if all our moral beliefs were highly doubtful,
we should still be confronted by moral choices which we
could not escape from making, and in such cases it would
clearly be the part of a rational being to act upon that
belief which seemed to be at all events the least doubtful
among all those he had been able to consider: in this
sense, clearly, one moral belief can be described with
perfect correctness as 'more reasonable' than another.

Of course it might be urged, not only that moral
beliefs are difficult to validate, but also that the
procedures to be used in validating them are far from
generally agreed; and furthermore, that there is disagreement about the very criteria by reference to which
one moral belief can count as 'less doubtful' or 'more
doubtful' than another. There is some truth in these
allegations, but again the question is surely one of
degree. Historians often disagree on the procedures to
be used in validating some assertion about a past event,
and even when all the available evidence is generally
known and accepted among them they may disagree about
whether the assertion can count as 'warranted', and in
what measure, in the light of this evidence. Moreover,
while there is certainly disagreement about criteria and
procedures in the moral sphere, it can hardly be denied
that there is also a fair measure of agreement, which
ought not to be underestimated. Plain men, taking actual
moral decisions, are seldom in the quandaries which moral
philosophers would seem to like to wish upon them. When
Smith is at variance with Brown about the gravity of some
particular act of delinquency, he knows that if Brown can
once be convinced that the particular disputed act is an
instance of a certain recognizable *type* of act (unauthor-
ized use of the firm's telephone as an instance of
'stealing', say) he will almost certainly come to view the
act in question with the same degree of seriousness that
Smith himself does; and although Brown does not accept
Smith's view of the matter, the two men are at least
likely to agree about the validity of this kind of

procedure, with the analogical and other perfectly reputable sorts of reasoning involved, as one clear method of trying to arrive at the moral truth. Even when two men explicitly differ about the intrinsic goodness or badness of some *type* of thing, on the empirical characterization of which they completely agree (racial discrimination, say) - and this, I submit, is a much less frequent species of moral difference - there are various relevant and often fruitful procedures which they can adopt, and which people commonly do adopt, in their efforts to determine which view of the matter is the right one. Thus John can invite James to *inspect* the disputed type of phenomenon more closely and from fresh standpoints, in an attempt to get him to see what the experience of being discriminated against on the ground of one's race is really *like,* perhaps by presenting him with concrete examples from real life or from imaginative literature for fuller and closer inspection. He can invite him to compare racial discrimination with other forms of discrimination which he already acknowledges to be evils, such as discrimination on grounds of sex or social class. He can invite him to consider whether it really is the phenomenon of racial discrimination which is eliciting his approval or whether it is not perhaps something else, some essentially distinct type of phenomenon which may indeed be genuinely good - a stable social order, perhaps, or a distribution of social rewards according to people's deserts - which he rightly or wrongly supposes to be a feature of societies based upon policies of racial discrimination and which he is mistakenly identifying with the latter. From the fact that two men diverge absolutely in their most basic feeling responses to some distinctive type of phenomenon it by no means follows that they are wholly without ways and means of trying to settle their differences. And since we cannot escape from the making of moral choices, even if the procedures for settling our moral differences were much more sharply disputed than they actually are and even if the degree of cognitive certainty attainable by our moral judgments was very much lower than it actually is this should still not deter us from trying to reach moral judgments which are as reasoned and discerning as within these limitations they can be held to be. Nor should it deter us from trying to improve our capacity to make such judgments: it should not deter us from undertaking the business of moral education and trying to carry it out as well as we can.

We have argued that the moral education of the adult will take place, not as a separate and distinct exercise, but as an offshoot of many different types of educational

experience, arising within the pursuit of widely different
activities and forms of knowledge. To this the objection
might be made that an undertaking so conceived runs the
risk of violating one of the fundamental proprieties which
every process of education has to observe if we are to
deem it worthy of being dignified and distinguished by the
name of 'education'. It runs the risk of failing to
ensure that the educand has a sufficient awareness of the
nature of the process in which he is participating, for
there is a risk that the educand may not perceive that the
experiences to which he is exposing himself are likely to
have the effect of shaping the patterns of his subsequent
development as a moral being.

Now, it is undoubtedly true that a man who has elected
to study literature, say, for reasons that are not
obviously connected with any desire on his part to foster
his development as a moral being, may nevertheless - as a
direct result of his involvement with literature - acquire
a deeper insight into moral problems and a heightened
appreciation of the many forms that good and evil can
take, and so may significantly advance his moral development without having explicitly set out to do so. But we
might well wonder how many adults in fact elect to study
literature, or philosophy, psychology, economics, history,
or any branch of the humanities, in total ignorance of, or
indifference to, the moral aspects of their intended
study; we might surmise that its acknowledged moral
relevance in fact figures largely among the reasons
inducing many adults to commit themselves to a study of
a subject of these kinds, supplementing and reinforcing
whatever interest they may have in the distinctive content
and procedures of the subject for its own sake. Certainly, when his study of such a subject is well and truly
under way, the adult will nearly always find himself
consciously accosted and swayed by the moral promptings
which arise from it. In coming to grips with the ideas
of Freud or Sartre, with classical economic theory or the
institutions of the welfare state, he will be led to
confront moral assumptions and patterns of moral thinking
which may place whole areas of his life in question, and
when this happens he will nearly always be intensely
aware, perhaps uncomfortably aware, that he is being led
to reappraise the grounds of his most basic moral
judgments and the matrix of values in which they have
hitherto been encased.

Admittedly, in the exceptional case of a man who was
not aware that his moral percipience and understanding
were being in various ways developed by the studies in
which he was engaged, we could not in strict propriety

say that the process he was undergoing was a process of
moral 'education'. We should have to express the matter,
rather more cautiously, by saying merely that the various
processes of education in which he was engaged (historical, literary, philosophical, or whatever they might be)
were in fact resulting in his further development as a
moral being. But provided that he really was refining and
not blurring his perceptions, that he really was extending
and not narrowing his understanding, it is obvious that we
should still have to consider this a highly desirable
result. We perhaps do well to remember that very many men
and women rise to considerable heights of moral attainment
in the course of their adult lives without the benefit of
anything that could remotely be called moral education and
indeed (since many adults take no part in any kind of educational activities properly so called) often without the
help of any kind of further or higher education at all.
The moral advances made by grown men and women - and also
of course their moral regressions - commonly result from
the fortuitous challenges and responsibilities, the
unforeseen opportunities and setbacks, of their daily
lives, not from processes of education or from any
conscious intention on their part to promote their further
development as moral beings. Until education comes to
occupy a central place in the lives of most adults, this
is how things are likely to remain. For this reason, and
also because the most careful projects of moral education
are attended by peculiar difficulties rendering them
uncertain of clear success, we seldom expect to find any
very close connection between a man's educational level
and the moral stature to which he has risen in the course
of his adult life. We all know morally outstanding people
who have received very little education either as children
or as adults, but who manifest the keenest moral percipience and display the surest grasp of delicate moral
issues; and we know many people who in other respects
are rightly considered to be very well educated indeed
but when confronted by a real moral problem show themselves up to be the most pathetic moral dunces.

However, none of this amounts to an argument against
moral education. In all education we are making a
conscious and deliberate attempt to develop in a man
various qualities of awareness which might indeed be developed in him by the fortuitous experiences of daily
life, but which life - if left to itself - would be likely
to develop in him slowly, fitfully, haphazardly, and at an
unnecessarily high cost (that is, if it enlarged his
awareness at all and did not instead shrink, distort, and
impoverish it). Underlying all education is the con-

viction that so pre-eminently worthwhile an outcome as the
building up of persons in their personhood is something
that we ought consciously to strive to bring about, not
passively leave to the blind workings of life's random
processes, and clearly it is this conviction which also
underlies and justifies our endeavours in the realm of
moral education. Because we cannot lay claim to an
organized, comprehensive, and unmistakably validated body
of moral knowledge which could be mastered and taught as
a single coherent system, and because values in abstraction from the things possessing value lack the
prescriptive force without which they cease to *be*
'values', we have to recognize that the moral education
of adults, when it takes place, will take place at a
thousand different points of their educational experience
and within the framework of widely different forms of
knowledge, and for this reason we shall seldom be able to
offer any very confident estimate of the kind or degree of
success that our hopes of moral education have met with.
The teacher of a subject will nearly always be conscious
of the opportunities for moral education presented when
some historical event, some incident in a novel, or some
situation in a drama confronts his adult students with
issues of general moral relevance. But because moral
issues can take so many different forms, and because the
life-experience of different individuals can differ in so
many subtle but crucial ways, only the individual student
himself can judge the precise kind and degree of relevance
which the topic studied has for his special moral doubts
and questionings; and this amounts to saying that only
the individual student himself can judge when the topic
studied is throwing light on his uncertainties, refocusing
his moral perceptions, and acquainting him with new
aspects of good and evil, justice and injustice, wisdom
and folly - in short, furnishing him with materials for
his continuing moral education. In every form of adult
education, as we shall see in Part Three, the responsibility for an individual's progress has ultimately to be
borne by the individual himself. But this is peculiarly
so in the case of moral education, with its peculiar
difficulties, in particular the difficulty of building
our accumulating moral insights into a clearly articulated
and fully demonstrated system. Of course, from the fact
that a man is ultimately responsible for his own moral
education it by no means follows that he, at least, is
capable of forming an exact and reliable estimate of the
progress he is in fact making, for we are all liable to go
very far wrong in our estimations of our own moral
stature. However, a man who is genuinely making an

attempt to deepen and extend his moral understanding and
sensitivity can at any rate be credited with one undoubted
moral virtue from the outset. To show concern, in a
clear-sighted and purposeful way, for one's development as
a moral being is at any rate to show one's determination
to take seriously that which, of all the things in one's
life, surely demands to be taken with the utmost seriousness. If we can seldom confidently assure ourselves that
our efforts in the sphere of moral education have been
successful in this or that respect and to this or that
degree, we can at any rate be sure that - whether viewed
as expressing a general moral aspiration or as a particular form of educational endeavour - our efforts are
supremely worth the making and are at least a sign of
some kind of emerging grace in those who make them.

Educational processes

Part **III**

Teaching and learning 6

So far we have analysed the concept of adult education
entirely in terms of its objectives. The education of
adults is the attempt to foster the development of grown
men and women as persons, and this, we have argued,
consists essentially in the fostering of their continued
growth as centres of awareness, as conscious selves who
perceive, feel, imagine, judge, appreciate, and understand
more fully, more sensitively, and more profoundly than
ever before. To develop a man's awareness is to put him
in closer and more meaningful touch with reality, to give
him a surer and more comprehensive grasp of his condition
and that of his fellows, and is thus best expressed in
terms of deepening and extending his *knowledge*: a man's
pursuit of education, we have claimed, is his pursuit of
knowledge in all its principal forms, for in building up
richer and more finely wrought structures of knowledge and
understanding a man is building up his very being as a
centre of awareness, as a mind. The dimensions of a man's
mental development to which we have given special attention are his development as a rational being, capable
of thinking clearly and consistently and with due regard
to standards of intellectual honesty and objectivity, and
his development as a moral being, capable of making
balanced and discerning moral judgments and of finding
his own way, by what we might call *sage feeling,* to the
manifold moral realities which make their imperative
demands upon him.

However, the concept of adult education is more than
the concept of certain characteristic objectives. In
speaking of 'education' we are not merely referring to
the fuller development of persons in their personhood:
we are also attributing this intrinsically desirable
outcome to the taking of certain appropriate measures.
As we saw in Chapter 1, there is a 'task' as well as an

'achievement' aspect to the concept of education. All
education, and therefore all adult education, involves the
mounting of operations, the following of procedures, the
initiation and pursuit of various activities which are
undertaken and carried out as ongoing patterns of events
unfolding in and across time. The concept of adult education, in short, is the concept of certain characteristic
processes which men and women can set in motion and in
which they can take an ongoing part, as well as of a
characteristic destination towards which, it is intended,
these processes will carry them. Naturally, only those
processes which carry the adult towards the right destination can even begin to be considered as processes of
adult education properly so called; the paths leading to
a given destination are the distinctive paths they are
partly because of the direction in which they distinctively lead; in other words, the measures taken by educators
only count as *educational* measures if they are directed to
a distinctively educational achievement. Obviously, then,
any processes of teaching and learning which we are
prepared to dignify by the name of 'educational processes'
must first of all satisfy the 'achievement' criterion of
an educational process. But in the second place they must
satisfy a quite different kind of criterion, one which is
more peculiarly connected with their nature as activities
or tasks and which we may therefore call the specifically
'task' criterion of an educational process. Thus in
Chapter 1 we saw that there are certain inherent proprieties, inseparably bound up with the values implicit in
personhood itself, which must be respected and upheld by
any process of education properly so called. Even if they
resulted in his development as a person, we should not
consider that the processes a man was undergoing were
educational processes if he was wholly unaware of the
nature of what was happening to him, if it was happening
to him against his will, if there was no kind of conscious
control or direction of the situations to which he was
being exposed, if these were utterly devoid of any kind
of interpersonal encounter, or if he remained completely
passive and inert throughout. In an educational process
properly so called the educand participates wittingly,
voluntarily, and actively, the whole process is under some
degree of formal direction and control, and to some degree
at least it partakes of the nature of a meeting of minds.
There are, then, we may conclude, two quite different
kinds of criteria, both of which a bona fide educational
process must satisfy in some sufficient degree. A bona
fide educational process must in the first place foster
the development of persons in their personhood; and,

second, it must perform this task in educationally acceptable ways.

We must now go on, in this chapter and the one that follows, to analyse the concept of an educational process in somewhat greater detail, giving special consideration to the ways in which the cognitive and ethical stipulations built into this concept receive new emphasis and sharper definition in their application to the education of adults. We shall not, of course, be concerned with empirical questions in educational psychology or with practical questions about teaching methods, but rather with the conceptual and normative questions which arise in connection with the education of adults when this is viewed as a set of activities in which people engage or a set of processes which they undergo. We shall, that is to say, be concerned with the requirements which any process of teaching or learning must satisfy if it is to count as a genuinely 'educational' process, and with the characteristic ways in which the processes of teaching and learning that go on in connection with the education of adults can be deemed to satisfy these requirements.

Clearly our first task - which will fully occupy us for the rest of the present chapter - must be to examine the concepts of 'teaching' and 'learning' in general. And of the two it is clearly the concept of 'learning' which is the logically primary one, since as a matter of logic learning can take place without any sort of teaching taking place but whenever we can correctly say that teaching is going on there must necessarily be some sort of learning going on. What precisely are we stating, then, when we state that a man has 'learned' something?

We are, of course, stating that a man has acquired knowledge of some kind, and it might seem obvious that we are therefore stating that, as a result of some relevant perception or inference on his part, (1) he has become aware of something of which he had not hitherto been aware. To learn, perhaps by hearing it from a neighbour or by seeing heavy equipment arrive, that road repairs are about to begin outside one's house is to become aware of the fact that road repairs are about to begin outside one's house. Thus written into the concept of 'learning' is the concept of a certain achievement - an extension of awareness - which is closely related to the distinctive achievement that we have already found to be central to anything that we are prepared to call 'education', but which nevertheless must, I think, be clearly differentiated from this latter. In becoming aware of something for the first time we may be correctly said to have 'learned' something even if what we have learned is completely

trivial (as when one learns that one has a mole on the
back of one's arm), but we do not count some extension of
our awareness as a contribution to our 'education' unless
what we have become aware of has some degree of real
cognitive value and can be thought of as in some degree
contributing to our overall mental development. The
cognitive achievement written into the concept of
'learning' in general is subject to no such normative re-
strictions, and therefore in general, we may claim, whenever it can correctly be said of a man that he has
'learned' something, of whatever character and for whatever reason, we can correctly say of him that he has extended his awareness, and whenever it can correctly be
said of a man that as a result of some relevant perception
or inference on his part he has extended his awareness, we
can correctly say of him that he has 'learned' something.

However, to this way of putting the matter there are
notorious objections. To analyse the concept of learning
in terms of an extension of awareness, it will be objected, is to base one's analysis far too heavily on those
types of learning which involve learning *that* something is
the case, the learning of truths, and to fail to do
justice to those other types of learning which involve
learning *how* to do something, the learning of skills.
Perhaps a man's learning that road repairs are about to
begin outside his house or that he has a mole on the back
of his arm can plausibly be rendered as his becoming-
aware-of these things, but surely, the critic will object,
any account of what it is to learn to tie a knot, to
dance, to drive a car, or to grow one's own vegetables
must centre on the learner's acquisition of the ability
to *do* these things, his acquisition of the ability actually to carry out a distinctive range of operations at or
above some minimum level of competence. In the learning
of skills at any rate (linguistic skills and the skills
involved in intellectual inquiry, as well as practical and
artistic skills) is not the claim that a man has learned
something essentially the claim that, as a result of
relevant perceptions or inferences on his part, a man has
come to *modify his behaviour* in some way signifying
greater efficiency? (2)

If by a man's 'behaviour' we mean his bodily movements
or patterns of bodily movement, this question is easily
answered. The answer is, No. Even with regard to physical skills, like the tying of knots, we can conceive of
learning taking place without any relevant modifications
of the learner's behaviour taking place. By dint of
careful watching and listening, a limbless man might well
learn how to tie many quite complicated knots, although

because of his handicap it was physically impossible that
he should ever actually tie any of them. He would know
how to tie a running bowline on Tuesday, having been
ignorant of how to do it on Monday; he might even be able
to teach others; and we should certainly have to acknowledge that he had 'learned' how to tie the knot; but
what we clearly could not say was that any relevant modification of his behaviour had occurred. (For the benefit
of a behaviourist who claimed that at least anything the
learner *said* about knots would be different from now on
and so his 'verbal behaviour' would have been modified,
let us turn our limbless man into a mute as well or - if
we feel compunction about doing this - let us simply
ascribe to him an invincible taciturnity on the subject
of knots.)

Thus, if we equate 'the modification of a man's behaviour' with the actual *occurrence* of changes in the way
he behaves we must not say that a logically necessary
condition of 'learning' having taken place is that a man's
behaviour shall have been modified. And indeed, even if
we equate 'the modification of a man's behaviour' merely
with his acquisition of the *ability* to behave differently,
we still cannot say that a logically necessary condition
of 'learning' having taken place is that a man's behaviour
shall have been modified, since - as our last example
shows - a man may have learned how to perform some physical task but may nevertheless remain quite unable to
perform it. Of course, the term 'ability' is extremely
ambiguous and no doubt there is a sense of 'ability' in
which some people might attribute to a man the ability to
perform some task which, because of physical incapacity,
it was manifestly impossible that he should ever in fact
perform. Our limbless man's teacher, in giving an account
of his pupil's progress, might say that he was now able to
tie a running bowline but not yet able to tie a clove
hitch. In such a case, however, the attribution of the
'ability' to perform the task carries no implications
about probable future behaviour but is simply a way of
saying that a man 'knows how' to do something which
nevertheless in fact cannot do - and this in turn, it is
now clear, must be taken to mean that he has a thorough
mental grasp of the procedures which the task involves,
that he is thoroughly *aware of* the·common pitfalls, and
that he is thoroughly *acquainted with* the measures by
which these may be avoided or overcome.

In an attempt to escape this conclusion, a behaviourist
will argue that the notion of 'being able' to do something
logically involves an allusion at least to what we might
call a man's hypothetical behaviour, that is, to his

tendency-to-behave-in-some-given-way-if certain conditions
are satisfied. The behaviourist will claim that a man who
has learned to tie a running bowline has acquired the
ability to tie running bowlines in the sense that *if* this,
that, and the other condition were satisfied he actually
would successfully tie a real running bowline. However,
this kind of claim in this context surely calls for two
obvious comments. First, it is in principle impossible
to specify all the conditions that would need to be
satisfied if a person was actually to behave in some way
hypothetically ascribed to him: no doubt our limbless
man would actually tie a first-class running bowline if
he were not limbless, but of course only if also he were
not struck down by paralysis or overcome by fatigue, and
if also his fingers were not numbed by cold or his brain
addled by drink or drugs, and if he did not happen to fall
victim to this, that, or the other disabling circumstance
... but clearly the specification of each and every relevant enabling or disabling circumstance cannot even in
theory be carried out. Second, it is hard to see what
considerations could possibly lead us to ascribe a
tendency-to-behave-in-some-given-way to a learner who has
never actually behaved in this way and perhaps manifestly
never will, other than our conviction that the learner in
question has *mentally* grasped what has to be done in order
to perform some given task, or in other words our conviction that he is thoroughly aware of what means need to
be employed and what steps need to be taken to attain some
given end. If we feel inclined to claim that in happier
circumstances our limbless pupil would have tied a first-
class running bowline, even although we know he never in
fact will, surely this can only be because we feel confident that when he runs through the whole task in his mind
he gets the whole thing right. In short, it can only be
because we feel confident that he has *learned* it - for we
do in fact rightly equate 'learning' how to perform a task
with acquiring a thorough mental grasp of how it should be
done, whatever our opinion concerning the learner's
probable future behaviour.

However we construe the notion of a 'modification of
behaviour', then, even in the case of physical skills we
cannot say that a logically necessary condition of
'learning' having taken place is that the learner's
behaviour shall have been modified in some relevant way.
No doubt it often proves to be the case that practising
the carrying out of the actual physical operations involved in some skill is by far the best method of bringing
learning about, but the excellence of a means does not
oblige us to count it as part of the end. No doubt, too,

by far the most conspicuous result of learning some skill
is generally that the learner will henceforth carry out
the physical operations involved in the skill with reasonable efficiency in most circumstances, but to say that one
thing is the result of another thing is to acknowledge
that what we have to do with is a relation between two
things quite distinct in themselves. And no doubt a
competent carrying out of the relevant physical operations
usually offers by far the best evidence that some given
skill has been learned; but from the fact that some occurrence offers excellent evidence of some achievement we
cannot conclude that the occurrence in question itself
constitutes part of the achievement in question.

Much the same considerations apply to the learning of
mental skills. If by a person's 'behaviour' we still mean
his bodily movements or patterns of bodily movement,
including speech and writing, we are bound to insist that
the idea of learning a language or learning to do quadratic equations does not have the idea of any sort of
behavioural modifications logically written into it.
There is nothing self-contradictory in the idea of someone
learning French but never going on to speak or write in
French or to read anything written in that language.
(Indeed this is all too common an outcome of much of the
learning done by schoolchildren.) There is nothing self-
contradictory in the idea of someone learning to work out
quadratic equations in his head but never expressing these
in speech or writing or using them for any practical
purpose. Of course, this is because the operations essentially involved in a distinctively mental skill are
essentially mental operations, essentially activities of
mind not pieces of physical behaviour: nevertheless,
there is still nothing self-contradictory in the idea of
someone learning how to carry out these essentially mental
operations but never thereafter carrying them out even in
his mind, for a man might learn how to do quadratic
equations but never give these a thought during the whole
of the rest of his life.

However, the concept of learning a mental skill does
diverge from the concept of learning a physical skill in
one crucial respect. Whereas a man may learn how to carry
out the operations involved in some physical skill while
in fact remaining physically unable to carry them out, it
does not make sense to speak of a man learning how to
carry out the operations involved in some mental skill
while in fact remaining mentally unable to carry out the
operations in question. It is logically possible to learn
how to tie a running bowline while remaining physically
unable to tie a running bowline, but it is not logically

possible to learn how to work out quadratic equations
while remaining mentally unable to carry out this essentially mental task. Of course, when we say that a man
'is able' to work out quadratic equations, what we are
saying is not that he actually *would* successfully work out
some quadratic equation *if* this, that, and the other condition were satisfied (if he were not acutely depressed,
if he were not subject to intolerable interruptions and
distractions, and so on), for a complete list of every
relevant condition which would need to be satisfied cannot
even in theory be compiled. What we are saying is that he
has some adequate degree of mastery of the rules governing
the correct working-out of quadratic equations, where
'mastery' consists in being fully and clearly aware of
what these rules are and of how and when they apply. We
may certainly agree, then, that a man cannot be thought of
as having learned to do quadratic equations unless he has
acquired the ability to *do* quadratic equations - but what
this amounts to saying is that he has not learned this
particular skill unless he has acquired a thorough mental
grasp of a certain set of procedures and the rules governing these, and what *this* amounts to saying is that he has
not learned the skill unless he has arrived at a clear
awareness of what constitutes and what does not constitute
a properly worked out quadratic equation. The cognitive
achievement logically enshrined in the concept of
'learning' a mental skill - and indeed also, for the
reasons we have seen, in the concept of 'learning' a
physical skill - can, we may submit, be fully defined in
terms of an active and systematic extension of the
learner's awareness.

Thus it cannot be a logically necessary condition of
someone's having learned some skill (whether physical or
mental) that he shall have come to modify his behaviour,
if 'modifying one's behaviour' is supposed to be contrasted with 'extending one's awareness'. A man might be
correctly described as having learned some given skill
although he might never subsequently put what he has
learned into practice; and if we felt inclined to credit
such a man with a tendency, or at least an ability, to
perform the various operations characteristic of the skill
he has learned, this could only be because we considered
him to be fully conversant with - that is, fully aware of
- the various instrumentalities or means-end connections
which these involve in the case of a physical skill, or
the various rules and principles of procedure by which the
operations in question are governed in the case of a
mental skill. The logically necessary condition of
someone's having learned some skill, we may conclude, is

not that his physical behaviour shall have been modified
but rather that his awareness shall have been extended in
some relevant way.

Given that this is so, however, it clearly follows that
an appropriate modification of someone's behaviour cannot
even be regarded as a logically *sufficient* condition of
his having learned some skill, if 'behaviour' is still
being contrasted with 'awareness'. It is not enough that
a man's fingers should come to move about in ways which
result in a running bowline making its appearance. Unless
the movements of his fingers are continuously informed and
directed by a guiding awareness, we are not entitled to
speak of him as 'acting' at all; and unless the movements
of his fingers are informed and directed by an awareness
of the distinctive means-end connections and instrumental
sequences which go to make up the tying of a running
bowline, we are not strictly entitled to say of him that
he is a man engaged in the distinctive act of 'tying a
running bowline'. This does not mean that the man tying
a knot has to be concentrating or pondering on what he is
doing, mentally reviewing every feature of the exercise
and going over each step in the exercise in his mind as
he executes it with his fingers. Obviously the more adept
a man is, the more the task on which he is engaged can
slip into the background of his awareness while his
attention is active elsewhere. But we can never be literally *unaware of* anything we are actually engaged in doing
(though no doubt we may carelessly put the matter in this
way when what we mean is that we are not at all heeding
what we are doing), and the proof of this is that the
moment we meet a slight check or obstacle or even
something slightly unusual - the moment our fingers touch
a frayed part of the rope we are vacantly knotting whilst
our attention is held by the interesting scene in the
harbour - our attention will veer sharply back to the task
in hand and to the particular item which has just an-
nounced itself to our hitherto relaxed and casual
awareness. The man who can dance, drive a car, cut hair,
or tie a running bowline while giving his mind to other
things is not unaware of the operations he is carrying out
or the circumstances affecting them; he may in fact be
aware of a great deal more than is the conscientious tyro,
brows knit as he strives to keep every feature of his
unfamiliar task in view. We may be tempted to think of
the skilled practitioner as unaware or scarcely aware of
the operations he is carrying out, when the truth is that
he is more fully aware, but *effortlessly* aware, of what he
is doing, taking in at a glance, as it were, everything
that the tyro has to laboriously pick out, identify, and
docket.

Thus in learning a skill a man is doing much more than replacing one set of bodily movements by another, more efficient, set of bodily movements. By adjusting the arm movements of a mechanical puppet we might cause it to produce a variety of knots in any piece of rope with which we fed it, but we could never say of a puppet that it had 'learned' how to tie a knot. Partly, of course, this is because a puppet cannot perceive or infer, and, as we have seen, all 'learning' properly so called results from some relevant perception or inference (or set of perceptions or inferences) on the part of the learner. But principally it is because the *achievement* logically enshrined in the notion of 'learning' is an achievement which is possible only for a conscious being, that is, for a being who can not only do things but can do them intentionally and with full awareness of what he is doing, and to whom alone therefore terms like 'skill', 'competence', 'mastery', and so on can be properly applied. In normal circum- stances, to be sure, we certainly expect the bodily movements of a man who has learned how to tie a running bowline to differ significantly from the bodily movements of a man who has not learned how to tie this knot. We should, however, be completely wrong to suppose that the difference between the two men was essentially a differ- ence in respect of their outward physical behaviour. On the contrary, the difference between the man who knows and the man who does not know how to carry out a given task is, I think we may now confidently claim, essentially a difference in respect of their inward mental condition.

When we say that someone has 'learned' something, then - be it a truth or a skill, be it a mental skill or a physical skill - we are not necessarily saying anything whatever about his past, present, or future behaviour. The connection between learning and behavioural change is empirical and contingent, not conceptual and necessary. Whether any behavioural changes have occurred or not, we are entitled to assert that learning has taken place when- ever someone has become aware of something he was not previously aware of (some set of rules or instrumentali- ties, in the case of 'learning how'), provided that the new knowledge he has acquired really is knowledge and not error, and provided that it has been gained by processes involving relevant mental activity on the part of the learner (seeing or hearing that something is so, for example, or working out that it must be so) not by processes by-passing relevant mental activity on the part of the learner (such as the administration of drugs or natural processes of maturation) - and we are entitled to assert that learning has taken place only when each and

all of these conditions have been fulfilled. The conceptual and necessary connection holds, not between
learning and behavioural change, but between learning and
awareness. In saying that a man has learned to tie some
knot, we are logically implying that he was in some degree
aware of what he was doing and what was happening to him
while he was learning, and that he is now in some degree
aware of what he is doing when he is tying this knot or of
what he would be doing if he were tying it. Learning, we
may conclude - of all kinds and at all levels - is essentially a becoming-aware.

Our analysis of the concept of learning has, I think,
supplied us with most of what we need for a correct
analysis of the concept of teaching. We may define
'teaching' quite simply as 'the stimulation of learning'.
To teach someone something is to foster his learning of
that thing. It is to take measures which may be correctly
regarded as contributing to a learner's mastery of some
body of knowledge or some skill. Of course, a man may
learn something without being taught. It is not a necessary condition of learning taking place that teaching
shall have taken place. However, it is, I suggest, a
logically necessary condition of *teaching* taking place
that *learning* shall be taking place, at least in the most
frequently used sense of the word 'teaching'. In its most
frequently used sense, 'teaching' is an achievement-word.
The concept of teaching - like the concepts of curing,
breaking, killing, or transporting but unlike the concepts
of running, talking, sneezing, or laughing - is the
concept of an activity which leads to a characteristic
outcome and which therefore has the concept of this
outcome logically built into it. From the sole fact that
running, talking, sneezing, or laughing is going on we
cannot infer that anything else whatsoever is happening
in the world as a consequence. But from the sole fact
that curing, breaking, killing, or transporting has taken
place we can validly infer that something once unhealthy
is now healthy, something once whole is now in parts,
something once living is now dead, and something once
located at point p^1 is now located at point p^2. For in
these cases the concept of the activity in question logically incorporates the concept of a distinctive outcome or
result. And from the sole fact that teaching has taken
place we can validly infer that someone once unaware of
something is now aware of that thing: we can validly
infer that learning has taken place, since the assertion
of this distinctive outcome is, I suggest, logically

incorporated in any assertion we may make that what has been taking place really does deserve the name of 'teaching'. For it would surely be self-contradictory to assert that Jones had taught Smith how to read a map but that Smith still did not know how to read a map.

Admittedly, ordinary English usage permits us to speak of Brown as engaged in teaching his subject to pupils who, for whatever reasons, are in fact learning nothing. However, all this shows, I think, is that ordinary usage is haphazard and unsystematic and that a clear definition of 'teaching', or of any other word, will inevitably fall foul of ordinary usage at some point or other. The most we can do is to try to frame a self-consistent definition which will capture as wide a range of the ordinary uses of the word as possible, and do as little violence to ordinary usage as possible. Thus in this particular instance we obviously can, if we choose, say that both Jones and Brown have been 'teaching' but that Jones alone has been 'successfully teaching' his subject to his pupil. Alternatively, we can say that only Jones has been 'teaching' his subject to his pupil, and that Brown has been merely 'trying to teach' his subject to his pupils. And nothing forces us to adopt the one usage rather than the other. Nevertheless for overall convenience we do well, I suggest, to prefer the latter usage, which preserves the achievement element in 'teaching'. For although in ordinary English we may say that a man successfully taught his pupils to speak Russian, we should not normally say of someone that he had unsuccessfully taught his pupils to speak Russian: we should undoubtedly prefer to say that he had *tried* to teach them (and failed - that is, failed to *teach* them). Nor should we normally want to say that someone had wasted a year teaching a class to appreciate good poetry, or to commiserate with such a teacher; if commiseration were called for, we should normally prefer to say that he had wasted a year *trying* (and failing) to teach his class to appreciate good poetry.

It cannot be too heavily emphasized that nothing of substance hinges on how we choose to use a word, as long as we are perfectly clear about the *idea* which that word is being used to express. No doubt the English word 'teaching' can be correctly used in either its weak sense, which does not imply learning, or its strong sense, which does. If we are opting here to use it in its strong sense, this is partly because we believe that in fact it is in its strong sense that the word tends to be employed in most contexts, and partly because the weak sense of the word would appear to be as it were parasitical on its

strong sense. For it is only because there are activities
which issue in people learning things that we are moved to
pick out activities which do not have this outcome but are
intended to do so. The strong sense of 'teaching' would
appear to be the logically primary one. And certainly in
the strong or achievement sense of 'teaching', which we
shall henceforth employ, it is self-contradictory to
assert that Peter has taught Paul something but that Paul
has learned nothing from Peter. As we shall use the term,
it is a logically necessary condition of teaching taking
place that learning shall be taking place.

Now, from this it follows that it is a logically
sufficient condition of learning taking place that
teaching shall be taking place. If Peter has taught Paul
that honesty is the best policy, ipso facto Paul has
learned that honesty is the best policy. However, it
would be absolutely wrong to conclude that Paul's learning
is therefore a *result* of Peter's teaching, if by a
'result' we mean a change produced as an *effect* by some
antecedent or accompanying event or process as its *cause*.
The necessity connecting teaching and learning is a purely
conceptual and formal necessity, not a factual and causal
necessity. The proposition that teaching entails learning
expresses a logical truth about the relation between
concepts, not an empirical generalization about the impact
of teachers upon learners. And in fact, of course, a
pupil who learns something from a teacher does so not only
because he has been the recipient of teaching but also
because he has to some extent responded to the teaching he
has received. In schoolrooms wooden, inattentive, or
hostile pupils may have altogether dropped out of the
business of learning, although their physical presence is
commanded by the State. They are not learning, and they
are not being taught. Adults who have no desire to engage
in systematic learning, on the other hand, do not generally present themselves to official teachers, and it is
generally safe to assume that those men and women who do
voluntarily enrol on courses of further study come prepared to make the kind of response which will match and
fructify the efforts of their teachers to create a genuine
learning situation. But whether the pupils are children
or adults, there has to be some kind of reaching out by
the pupil to accept what is being offered before learning,
and therefore before teaching, can even begin to take
place. The measures taken by the teacher cannot of
themselves cause learning to occur. Although, then, we
may say that teaching acts as a *stimulus* to learning - and
by definition as an effective stimulus, for if the pupil
does not respond the stimulus has not stimulated, nothing

has been learned and therefore nothing has been taught -
we must not say that teaching is the 'causing' or
'bringing about' of learning, if by this we may be understood to imply that the learning done is entirely the
result of certain characteristic measures taken by the
person or persons acting as teachers.

Nor must we make the mistake of writing into the
concept of teaching in general (as distinct from whatever
special forms of teaching we may be entitled to pick out
and dignify as 'educational') any kind of *normative* stipulations apart from those which we have already seen to be
incorporated in the concept of learning. When Downie,
Loudfoot, and Telfer seek to characterize teaching in
terms of its 'intrinsic aim' and go on to define this as
'the creation of the educated man', (3) they forget that
Fagin, while clearly not engaged in educating his pupils,
was undoubtedly engaged in teaching them. When Scheffler
characterizes teaching as 'an activity aimed at the
achievement of learning, and practised in such a manner
as to respect the student's intellectual integrity and
capacity for independent judgment', (4) the indignant
wraith of Fagin again rises up to refute him, joined this
time perhaps by an angry Prussian drill-sergeant who has
taught thousands of recruits to goose-step. All educators
properly so called are teachers, but not all teachers
properly so called are educators. The normative stipulations which are written into the concept of education
are not written into the concept of teaching in general.

While we may define a teacher as someone who takes
measures designed to stimulate learning, this must not be
taken to mean that the concept of teaching is the concept
of some particular measure or set of measures which have
been found to be specially suited for this purpose.
Certainly, teaching necessarily involves the taking of
some measures or other. Teaching is an activity, and a
teacher is an agent of learning, not a passive spectator
of learning which is mysteriously going on in his
vicinity. (5) But 'teaching' is not the name of a
particular method of stimulating learning, or of a
particular set of methods. When we have said that Brown
has been teaching all afternoon, we have neither stated
nor denied that he has been instructing, demonstrating,
lecturing, using audio-visual aids, conducting a controlled discussion, supervising his students' practical
work, or directing their private study, for he might have
been doing none, any, or all of these things. We might
want to contrast *good* teaching with, say, instructing or
lecturing: but the bare notion of teaching in general
does not of itself prescribe this or that particular
method or set of methods.

However, having acknowledged this, we must not forget
that written into the concept of 'learning' there are the
stipulations that what is learned must be knowledge and
not error and it must be learned by processes involving
relevant mental activity on the part of the learner;
and, since the concept of learning forms an essential
ingredient in the concept of teaching, what this means is
that built into the concept of teaching at one remove, as
it were, there are stipulations which logically *exclude*
certain kinds of activity from the category of 'teaching'
activities. Thus conditioning, at least in the stricter
senses of this term, is a process or set of processes
completely by-passing relevant mental activity on the part
of the conditioned subject, and for this reason alone we
are bound to differentiate between conditioning and
teaching. For the same reason, 'brainwashing' and many
forms of propaganda must surely be excluded from the
category of teaching activities. And of course, when
conditioning, brainwashing, and propaganda (as is often
the case) are used to inculcate beliefs which are in fact
false, this clearly gives us another absolutely decisive
reason for refusing to count these activities as forms of
teaching.

Moreover, because of this stipulation that learning
must involve some form of relevant mental activity on the
part of the learner, it follows that any measures which
are to count as *teaching* must be capable of stimulating
mental activity that is at least of some definite cognitive relevance to the subject being learned. In other
words, the learning done has to be in some appropriate way
grounded in whatever the teacher is presenting to the
learner, if the learner's extension of awareness is to
count as 'learning' and the measures taken by the teacher
are to count as 'teaching'. There has to be a rational
connection between what the teacher says or does and the
knowledge, insight, or skill which he intends his pupil to
acquire. This is why we demand, as a matter of logic,
that measures properly styled 'teaching' shall in some
way, directly or indirectly, pick out and *indicate* the
content to be learned. Obviously there are very many
different ways in which this can be done, some involving
explicit and formal instruction, others relying more
heavily on the initiatives of the pupils themselves. But
at some stage, and in some way, if 'teaching' is to occur,
the materials, the data *from* which it is intended that
learning shall proceed - the foreign words, zoological
specimens, maps, newspaper reports, statistics, paintings,
symphonies, arguments, concepts, and so on - have to be
put on offer to the pupils, and the pupils have to be

induced to encounter this material in ways which will in
fact enable them to learn from it. (6)

It is also because the concept of 'teaching' is logically dependent on the concept of 'learning' that a
teaching activity has to stimulate the pupil to acquire
knowledge or skills which, at the time of teaching, are
genuinely *new* to him. We logically cannot teach people
things which they already know. They may have forgotten,
in which case we can teach them anew. But if a man
already knows what his teacher is trying to impart to him,
he clearly cannot be said to be learning and his teacher
cannot be said to be teaching him.

From the last two formal requirements of a teaching
activity there follows another one, which is also formal
in character although it is often stated as if it embodied
a substantive prescription about teaching method rather
than a purely logical truth about the concept of
'teaching'. This is the requirement that the teacher
shall take explicit account of the cognitive state of his
pupil - his intelligence, aptitudes, and limitations, and
the existing level of his knowledge, understanding, and
skill - in relation to the subject which is being taught
to him. For unless the subject, as the teacher intends to
present it, falls within the mental grasp of the pupil,
there clearly cannot occur anything that could be correctly deemed 'relevant mental activity' on the part of the
pupil, and hence there cannot occur anything that could be
correctly deemed 'teaching' on the part of the teacher.
And unless the subject, as the teacher intends to present
it, offers the pupil some sort of knowledge, understanding, and skill which he does not as yet possess,
what the pupil is doing clearly cannot be described as
'learning' and what the teacher is doing cannot be described as 'teaching'. The material presented by the
teacher must be intelligible to the pupil, and it must be
as yet unmastered by the pupil. To say this, however, is
not to proffer a piece of advice, which every sensible
teacher already acts upon but which perhaps a very foolish
teacher might neglect at the cost of bewildering or boring
his pupils. It is merely to draw attention to yet another
feature of our concept of teaching, yet another purely
formal condition which any teaching activity, however
competent or inept, *logically* must satisfy if it is even
to count as a 'teaching' activity in the first place.

There are various other logical requirements built into
the concept of teaching on which there is perhaps no need
for us to dwell. Thus it is obvious that for teaching to
go on there must always be someone, namely the teacher,
who already possesses whatever knowledge, understanding,

or skill the learner is being taught. (7)   (Classes which
are engaged in projects of research or discovery - local
history classes, for example, burrowing away in parish
registers or Victorian newspapers for knowledge not
possessed by any living person - do not form an exception
to this rule;   in classes like these such teaching as is
going on concerns research techniques, principles of
interpretation, and so forth, and it would not be claimed
that the specific factual knowledge unearthed by the
students themselves was being 'taught' to them by their
tutor, although of course they might well be engaged in
teaching it to one another.)   And there are various other
purely formal implications that follow from our definition
of 'teaching' as 'the stimulation of learning' which,
however, it would probably be quite superfluous for us to
trace and spell out here.   For we have now, I think, noted
most of the main features of the concept of teaching with
which we need at present to be concerned.   We have seen
that, in describing Jones as having 'taught' Smith
something, what we are asserting is that Jones has taken
certain measures, as yet unspecified, designed to help
Smith to become aware of something of which he had not
hitherto been aware (some set of rules or instrumentalities, when it is a case of teaching a skill).   We are
further asserting that these measures, whatever their
specific nature, have been devised not only in the light
of Jones's own knowledge of the subject he is teaching but
also with due regard to the existing cognitive state of
Smith his pupil, and that they have been to some extent
successful in eliciting some form of relevant mental
activity on the part of Smith.   And finally we are asserting that, as an outcome of the whole process, Smith's
awareness has in fact been extended in the direction
proposed by Jones (although not necessarily in any educationally worthwhile direction).

Now, given that this is what we mean by 'teaching'
someone something, several widely influential and perennially recurring models or analogues of the teaching process
can, I think, be seen to be seriously misleading, in
particular those which contrive to suggest that teaching
is entirely a matter of performing various operations ab
extra on the docile mind of an essentially passive recipient.   Teaching cannot be a matter of mere 'input', of
packing, feeding, loading, pumping, stoking, or otherwise
inserting some new truth into some kind of mental recepta-
cle or tank.   It cannot be a matter of inscribing new
truths in the blank spaces remaining on some sheet of
paper already partly covered by earlier writing.   Nor can
it consist in working up some more or less rudimentary

material into some sort of desirable shape - whether this be thought of as the kneading, moulding, stamping, and sculpting of an originally formless and completely plastic stuff, or as the strengthening, tightening, stretching, and exercising of a kind of mental sinew or muscle.
Models or analogues of the teaching process which suggest that the mind of the learner is akin to a container or storeroom, to paper or wax waiting for an imprint, to clay or dough waiting to be pressed into shape, or to a muscle or tendon waiting to be quickened and built up, are all in their various ways profoundly misleading because they lead us to speak and think of human awareness as if it were that which it precisely is not - namely a closed and inert quantity, an object rather than a subject, in fact a *thing,* and moreover an essentially *mindless* thing which can only be brought to shift and stir by dint of impulsion from without.
If we are to do justice to the character of awareness as a free active reaching-out-towards the objects of which it makes itself aware, we shall have to employ imagery which makes it clear that teaching is a collaborative process, involving exchanges, outgoings, and interaction between two separate and independent centres of consciousness, and converging on to some objective and accessible reality which offers itself as the common focus of the teaching done by the one consciousness and of the learning done by the other. Perhaps the kind of imagery used by Heidegger to convey the nature of man's relation to truth could be used to portray the inner character of the teaching process with at least a greater degree of verisimilitude and fidelity than can be credited to most of the imagery that has typically been used for this purpose. (8)
Teaching might be thought of as a 'clearing of the way' to the truth, which the teacher 'unveils' and 'illuminates' for the pupil. We can think of teaching as an opening up of that which has been closed off, a laying bare of that which has been concealed, a dis-covering of that which has been shrouded and obscure. In teaching someone something we are not injecting a truth his passive and waiting consciousness. Rather, we are making a truth visible to him by placing it before him, manifest and uncovered, and inviting him to contemplate it. The relation between the measures taken by a teacher and the learning done by a pupil is not like the relation between cause and effect. It is more like the relation between an invitation and its acceptance, and of course the invitation may be refused: the path may be cleared, but the pupil may refuse to take it; that which was hidden may be revealed, but he may avert his eyes from it. If teaching is a

dis-closing, a putting-forth-to-be-seen of that which has been screened and shut off from the pupil's consciousness, it requires the free consent and active collaboration of him whose consciousness is being beckoned.

Looked at in this way, teaching is essentially a matter of bringing the pupil up to some reality and setting it before him that he may see it. Teaching is a kind of presenting or making-present. It is a matter of presenting the pupil with what is there to be perceived, felt, and understood, or of leading him, by one route or another, into its presence. What is there to be known and experienced needs to be brought within the pupil's range of vision. The metaphor of vision, which forms an indispensable part of this whole way of thinking and talking about the teaching process, of course has its roots in much older conceptions of teaching and learning and indeed of human knowledge in general. Thus in Book VII of the 'Republic' Plato likens teaching to a turning round of the learner's soul from the darkness of ignorance to behold the daylight of truth. (9) And St Augustine, in his dialogue 'De Magistro' and elsewhere, describes teaching in terms of an illumination of the learner's soul, a turning of the eyes of his mind towards the light. In fact it is in the course of criticizing what he calls Augustine's 'insight model' of teaching that Israel Scheffler puts forward his objections to 'the notion that what is crucial in knowledge is a vision of underlying realities', a notion which he unhesitatingly declares to be 'far too simple'. (10) The concept of a 'vision of reality', he alleges, is quite inadequate as a mode of characterizing our knowledge of the kinds of proposition which figure in practical affairs, the sciences, politics, history, law, and other spheres of knowledge where the emphasis is on processes of deliberation, argument, judgment, on the appraisal of reasons, the weighing of evidence, and the appeal to principles, rather than on processes resembling a direct observation or inspection of reality. 'Vision', says Scheffler, 'is just the wrong metaphor.' However, surely vision - properly understood - is in many ways just the right metaphor. Certainly Augustine did not understand by vision (as Scheffler seems to suppose) a passive and immobile staring at some stationary external object, for he recognized and indeed emphasized that sense-perception is essentially an active response on the part of the mind, a response made to the external stimuli by which our sense-organs are affected but a response which calls for effort, exertion, attention, and discrimination on the part of the perceiver, who may after all be engaged, not in gazing at some fixed and homogene-

ous object, but in following the progress of some complicated and fast-developing situation or train of events
that requires, not a petrified staring, but an active and
continuous focusing and refocusing, watching, scanning,
descrying, and reviewing of everything that is coming to
pass in the unfolding scene before him. There is no
reason whatsoever why we should not apply the metaphor of
vision to discursive mental processes involving deliberation, reasoning, and judgment, theoretical and practical,
and in fact we habitually do precisely this. We speak of
looking at the evidence, of overlooking or being blind to
important pieces of evidence, of viewing a question from
all sides or from certain sides only, of seeing the force
of an argument or the drift of a narrative, seeing how
some belief is proved or some policy justified, seeing
how some task is performed, envisaging how some proposal
would work out in practice, and so on. If we think of
teaching as an opening up or unveiling of some reality, a
setting of some reality before the learner for him to see,
then that which is displayed for the learner to see may of
course be some simple, isolated, self-contained, and homo-
geneous fact - but equally it may be a principle, a rule,
a value, a body or constellation of these, a logical or
causal connection, a sequence of logical connections or
a whole evolving pattern of causal connections, or indeed
any series or organized system of truths, particular or
general, of any kind or on any scale.

As a philosophical model of the teaching process, this
ontological-existential interpretation of teaching in
terms of a dis-closing, a making-visible of some objective
reality can, I think, be applied to any kind of subject-
matter with which a teacher may be concerned. (11)   It
has, I think we can also claim, the merit of remaining
true to the inner character and general spirit of the
teaching process, as this is directly experienced by both
teacher and learner. And in addition it has the merit of
bringing out and emphasizing certain specific features of
teaching which do need to be clearly brought out and
strongly emphasized and which are perhaps most vividly and
aptly evoked by a model impregnated with the imagery of
personal interaction and mutual awareness. The ontological-existential model serves to remind us, for example, of
the fact that teaching is an *activity* and that therefore -
like any other activity properly so called - it is
something which has to be done *intentionally,* by someone
who is aware of the nature of what he is doing. A mechanically gifted youth who, unnoticed, stood watching his
father change a tyre might in this way learn how to carry
out this operation; he might learn how to do it, whether

his father's performance was skilled and successful or
whether it was clumsy and abortive; but in neither case
could we correctly say that the father had 'taught' the
son how to change a tyre, since he had in fact done
nothing that was consciously directed to this end.
Teaching, unlike learning, cannot happen by accident, and
while no harm is necessarily done by figurative language
which implies that it can - 'his angry explosion taught me
to stay well clear of political arguments', and so on - we
should never allow ourselves to forget that, strictly
speaking, the activity of teaching someone something logically involves at least some degree of conscious concern
and purposiveness on the part of the teacher.

The ontological-existential model of teaching also, I
think, serves to remind us how very *basic and pervasive* a
feature of all human relationships the generic activity of
teaching is. We ought always to remember that the relationship between teacher and learner is essentially one
of *communication,* a coming-together of two distinct selves
(converging on a common object of awareness), and that
this relationship, one of the most fundamental if not the
most fundamental into which conscious selves can enter, is
by no means restricted to the official occupants of a
formal role but is open to anyone who is capable of stimulating or capable of responding. Of course, not all
communication is teaching. John may communicate with
James merely in order to amuse, reassure, persuade, in-
timidate, interrogate, command, inspire, or demoralize
him. It is only if his intention lies in James *learning*
something, and if he succeeds in this intention, that we
can say he has been 'teaching' James. (12) And of course,
communication need not be face-to-face, nor need those
communicating even know the identity of those with whom
they are communicating. A lecturer appearing on television for the Open University and the writer of a correspondence course or a textbook are engaged in teaching,
and so is someone who writes an informative article for
his local newspaper or even someone who writes a letter
to his local newspaper if he intentionally succeeds in
guiding his readers to acquire new knowledge or a better
understanding thereby. But whatever the form of the
communication, if the person communicating intends that
it shall have the outcome of *people learning,* and it
actually has this outcome, then we can correctly say of
him that on this occasion what he has been doing has in
fact been *teaching,* whether he himself and others realize
this or not. Certainly, there is a narrower sense of
'teaching', in which we only count someone as a teacher
if he is fairly regularly engaged in the activity of

teaching; a 'teacher' in this specific sense is someone
charged with stimulating the learning of a particular
pupil or group of pupils, usually over a continuous period
of time, and he will certainly see himself, and be seen by
others, as someone who is distinctively occupied in
fulfilling a definite role. However, we must never forget
that teaching in the generic sense of the term is an
activity that all men may and do engage in from time to
time, in connection with almost any matter, serious or
trivial, with which they or others may happen to be concerned and on which it is possible for one person to learn
from another. Perhaps particularly when we are thinking
of the teaching of adults, we do well to remember that
teaching is something which is going on all the time in
many different kinds of situation, not something which
happens only within the settled framework of acknowledged
teaching institutions.

Another feature of teaching which the ontological-
existential model brings to the fore, and which it is also
particularly desirable to emphasize in connection with the
teaching of adults, is *the ultimate sovereignty of the
pupil*. The teacher can offer access to that which has to
be learned, but as we have already seen he cannot literally 'bring about' learning; he cannot cause or constrain
the pupil to reach out and grasp that which has been set
before him. When learning occurs, it results from the
complex interplay of teacher, learner, and the objective
material to be presented and grasped. The measures taken
by the teacher consist in identifying, demarcating,
selecting, arranging, bringing forward and displaying the
material to be learned, but before teaching and learning
can take place the learner has to gather himself, compose,
focus, and direct his attention, and open himself up to
receive what has been plucked and offered to him. The
teacher can prompt, suggest, point out, appeal, invite,
solicit, and guide. The decisive act, however, must
emanate from the will of the learner, for if he does not
exert himself to inspect and hold in view that which has
been uncovered and exhibited to him, the measures taken
by the teacher will all have been to no avail.

Those models or analogues of the teaching process which
liken teaching to the filling up of a container, the
imprinting of messages on virgin wax, the moulding of a
hitherto formless clay, or the building up of a muscle or
sinew, surely owe whatever plausibility they have to our
ingrained tendency to think of teaching as an activity
which mainly goes on in connection with children, with
the growing and the half-formed, the immature and the
not-yet-fully-awakened. But when we recall that 'teaching

someone something' is one of the most basic and universal
of human activities, and indeed one that is virtually
inseparable from all personal interaction and that is more
or less pervasive of all personal relationships; and
when, therefore, we bear in mind that most teaching, in
the fundamental and generic sense of the term, in the
nature of things takes place in and across the wide world
of adults and involves transactions between men and women
who are presumed to be mature and entitled to all the
rights and privileges of maturity; then we shall, I
think, be less likely to be seduced by models which depict
teaching as an external operation performed on a con-
veniently passive and pliant stuff, and we shall be
correspondingly more likely to demand a conception of
teaching which does full justice to the independence and
self-determination of the learner. In constructing a
philosophical model of teaching, we have to take care that
it will apply with equal validity to those situations
where the recipients of teaching are children and to those
where both teachers and learners are adults, but we may
well feel that it is in the latter situations, where
everyone involved can be treated as a fully developed
human person, that the distinctive features of the
teaching process are likely to be most fully and accurately brought out and most vividly and incontrovertibly shown
forth.

Of course, whatever model of teaching we favour, it
will have to apply with equal validity, not only to the
teaching of every kind of learner, but also to the
teaching of every kind of subject-matter, in every kind
of way, and for every kind of reason. Clearly, any model
of teaching that is going to be in any degree adequate
will have to be drawn up in the light of the features
shared by *all* teaching, the features characteristic of
teaching in general - not merely in the light of the
features characteristic of those teaching processes which
we can distinctively think of as processes of 'education'
properly so called. And in fact everything that we have
said so far applies equally to those sporadic and unpre-
meditated cases of teaching, so common in life, where one
man simply finds himself learning something from another;
to the vast body of organized teaching which goes on in
connection with training programmes in business, industry,
and the professions, most of which is purely vocational
and makes no pretence to be at all educational in character; and even to those forms of teaching which go on in
connection with what most of us would consider to be
processes of indoctrination (and which are therefore
positively anti-educational in character); as well as to

those forms of teaching which are undoubtedly directed to
the fuller development of persons in their personhood,
which employ only such measures as may be deemed proper
for this purpose, and which we can therefore dignify by
the name of 'educational processes' in the strictest sense
of the term. However, it is now high time for us to look
more closely at the conditions which processes of teaching
and learning must satisfy if we are indeed to be entitled
to refer to them as 'educational processes', since
manifestly it is on the *education* of adults, not just on
any and every kind of teaching and learning in which
adults may for one reason or another engage, that our
interest must continue to focus. It is to this central
question, and to the congeries of normative and conceptual
issues which cluster around it, that we must therefore
address ourselves in the chapter that follows.

The uses of maturity 7

It is safe to conjecture that most of the teaching and
learning in which men and women find themselves engaging
forms no part of anything that could remotely be called
'education'. The new employee who is taught how to clock
on and clock off on his first day in the factory, and who
spends that day learning how to service and repair the
packing machine of which he is to be placed in charge,
would probably be very surprised (and in fact ought to be
scandalized) at the suggestion that he should regard any
of this as a contribution by his new employers to his education. Most of the teaching and learning processes to
which adults are exposed are not even remotely intended to
develop the learner as a person by enlarging his awareness
and building up in him richer and more extensive
structures of knowledge and understanding. That is to
say, they do not come anywhere near to satisfying what we
have called the 'achievement' criterion written into the
concept of education, and for this reason alone,
therefore, such processes cannot be regarded as *educational* processes even when they are conducted under the
auspices of bodies officially described as educational
bodies.

There are two main respects in which some process of
teaching or learning may fail to satisfy the 'achievement'
criterion of an educational process. In the first place,
the experience or knowledge acquired by the learner may be
more or less devoid of intrinsic value. As we saw in
Chapter 2, (1) much of the knowledge imparted and acquired
in courses of vocational study can only be justified in
terms of its social or economic utility (company ac-
countants mastering the complexities of new taxation
procedures, for example, or safety officers learning how
to use the latest types of mining rescue equipment), for
few normal men or women would wish to acquire such

knowledge purely for its own sake, and indeed most normal
people would be glad to think that with technological
progress human beings might be increasingly liberated from
the need to spend their time acquiring such knowledge,
which - whatever its transient utilitarian value - is
clearly quite worthless judged as a contribution to the
inner assets of a freely functioning human mind. A good
deal of what passes for adult education in evening institutes and community centres contains equally little that
is genuinely worth mastering for its own sake, and much
of it can only be justified as an exercise in indirectly
helping individuals to improve their material standards of
living: courses in cookery, dressmaking, and motor car
maintenance, for example, notoriously attract students who
are primarily looking for ways of reducing the money they
have to spend in butchers', bakers', grocers', dress-
shops, or garages, or of reducing their reliance on
ordinary trade channels for the particular goods or
services which they or their families happen to want,
simply in their capacity as consumers. And from the fact
that other evening institute courses - in flower arrangement, for example, or contract bridge - seem to
contain little or nothing of obvious utilitarian value we
cannot, unfortunately, infer that what they do contain is
therefore likely to have some significant degree of intrinsic cognitive value and so to be of real educational
worth: on the contrary, when we objectively appraise the
educational worth of the knowledge, experience, or skills
imparted by such courses, that is, when we judge these as
examples of knowledge, experience, or skill to be acquired
purely for their own sakes by free, responsible, and
intelligent beings, we are often bound to admit that their
educational worth is in fact so slight as to be practically negligible; and when we go on to reflect how much
there is all around us in the universe to stir, delight,
and absorb the minds of mature men and women, we might
even find ourselves wondering whether courses which deliberately foster an interest in such relative trivia
ought not strictly to be regarded as *anti-educational*
activities along with the activities of the bingo-hall,
the bowling alley, and the amusements arcade. Of course,
we may readily accept that classes in ballroom dancing or
soft toy making often help to satisfy an important type of
public need where, for instance, they help to relieve the
claustrophobic monotony of people's lives in isolated
villages or dreary housing estates; but there is no
reason whatsoever to describe measures which undoubtedly
help to satisfy important personal or public needs as
'educational' measures unless they are also plainly
intended to promote the development of men and women as

persons by systematically enlarging their awareness of
themselves, their fellows, and the world in which they
live, and unless the measures in question do to some
significant extent actually accomplish this. We may
readily accept, too, that courses which seem educationally
trivial and which in terms of what we might call their
'specific overt content' really are educationally trivial
- millinery, winemaking, water-skiing - can sometimes give
students access to dimensions of experience and understanding which, far from being trivial, undoubtedly lie
at the very heart of all true educational achievement. A
course on winemaking, for example, might lead students to
examine seriously and systematically, and against a
background of relevant knowledge, a whole developing range
of complex aesthetic, ethical, historical, and scientific
questions, and when this happens what we might call the
'ultimate actual content' of the course is immensely
richer than its specific overt content and, since clearly
we must judge a course by its ultimate actual content, we
are bound to conclude that such a course is in fact providing its students with knowledge and understanding of
high educational value. However, we must be careful not
to exaggerate the extent to which this sort of desirable
result actually tends to occur in practice. In practice
by far the best clue to the ultimate actual content of a
course is nearly always its specific overt content. Thus
most independent onlookers would be very surprised, to say
the least, if a woman who had professed herself eager to
sharpen her aesthetic insight and sensibilities, for
example, were to be advised by an evening institute
principal to join a course on cake decoration or country
dancing when suitable courses on, say, art appreciation
or contemporary poetry were equally available for her to
join, and such a principal would, I think, need remarkable
ingenuity if he were to have much hope of convincing us
that his advice had been based entirely on his sincere
judgment that, all things considered, cake icing and the
eightsome reel tended to be better vehicles of aesthetic
education than the paintings of Goya and the poems of
Philip Larkin. (2)
    A process of teaching or learning, then, may in the
first place fail to satisfy the 'achievement' criterion
of an educational process because, objectively assessed,
the experience or knowledge acquired by the learner appears to be more or less devoid of intrinsic value and
therefore of real educational worth. Second, a process of
teaching or learning may fail to satisfy the 'achievement'
criterion of an educational process because it results in
what can best be described as a crucial *narrowing* or
abridgement of the learner's awareness, perhaps by making

him blind to certain kinds of truth or unresponsive to certain kinds of experience: the learner may indeed be taught much that has high cognitive value, but this is achieved at the cost of systematically constricting his perceptions and perhaps even blurring his judgment in other directions. (The fact that the learner is of course never literally a passive victim, but always has to be at least an accomplice - and may sometimes even be the instigator - in his own cognitive impoverishment, makes no relevant difference to the character of the process.) A protracted and intensive study of the physical sciences, for instance, without any accompanying grounding in other forms of knowledge, can sometimes render a man incapable of recognizing and adhering to any standards of intellectual rigour other than those to which he habitually conforms in his scientific pursuits, and so can render him naive and clumsy when he is faced by philosophical, ethical, religious, or aesthetic questions which demand an altogether different type of approach. This is in fact what we usually have in mind when we speak of 'over-specialization', which can of course occur in connection with any form of knowledge, and which we rightly contrast with education properly so called. And when we speak of 'training' - as we saw in Chapter 2 (3) - we usually have in mind processes which also involve a certain constriction of a man's awareness and which we also contrast for this reason with educational processes properly so called. To be sure, unlike over-specialization, the constriction of awareness produced by training is something aimed at deliberately by those who engage in the training; moreover, while it may be undertaken for good or bad purposes, and be well or ill done, the notion of 'training', unlike that of 'over-specialization', is not the notion of something per se undesirable, perhaps because training, unlike over-specialization, does not necessarily deter the learner from subsequently exploring and responding to those dimensions of knowledge and experience which the process of training nevertheless itself by definition neglects (for example, the wider scientific and social aspects of telecommunications which are by definition excluded from anything we should call the mere 'training' of a telephonist, but which a telephonist is unlikely to be positively *deterred* by his training from appreciating if he should ever be subsequently led to consider them); and so, although clearly processes of 'training' have to be sharply distinguished from processes of 'education', unlike 'over-specialization' the notion of 'training' is not the notion of something which is positively *incompatible with* a man's pursuit of education in the full meaning of the term.

What over-specialization and training have in common,
however, is that they characteristically turn their backs
on all forms of knowledge and experience which are not directly relevant to the specific purposes they have in hand
and thus, although in very different ways, they can both
be described as inducing the consciousness of the learner
to run along comparatively narrow channels and to focus
upon a comparatively restricted range of objects. (4)
    This is also, I think, the basis on which we dis-
tinguish processes of 'indoctrination' from bona fide educational processes. It is not because some teaching
process fails to satisfy the 'task' criteria of an educational process that we deem it to be a process of indoctrination, for those who are receiving the indoctrination may in fact take part wittingly, (5) voluntarily, and
actively in the whole process, and sophisticated forms of
indoctrination may well satisfy each and all of the proprieties that we require of a genuine process of education. The difference between political or religious
education and political or religious indoctrination is,
I think, that indoctrination fails to satisfy the
'achievement' criteria of an educational process - not,
however, because the knowledge imparted by the indoctrinator is devoid of intrinsic value (for what is imparted
in a course of political or religious indoctrination may
be of very high cognitive value), but because, like over-
specialization and like training, indoctrination distinctively involves a significant narrowing of the
learner's mental horizons, a definite contraction or
curtailment of his capacity to grasp and respond, which
the indoctrinator induces to operate within certain
selected areas of experience and belief only. Unlike
over-specialization, indoctrination is something done
intentionally by someone who is at least in some degree
aware of what he is doing; (6) unlike training, indoctrination positively deters its victims from exploring and
appreciating this, that, and the other domain of knowledge
and experience which the indoctrinator strategically
neglects or disfavours, and so, unlike training, indoctrination is positively incompatible with a man's pursuit of
education in the full meaning of the term. Unlike
training, therefore, but like over-specialization, the
notion of 'indoctrination' is the notion of something per
se undesirable; but unlike over-specialization, which
happens fortuitously and at worst by culpable omission,
indoctrination, being intentional, is actively *malign*.
However, like over-specialization and training, the
concept of 'indoctrination' is essentially the concept of
a teaching process or set of teaching processes which have
as their central feature a confinement of the learner's

awareness within relatively close and rigid limits, dis-
tracting and divorcing it from much else which a man's
education ought properly to include.

Of course, as the term itself implies, the constriction
of awareness which 'indoctrination' distinctively induces
is essentially a matter of the canalization or hedging-in
of the learner's *beliefs*. This by no means rules out the
possibility - indeed the likelihood - of the indoctrinator's being chiefly concerned to transmit a particular
range of *attitudes*, since the concept of an attitude
(hostility to Jews, unswerving obedience to the Party, and
so on) is the concept of a phalanx of habits, inclinations, feelings, and emotions which are permeated and
shaped by a more or less clearly held set of beliefs, and
the task of altering a man's attitudes is therefore one
which can only be carried out if the teacher can bring his
pupil to alter his beliefs in this or that appropriate
way. Nevertheless, it is important not to lose sight of
the fact that the manipulation of a man's attitudes logically counts as 'indoctrination' only when, and because,
it involves a manipulation of his beliefs. As Antony Flew
tersely puts it: 'No doctrines, no indoctrination.' (7)
The beliefs with which a man is indoctrinated may be
false: this is how most people would view the central
beliefs of Scientologists and of the Jehovah's Witnesses,
for example, who are often accused of indoctrinating their
members. (8) Or they may be wholly true: in saying that
a country at war is indoctrinating its soldiers with its
own version of the incidents which precipitated the war,
we are in no way excluding the possibility that its
version may ultimately turn out to have in fact been
true in every particular. They may be beliefs of any
kind. They may be 'doctrines' in the narrower sense,
that is, beliefs of low cognitive certainty which form
part of some distinctive moral, political, or religious
creed or ideology demanding a high measure of loyalty from
its adherents. For obvious reasons those who are interested in spreading such beliefs are often tempted to
resort to indoctrination, and often yield to the temptation; and this, surely, is why the activity of indoctrinating tends to be associated with 'doctrines' in
this narrower sense. As I.A.Snook points out in his
admirably thorough monograph on the subject, the connection between indoctrination and 'doctrines' is not
conceptual but motivational. (9) But from this it follows
that the beliefs with which a man is indoctrinated may as
a matter of fact have no relevant connection with any
doctrinal system, and in any case it clearly makes perfect
sense to speak of indoctrinating someone with, say, the
belief that sleeping with the windows open is harmful to

one's health or the belief that Sir Philip Francis wrote
the Letters of Junius.

The necessary and sufficient conditions of Brown's
having indoctrinated Smith with some belief about some
subject are that Brown's teaching of Smith shall have been
intended to induce Smith to regard the belief in question
as the only belief worth considering about the subject in
question, although there are in fact other beliefs objectively worthy of serious consideration; and that
Brown's teaching shall to some significant extent actually
have induced this state of mind in Smith. (Where there
are no serious alternatives to the belief taught, for
example the belief that the Battle of Waterloo was fought
in 1815, or where the teacher has no reason to believe
that there are any serious alternatives, for example a
mediaeval teacher teaching his pupils that the earth is
flat, we plainly cannot describe what the teacher is doing
as 'indoctrinating'.) When it is said, as it often is,
that indoctrinating means instilling beliefs which the
indoctrinated person comes to hold undiscriminatingly or
uncritically, this is of course perfectly correct, since
any criticism to which we subject our beliefs must be
based on some other belief or beliefs and thus to speak
of a man who refuses to consider any beliefs directly or
indirectly opposed to the beliefs which he has been taught
is necessarily to speak of a man who refuses to subject
his beliefs to criticism (and vice versa). And when Snook
asserts that indoctrinating means instilling beliefs which
the indoctrinated person comes to hold 'regardless of the
evidence', (10) this too is perfectly correct, since
basing one's beliefs on the evidence entails exposing them
to possible refutation by the evidence and thus to speak
of a man who refuses to consider, or who only pretends to
consider, any facts or arguments which threaten to under-
mine the beliefs he has been taught is necessarily to
speak of a man who refuses to base his beliefs on the
evidence; such a man may be sincerely indifferent to the
whole question of evidence, perhaps professing to base his
beliefs on 'faith' or some other foundation supposedly
impervious to logical or empirical scrutiny; even if,
however, he has learned to attach importance to whatever
facts or arguments may be adduced *in support of* his
beliefs, we are still bound to describe him as believing
'regardless of the evidence', since he still refuses to
weigh these favoured facts and arguments (which would
entail weighing them *against* the counter-evidence that he
refuses to take seriously) and so the status which they
occupy in his mind is manifestly not genuinely evidential
but merely pseudo-evidential.

To indoctrinate someone, we may conclude, is to inflict

a kind of blindness upon him, for the indoctrinator's aim
is to screen rival beliefs from his victim's attention and
sympathies, not necessarily by shutting out all knowledge
of their existence but by employing whatever means will
best ensure that his victim will fail to perceive their
merits or grasp their relevance even when the rival beliefs are set plainly before him by their most patient and
eloquent advocates. The beliefs of the indoctrinated man
have been severed and mentally sealed off from the matrix
of moral, social, scientific, historical, religious, or
other beliefs in which they are logically rooted, and they
float before his mind, needing no rational support and
beyond the reach of rational criticism, monopolizing the
responses of his blinkered intelligence. It is in this
sense that we can aptly think of indoctrination as essentially an abridgement, an intentional and fatal contraction or narrowing, of the learner's awareness, and so
as the very antithesis of an educational process.

So understood, there can clearly be no reason whatsoever for attempting to restrict the concept of 'indoctrination' to what is done to children. When Snook asserts
(11) that the indoctrination of adults is very difficult
to carry out unless it is the continuation of a process
begun in youth or unless it is strongly reinforced by
propaganda and censorship, most of us will probably be
inclined to agree that this is generally so as a matter
of empirical fact. At least in comparatively sophisticated, economically advanced, liberal democratic, and
'open' societies like our own, it is doubtful whether any
attempt to impose some belief or set of beliefs on any
sizeable part of the adult population solely by processes
of indoctrination could ever expect to meet with any very
high degree of success. Such serious programmes of adult
indoctrination as are carried out in this country tend to
be confined to the members of tightly-knit and inward-
looking religious or quasi-religious sects or to the
adherents of small, rigidly disciplined, and highly motivated political organizations, and of course in both types
of case the recipients of the indoctrination participate
in the process for the most part wittingly and voluntarily. And we find that when a comparatively sophisticated
and advanced society is subjected to a Communist dictator-
ship, for example, it is usually not until a whole new
generation of suitably indoctrinated citizens have been
produced by the State schools that its rulers can begin
to hope that their teachings will be received with due
reverence and enthusiasm among the adult population at
large, even although during the first few years of the
régime massive attempts at adult indoctrination have been
heavily reinforced by absolute State control of the press,

broadcasting agencies, publishing houses, and indeed every
other important organ of large-scale public communication.
However, it is perhaps desirable to emphasize that whether
this or that society, this or that group of adults, or
this or that individual adult can or cannot be indoctrinated with some given belief or set of beliefs is always
an *empirical* question, which can only be answered (always
with a higher or lower degree of probability, never with
absolute certainty) in the light of the relevant empirical
facts; and - while our experience may strongly suggest
that the indoctrination of adults is normally a very
difficult and problematic undertaking - it perhaps needs
to be emphasized that there is certainly nothing in the
concept of 'indoctrination', or in the concept of an
'adult', which makes it *logically* impossible that adults
should become victims of indoctrination, either as individuals or as members of an indoctrinated society. It
would obviously be inappropriate for us to try to general-
ize here about the kinds of empirical conditions which
tend to make the indoctrination of adults easier or more
difficult. But there is one relevant *normative* truth
which we might usefully take note of here. Among the
requirements which must be met if someone is to be rightly
considered an 'educated' person are the requirements that
he should have acquired some measure of breadth of mind
and cognitive perspective and that he should in some
measure have developed those moral and mental qualities
which constitute reasonableness in a human being; this
being so, however, it is clear that the more highly educated a man, the less vulnerable he will be to attempted
indoctrination. The connection between being well educated and being to that degree less vulnerable to indoctrination is not an empirical connection, like the
connection between being adequately fed or emotionally
secure, say, and being correspondingly less likely to fall
prey to would-be indoctrinators. It is a contingent fact
that the adequately fed and the emotionally secure are
less vulnerable to indoctrination than the hungry and the
emotionally insecure. In stating that better educated
people are less vulnerable to indoctrination than poorly
educated people, however, what we are stating has the
force of a necessary truth, since the concepts of
'reasonableness' and 'cognitive breadth' are concepts of
mental attributes which are *by definition* antagonistic to
the kinds of cognitive narrowing and disregard of evidence
signified by 'indoctrination' and in judging someone to be
a 'well educated' person we largely base our judgment on
the breadth of knowledge and understanding which he
displays and the degree of overall reasonableness which
we feel entitled to ascribe to him. The *inherent* diffi-

culty of indoctrinating well educated people no doubt goes
a long way towards explaining the deep animosity towards
anything resembling liberal education which is one of the
most characteristic features of totalitarian governments
and totalitarian institutions of every kind.

We have dwelt for some time on the subject of indoctrination because it is an important and sinister example of
a teaching process (or set of teaching processes) which
fails to satisfy the 'achievement' criterion of an educational process for the second of the two main reasons
that we earlier mentioned - namely, because it results in
a crucial narrowing or abridgement of the learner's
awareness. Before leaving this whole question of the
range or scope of the learner's awareness, however, we
must briefly touch on a particular difficulty which arises
here specifically in connection with the education of
adults and which ought to cause some concern to those
responsible for the provision of liberal adult education
when they recollect that an educational process, properly
so called, should foster *breadth* as well as depth of
understanding in the educand and should *extend* as well as
intensify his sympathies, tastes, insights, and perceptions. Apart from the very small number of institutions (in effect, the handful of long-term residential
colleges) which provide full-time courses of education for
mature students, most adult education agencies in this
country operate with little or no commitment to anything
that could be described as a 'curriculum' in the sense of
a scheme of progressive study expressly designed to equip
each individual student with a broad and balanced understanding of all the main forms of knowledge. An educational centre may try to provide a comprehensive range
of studies within its walls. A university extra-mural
department may try to make a comprehensive range of
studies available, at an appropriate level, within the
geographical area which it serves. It must indeed be
admitted that not all adult education agencies make a
real attempt to offer a broad and balanced provision even
in this very limited sense: the ragged and limping provision of some extra-mural departments, with their
plethora of courses in local history and their almost
total lack of provision in mathematics and the more
rigorous branches of physical science, bears sad witness
to this fact. However, even when a highly conscientious
adult education agency succeeds in making a consistently
broad and balanced range of studies regularly available
to the population it exists to serve, this of course by
no means ensures that the *individual* student, exercising
his legitimate freedom of choice, will not often confine
his studies to some one particular subject or group of

subjects only, evincing little or no interest in or regard for the many other forms of knowledge and experience which are being offered to him. Now, does this mean that many adult students all over the country who are regularly and enthusiastically engaged in studying history, literature, art, music, theology, and so on, in serious classes and courses provided by recognized educational bodies, but who remain largely ignorant of and indifferent to any realms of knowledge and experience which seem irrelevant to their favoured subject of study, are in fact not really engaged in *educational* pursuits at all but rather in what it might be safer and less misleading to refer to simply as intellectual, scholarly, literary, or artistic pursuits of one kind or another - pursuits of very great value to all concerned, no doubt, but not in the case of these students of any distinctively educational value and significance?

It is, I think, fairly obvious that we do need to make some kind of a distinction between a man's attempt to acquire an education and his attempt merely to acquire greater knowledge about some admittedly interesting and worthwhile subject. Someone who already knew a very great deal about British birds or railway history would not be thought to have become a significantly better educated person simply because he had learned yet more about British birds or railway history or even because he had learned to structure his knowledge of one of these subjects in more sophisticated and discriminating ways (unless, indeed, - as might well be the case - his attempts to do this had led him into much wider perspectives and put him in living touch with much richer dimensions of knowledge and experience). A man who had learned everything there was to be learned about the flora of the Isle of Wight would be rightly regarded as a man of great if narrow erudition: but if his judgments on every other subject turned out to be confused, ignorant, naive, and crude, we should hardly be inclined to think of him as a well educated human being. If we were to apply the term 'education' to every increase in a man's knowledge of some worthwhile subject in which he took a serious interest, we should clearly run the risk of robbing the term 'education' of its distinctive meaning by obliterating the distinction between what are simply processes of worthwhile learning and processes which explicitly set out to foster the development of a man in his whole being as a conscious self by helping him to perceive, understand, and respond to the fuller texture of reality in all its most fundamental and pervasive forms. Very many people find their attention caught and held by subjects and themes - the First World War, canals and bridges, church music, North Country folklore, numismatics, or

anything else from life's limitless treasury of interest -
which they will pursue for years on end, in solitude or
with other enthusiasts, sometimes joining a course on
their cherished topic when one happens to present itself;
but we ought not to embroider and inflate what such people
are doing, even when they are members of a course, by
representing them as engaged in 'advancing their education'; and indeed, while the pursuit of an intellectual
or artistic hobby may of course contribute greatly to a
man's education, we must also recognize that a man's
pursuit of his hobby can easily take place *at the expense
of* his further education, by consuming time and energy
which might have been devoted to enlarging his awareness,
not just of one tiny corner of the world and its riches,
but of life's whole vast pageant with its inexhaustibly
varied materials for contemplation and enjoyment.

What, then, are we to say of some adult student who,
without having any desire or feeling any need to enlarge
his knowledge and understanding of himself, his fellow
men, and the world in general, is nevertheless passionately and intelligently interested in some specific subject
of real but limited cognitive value and for this sole
reason joins some course devoted exclusively to that
subject arranged by some agency of adult education? If
his concern with this one particular subject were to have
the result of deterring him from exploring and appreciating other realms of knowledge, taste, and experience,
then clearly what we should have to do with would be a
case of over-specialization in the sense already discussed
and clearly we could not describe the student in question
as engaged in an *educational* activity, since his studies
would in fact be *anti-educational* in character. If his
pursuit of his special interest simply failed to make him
aware of other, wider realms of knowledge, taste, and
experience (while not actually deterring him from exploring and appreciating these, that is, not positively
inflicting educational disabilities upon him), we should
still have to deny that he was engaged in an educational
activity properly so called, since no amount of knowledge,
no depth of understanding, no keenness of perception,
which is confined to some one, particular, limited subject
can ever make the narrow specialist into an educated man.
Of course, the firmness of our denial will depend on the
narrowness of his specialism. We could not say that a man
whose studies centred exclusively on, say, the history of
military uniforms was engaged in acquiring an education
even if he joined a whole series of courses on this
somewhat limited subject; if his studies centred exclusively on a rather wider subject, say the history of
warfare, it would surely still be misleading to describe

his attendance at courses as a process of education; but
if he took the whole of history for his province, im-
mersing himself with great thoroughness in this whole
basic form of human knowledge, then any description we
gave of his studies ought, I think, to recognize their
kinship with educational activities in the full sense of
the term, even although his exclusive study of history had
led him to neglect all the other major forms of human
knowledge and awareness. The broader the special subject
which a man is exclusively engaged in studying, that is,
the more appropriate it becomes to regard his studies as
partaking of the nature of an educational process. And it
obviously becomes still more appropriate to regard his
special studies as processes of education, the more they
link meaningfully up with other dimensions of experience,
the more they open doors leading into other forms of
knowledge and awareness, in short, the more they have the
result (even if unintended) of generally widening the
student's mental horizons. Thus in and through his exclusive attachment to historical studies a man might be
led to explore the history of ideas, the history of
science, the history of religion, the history of art, and
so on, and in this way might come to grasp and appreciate
the distinctive values, principles, issues, and methods,
and the distinctive kinds of insight and truth attainable
in these different realms; and in such a case, even if
the student never at any time explicitly devoted himself
to philosophy, natural science, religion, or art as
subjects of study in their own right but confined his
interest in these forms of knowledge to the parts which
they have played in human history, we should nevertheless,
I think, be very willing to allow that his study of
history had gone a considerable way towards establishing
a claim to be regarded as a genuine process of education,
on the grounds that the ultimate actual content of his
studies had turned out to be considerably richer and
cognitively more balanced than their specific overt
content.

Whether a process of study is at the same time a
process of education is not an all or nothing affair.
There can be no hard and fast rules for applying the term
'education' or the phrase 'liberal education'. Clearly,
words should be used to indicate distinctions, not to obscure them, and since there clearly is a distinction
between someone engaged in advancing his understanding
of one form of knowledge only and someone engaged in advancing his understanding of reality in all its basic
forms, it would seem reasonable to mark this distinction
by describing as *liberal* education' only those studies
which came somewhere near to realizing the latter type of

educational engagement. But to refuse altogether to apply
the term 'educational' to studies which developed a man's
awareness in one of its most fundamental forms, and in so
doing gave him a genuine if indirect insight into several
other basic forms of human knowledge, would surely - as
was suggested in Chapter 2 (12) - be puritanical to the
point of ineptitude. Whether a process of study can be
justifiably regarded as a process of education is surely
very much a matter of degree. We must allow a certain
amount of latitude in the use of the phrase, 'process of
education', and even in the use of the phrase, 'process of
liberal education' (although obviously our use of this
latter phrase needs to be subject to notably more rigorous
criteria, since the whole distinctive force of 'liberal'
when prefixed to 'education' - as was also suggested in
Chapter 2 (13) - consists precisely in the assurance which
it offers that the criteria of a genuine process of education are being abundantly satisfied). The important
thing is that we should be clear about *why* some process of
study can be correctly thought of as *more fully* 'a process
of education' than some other. To the extent that through
his studies a man can be correctly said to be acquiring a
broad and balanced knowledge and understanding of himself,
of his fellows, and of the world in which he lives, *to
that extent,* we may claim, his studies can be correctly
thought of as genuine processes of education. Of a
providing body like an evening institute or a university
extra-mural department we can, I think, say that it is
genuinely functioning as an agency of adult education to
the extent that it provides a range of courses wide enough
to give each individual adult the *opportunity,* over a
period of years, to enlarge his knowledge and understanding in ways which keep faith with the fundamental
educational requirements of breadth and balance. Of any
particular course of study we can say that it is genuinely
providing an educational experience to its members to the
extent that it *contributes* to their acquisition of a broad
and balanced body of worthwhile knowledge, either directly
by way of its specific overt content or indirectly by way
of its ultimate actual content. It perhaps needs to be
emphasized, however, that in the nature of the case no
single course or series of courses in history, philosophy,
literature, music, astronomy, or any other one form of
knowledge, branch of knowledge, or field of knowledge,
however generously construed, can possibly hope to do more
than *make a contribution* - perhaps a very big contribution, but still only a contribution - towards what its
members need if they are to be correctly thought of as
'advancing their education' in the truest and fullest
sense. Moreover in the last analysis, we must remember,

it is to the actual achievement of the individual learner
that we have to look if we are to discover whether anything that we are prepared to call 'education' has in fact
come about. And so we are, I think, bound to conclude
that the extent to which the processes of study engaged in
by adult students can be correctly thought of as processes
of education will ultimately depend on the extent to which
each individual student shows himself willing and able to
use the heterogeneous and competing educational opportunities placed before him, by judicious discrimination and
selection, to preserve some kind of overall breadth and
balance in the continuously growing measure of knowledge
and understanding to which he is aspiring.

This amounts to saying that in the last analysis the
responsibility for the mature John Smith's education has
to be borne by John Smith himself. In the case of the
child, it is primarily the school which must be held
responsible for ensuring that he is put in touch with a
range of knowledge sufficiently wide to give him some
understanding of what the world is like. In the case of
an adult, however, the educand is someone deemed to be
mature and therefore entitled to all the rights of
maturity and subject to all its obligations. At forty
or fifty years of age, it is John Smith who must have the
final say in determining the general shape and direction
of his continuing education. An individual's total life-
experience, the range of his insights, the shifting sum of
his knowledge, form a unique ensemble which becomes more
difficult to define and assess as each passing year adds
its new emphases and states its new demands. If it is
difficult for the mature John Smith to identify his
overall educational needs and establish relevant priorities among them, we can readily suppose that this would
prove an extremely difficult task for even the wisest,
most skilled, and most patient of educational counsellors.
In fact the individual adult is extremely unlikely to
enjoy close personal attention from a wise, skilled, and
patient counsellor, but even if he were lucky enough to
receive the most carefully thought out and personally
tailored educational counsel it would of course remain
his clear right, as an adult, to ignore it and set it
aside completely and to settle his own educational priorities according to his own unaided lights. This is not
simply because it is John Smith himself who has the
biggest stake in John Smith's education and should
therefore have the biggest say, for this argument applies
equally to the education of children. It is above all
because the adult is morally charged with the responsibility for his development as a person in a way that the
child is not and because, in presuming him to be a mature

human being and therefore an independent moral agent, we
are bound to accord him the ultimate right to fix his own
educational goals and choose his own paths to them. The
mature John Smith, we may say, has the *right* to take
overall command of his own education because it is on the
mature John Smith himself - not on some other person or on
some impersonal organization - that the *duty* to promote
John Smith's development as a person must ultimately rest.
    What this means is that, in a free society where for
the vast majority of adults participation in continuing
education will nearly always be voluntary and part-time
and where one man's life-experience and mental attainments
and requirements may be radically different from the next
man's, the construction of anything that we might call a
'curriculum' for an individual's continuing education at
some given stage of his life must in the last analysis be
left to the individual himself. Others may have excellent
advice to offer, based partly on their superior knowledge
of the inherent educational value of this or that possible
subject of study, partly on their estimate of what constitute the most serious gaps in this particular person's
knowledge, taste, and experience, and of course if he is
sensible he will listen to the advice they give him. But
the decision that at this particular stage of his life it
is right for him to be studying economics or zoology or
Italian, thus giving his continuing education this or that
general shape and propelling it in this or that general
direction, is in the last analysis an educational decision
which, morally, only the individual student himself can
make. In the case of children, even those educational
theorists who have advocated for the pupil the widest
possible freedom to determine his own curriculum have
tended to base their advocacy of this approach on its
supposed instrumental value as a learning strategy; when
they have appealed to ethical considerations rather than
considerations of practical pedagogy, they have seldom
tried to argue that we ought to presume a sufficient
degree of moral and mental maturity in the twelve-year-old
to justify making him the ultimate arbiter of his curriculum; and it has nearly always been obvious that they have
continued to regard the school, or perhaps the teacher,
but at any rate some adult agent or agency, as carrying
the ultimate *responsibility* for the overall education of
even the freest child. In the case of grown men and
women, however, the freedom of the individual student to
determine his own curriculum can be justified entirely by
reference to that distinctive constellation of moral
rights and duties which we are bound to ascribe to anyone
deemed to possess, in some sufficient degree, all those
various moral and personal attributes and competencies

which together make up 'maturity' in a human being. To
say that it is the individual adult student himself, not
his teachers or any of the course-providing institutions,
who must ultimately control the overall shape and
direction of his own continuing education is of course
not to say that the educational choices which he makes
will necessarily be the right ones; we are certainly not
asserting, in a spirit of educational relativism, that the
normative concept of 'educational value' can be reduced to
the descriptive concept of 'educational preference' and
that a suitable education for John Smith is therefore
always identical with whatever John Smith freely elects
to study; it is always perfectly meaningful to claim that
the overall mental development of some given individual,
who has elected to study, say, astronomy or archaeology,
would in fact have been best fostered, at this particular
stage in his life and in his particular circumstances, by
the study of, say, English language and literature, and
indeed in many cases claims of this kind are unfortunately
also perfectly true. A man's maturity does not prevent
him from making serious mistakes about his own best interests, mistakes which his teachers might well have avoided
if they had been charged with taking his educational decisions for him. On the other hand, his teachers too are
only human, and liable to make serious mistakes. If we
correctly insist that in the last analysis every adult
must be recognized to be individually responsible for the
overall pattern of his own continuing education, is this
not because we correctly judge that the right to make
one's own mistakes is one of the basic rights inseparable
from everything we understand by the word 'maturity'?

We have seen that whether the processes of study engaged
in by adults satisfy the 'achievement' criterion of an
educational process - and thus whether they can properly
be regarded as 'processes of education' in the full sense
of the term - rightly depends on the free choices made by
the individual adult student himself as, with a greater or
lesser degree of stable educational purpose, he organizes
or fails to organize his studies into a coherent, meaningful whole which will systematically foster his continuing
development as a conscious self capable of grasping and
responding to the world in which he finds himself
alongside his fellows. It is in the light of this basic
principle of the educational sovereignty of the individual
adult that we must also view what we have called the specifically 'task' criterion (or set of criteria) governing
processes of adult education properly so called: namely
those features of an educational process - wittingness,

voluntariness, conscious control, interpersonal encounter,
and active participation by the educand - which are
peculiarly connected with its nature as an activity or
task and which any educational process must evince if it
is visibly to respect and uphold the dignity as persons of
those to whose further development as persons it is essentially directed. Where the educands are children, with
comparatively limited responsibilities and rights and with
their briefer and narrower experience of life, it is often
questionable whether the proprieties characteristic of a
genuinely educational process can be observed or given
much substance in actual practice. To what extent is a
six-year-old aware of the overall purpose of his school
experiences? To what extent do fifteen-year-olds attend
school voluntarily? Despite his satchel and shining
morning face, the learning done by the whining schoolboy
after he has crept like snail unwillingly to school may
well not be done in any very educational spirit. Where
the educand is an adult, however, we judge it right that
in his educational decisions, as in other key decisions
affecting the pattern and quality of his personal life, he
should enjoy the greatest possible liberty with the least
possible interference by others, because we judge that as
a full moral agent it is he himself who ultimately has to
take responsibility for his own evolution as a person, and
we frame our expectations of him accordingly. We realize,
of course, that there are men and women of fifty who are
in fact morally and emotionally less mature than some boys
and girls of fifteen, but it is because we are entitled to
expect the adult to be capable of taking responsibility
for his life that we feel bound to *treat* him as someone
who can in some adequate degree measure up to this duty.
Now, in treating someone as an adult, we are treating him
as someone who is capable of taking serious decisions in
a serious spirit, and thus when he comes to take part in
processes of education the whole way in which he takes
part, it seems clear, must throughout be presumed to
reflect this generally deeper concern and sense of purpose
which we feel bound to ascribe to him.

We are, I think, in the first place entitled to presume
that the normal adult who is in process of being educated
will have a truer and more complete understanding of the
nature of what is happening to him than we can normally
presume in the young child or even the adolescent. He may
be unlikely to say, 'This course of study is advancing my
education'. He is extremely unlikely ever to say, 'This
course of study is developing me as a person by enlarging
my awareness' (although if he ever makes the former
statement, he is in fact making this latter statement,
whether he knows it or not). But there are obviously

very many ways, other than by giving a verbal description,
in which a man can plainly show that he is aware of the
nature of what he is doing or of what is being done to
him. This is evident in every sphere of human activity.
The man who grasps the nature of the task he is engaged on
will, for instance, repeat the successful steps he has
taken and try to build on them; he will try to modify
whatever unsuccessful measures he has taken or will drop
them from his repertoire altogether; he will acquire
collateral arts, ancillary to those he already deploys;
he will recognize opportunities and obstacles, distinguish
fellow workers, rivals, and adversaries, and confidently
identify situations which he can put to creative use; we
can watch him checking, correcting, altering direction,
taking stock, retracing his steps, but headed all the time
consistently forward; and in numberless other ways we can
be perfectly sure that what we are observing is someone
who is well aware of what he is about. And so when some
adult student is not content with joining courses but is
plainly determined to extract from them the last drop of
knowledge and insight they can offer, which he then
endeavours to hold as a living element in his mind and to
build upon; when through his use of libraries, museums,
theatres, broadcasting, and so on, he continually tries
to extend, in systematic and integrated ways, what he has
learned from more formal study; when he shows himself
alert to and excited by the connections which hold between
his different interests and keen to identify the wider
significance of whatever new knowledge he has acquired;
when he persists in his pursuit of knowledge through every
change in his personal fortunes, undeterred by adverse
circumstances and uninfluenced by any extrinsic advantages
which may accrue to him; then we are surely justified in
claiming, when such a man enrols on some fresh course of
study, that he is likely to have a pretty fair idea of the
nature of the exercise on which he is embarked. There
would be little point in speculating about the extent to
which a high degree of conscious educational purpose is
actually present in the minds of students enrolled on
courses of adult education in this or any other country.
It obviously always will be very much a matter of degree.
It may be present only in a very low degree. However,
what we can and must insist on is that the student shall
be in *some* degree aware that his studies are figuring as
part of his general education, and indeed it will be only
to that degree that we can correctly regard them as
constituting 'educational' processes properly so called.
He may not be aware that he is aware of this. When he
tries to formulate the purpose of his studies, he may
lapse into all kinds of circumlocutions and may completely

fail to do himself justice. What matters is not that he
should describe what he is doing as 'advancing his education' (since a schoolboy who totally failed to grasp the
point of his schooling might nevertheless be capable of
producing this stock reply when asked) but rather that he
should testify by his whole demeanour, by the ways in
which he actively responds to the situations and experiences before him, that the activity of developing his
knowledge and understanding and of building up his being
as a mind is in some degree meaningful and real to him.

This perhaps gives us the answer to the question which
was raised earlier in this chapter (14) concerning courses
where the ultimate actual content is significantly different from the specific overt content and of much greater
educational value - a course on stamp-collecting, for
instance, which is thought to justify its place in an
evening institute's educational provision because of the
geographical, historical, or anthropological knowledge
which it imparts - and where the providing body's professed aim is to educate students by stealth who would
otherwise not participate in adult education at all. Of
course, this kind of condescension is often pointless
anyway, since most adults can tell a hawk from a handsaw
and will either shun such courses altogether or join them
quite avowedly for the very purposes which remain officially unavowed; but even in the case of those students
who would sincerely avow themselves to be simply 'studying
stamp-collecting', when we observe the quality and complexity of their responses to the subject-matter actually
put before them it will often in fact be apparent, from
the ways in which they come to terms with it, explore its
ramifications, and rise to its unexpected demands, that
at a deeper level of their awareness they have in varying
degrees perceived, and by implication assented to, the
wider educational purposes of their studies. Naturally,
where this does not happen to any appreciable degree and
we are accordingly unable to credit students with any significant awareness of the nature of what is happening to
them, we are clearly bound to insist that one of the
fundamental proprieties of an educational process has not
been upheld and therefore that what these students have
taken part in cannot properly be styled a process of 'education'. It by no means follows that such students have
not been doing something very worthwhile. They have,
after all, unintentionally and unwittingly acquired
knowledge of considerable intrinsic value. They may at
some stage become aware of the value of what they have
unwittingly learned and begin to develop an active interest in the pursuit of worthwhile knowledge for its own
sake. The only reservation we must nevertheless insist on

making is that these highly desirable consequences have
not come about as a result of processes which meet the
full ethical requirements of a genuine process of education.

If we are entitled to presume that on the whole someone
whom we consider to be an adult is more likely than a
child or an adolescent to have a real awareness of the
nature and purpose of the educational situations in which
he is placed, we are surely entitled to make a similar
presumption with regard to the degree of willingness with
which he enters into these situations. The more mature
the educand, the more witting and also the more willing we
may presume him. Our presumption is of course primarily
an ethical not an empirical presumption. We have a
greater right to regard the grown man whom we find in an
educational situation as being there voluntarily than we
do the child; and he in turn has a greater right to take
part in education only by his own consent than does the
child. To be sure, every process of teaching or learning
which deserves the name of education ought to be undertaken only with the consent of the educand, whatever his
degree of maturity. However, mainly because of the intimate conceptual connection between the voluntariness of an
action and the agent's awareness of the nature of what he
is doing, it is to say the least somewhat implausible to
describe, for instance, a five-year-old in an infants
class as voluntarily embarked on a process of education.
(He may be voluntarily doing something, but it does not
follow that he is voluntarily seeking to develop himself
as a person by extending and enriching his awareness.)
Moreover, whatever his will in the matter, a child is
compelled by law to undergo education up to the school
leaving age, and when he goes on to further or higher
education his educational will is still dominated by extrinsic considerations of one kind or another - above all
the need to gain qualifications as a means to his personal
economic and social advancement. The adult student on the
other hand (at any rate in liberal adult education) is not
normally subject to educationally extrinsic pressures of
such definite and powerful kinds. As a matter of
empirical fact, therefore, his pursuit of education is
more likely to be voluntary, since it is in practice so
much easier for him to put education aside (as very many
adults manifestly do). And in any case, purely as a
matter of ethical principle, we both have a greater right
and are under a greater obligation to treat the adult
student as essentially a free agent, first, because as
someone deemed to possess the basic attributes and competencies of maturity we may and must presume in him a
greater capacity for autonomous choice than we can reason-

ably presume in the child, and second, because as someone
deemed to be a fully responsible moral being we are bound
to view his participation in educational pursuits as being
at least prima facie a specific actual exercise of his
maturer capacity for autonomous choice.

If we were to set out to analyse the concept of a
'voluntary action' at all adequately, we should of course
have to distinguish and elucidate a large number of
distinct if related senses in all of which a human action
can correctly be said to be 'voluntary', and it would
obviously be quite impossible for us even to begin to
undertake so complex and far-reaching a task here. Fortunately it is also unnecessary. Here we need only distinguish the particular sense in which a man's participation in education has to be 'voluntary' if the processes
in which he engages are to count as genuinely 'educational' processes.

What, then, is the educationally relevant sense in
which we can assert that a man's participation in education has to be 'voluntary'? We can, I suggest, correctly say that a man's participation in education is voluntary in an educationally relevant sense if and only if he
participates in education *for the sufficient reason that
it is what it is*. Or in other words, of a man who can be
correctly said to be participating voluntarily in education we must be able to say that he is doing so because
he aspires to a greater fullness of personal being by
enlarging his awareness, by developing his knowledge and
understanding, as something worth doing *for its own sake;*
and whenever we can make the latter statement, we can also
make the former. The important thing, therefore, is that
the student should sincerely feel that the pursuit of education is something *intrinsically* worthwhile. Once again,
however, we have to acknowledge that the question is
necessarily one of degree. A man's motives are nearly
always mixed. A teacher of English may join a university
extra-mural course in French literature because he judges
that of all the studies in which he can engage at this
point in time these are intrinsically the most worthwhile
in terms of his overall mental development; and this is
in no way incompatible with his also being motivated by a
desire to acquire knowledge of a related literature which
he hopes will be of direct practical use to him in his own
professional work, and perhaps even also by a simple
desire to go out a bit more and meet some congenial
people. There is no reason why strictly educational
motives, frankly vocational motives, and obscurer personal
motives of one kind and another should not live side by
side in the same student's mind, and indeed fructify and
reinforce each other. When someone participates in edu-

cation solely from motives of a strictly educational character, we are clearly entitled to say that his participation is 'entirely voluntary'. But we can still with perfect accuracy say that his participation is 'voluntary' even when he participates from a mixture of motives, provided of course that these include strictly educational motives and provided that the strictly educational motives would of themselves have been sufficient to ensure his participation had his other motives been for some reason inoperative. Even when his strictly educational motives would not of themselves have been sufficient, however, we are still not bound to describe his participation in education as 'involuntary' tout court: we know from experience that there are many adult students who are motivated by genuinely educational considerations to some degree albeit not to a sufficient degree, and where this is the case we are surely not just entitled but in accuracy obliged to describe the student's participation as at least 'not wholly involuntary'. (15)

It is perhaps desirable to re-emphasize that we are here considering the 'voluntariness' of a student's participation in education in one particular sense only, namely the sense in which a student's participation has to be voluntary if the processes of study in which he engages are to count as processes of education in the fullest sense of the term. There are undoubtedly many students, of very poor educational motivation, whose enrolment on worthwhile courses of study is nevertheless 'voluntary' in a wider and less educationally relevant sense - the owner of a small business, for example, who undertakes the study of economics in the hope that the knowledge he acquires will help him to run his business more successfully but who has little or no appreciation of the general educational value of his studies and would not be stirred by that reason alone to engage in them even if he had. While such a man's enrolment on his course is in a clear sense 'voluntary' (by contrast with, say, a junior bank employee who was directed by his superiors to enrol on the same course), it is clearly far from being voluntary in the sense required if the relevant 'task' criterion of an educational process is to be properly satisfied.

We may conclude, then, that while we are ethically obliged and empirically entitled to presume a generally higher degree of wittingness and willingness in the adult student than in the schoolchild (on the basis of which we may infer that in these respects the processes of study in which adults engage have a generally better claim to be regarded as processes of education properly so called), the actual degree to which these two ethical conditions are satisfied by individual adult students may vary

enormously from individual to individual. It would be
foolish, because futile, to try to draw a hard and fast
line below which the processes of study in which a man
engaged ceased to be processes of education altogether.
What we can confidently assert, however, is that *the
greater* a man's awareness of the overall educational
purpose of his studies and *the greater* his willingness
to commit himself to this purpose, *the more justification*
we have for regarding the processes in which he is engaged
as constituting 'processes of education' in the fullest
sense of the term.

Much has been heard in recent years from writers like
Ivan Illich and Everett Reimer about the miseries and
evils of compulsory 'schooling'. No doubt as public provision of adult education increases there will be some
losses as well as many benefits, and no doubt among the
risks which will have to be faced are those attendant on
any form of 'institutionalized education'. Thus the increasing professionalization of adult education can too
often mean a transformation of educators into bureaucrats
and a subordination of genuinely educational concerns to
the expediencies required by any system of close superintendence and control. However, as some followers of
Illich seem themselves to have recognized, (16) the education of adults is in some ways much less liable than the
education of children to be held down and compressed
within the narrow, mechanistic, factory-production-line
mentality which Illich considers to be endemic to
'schooling'. Of course in any large and highly organized
society in the modern world there will be inbuilt tendencies to regimentation and the direction of people into
slots and grooves, and it would be surprising if education
somehow managed to remain altogether exempt from these
tendencies. But we are entitled to expect that adults
will offer more resistance to all these subtly coercive
and depersonalizing tendencies when they threaten to
stifle the individual's freedom of educational choice and
educational evolution in later life, and that grown men
and women will fight them with greater skill and conviction than we can possibly expect of children or adolescents. And as a matter of fact we do find very much
less deliberate direction and control of students' choices
and styles or patterns of study in the domain of adult
education (at least in Western democracies) than in
schools, colleges, and universities where children and
young people are in one way or another subjected to the
constraints of a much more rigid system of educational
options with much narrower and more short-term definitions
of educational progress and much more immediate and
sharply felt penalties for educational failure. This is,

I think, largely because liberal adult education in the
West already observes many of the principles which Illich
(wisely or foolishly) would like to see governing the education of the young. In England, for example, there is
completely open access to most of the educational facilities offered by university extra-mural departments, the
Workers' Educational Association, and local authority
evening institutes, none of which normally demands any
kind of formal qualifications from prospective students;
the WEA (and some other organizations) still try to uphold
the principles that tutors should be chosen by the student
body and that syllabuses should be worked out by agreement
between the tutor and those who have opted to be his
students; and in the last resort adult students can
always 'vote with their feet' and so exert with impunity
one of the most practical and potent forms of student
pressure to which educational agencies - whose very raison
d'être, after all, is to provide classes for people - can
possibly be subjected. Admittedly, the average adult
student's enviable freedom from extrinsic constraints may
seriously diminish if English adult education ever becomes
engulfed by a demand for certificates, diplomas, and
degrees, or if it ever comes to be mainly provided in the
form of day-release or paid educational leave, since part
of his educational initiative will then in practice have
to be surrendered, to the examining and awarding institutions in the one case, and to both the educational
agency and his employers (or trade union) in the other.
But at present, at least, English adult education might be
said in many ways already to resemble the 'educational
free market' which Illich advocates as an ideal for the
future in opposition to the paternalistic and managerial
attitudes which prevail wherever education has become
institutionalized. We have seen that in the sphere of
education as elsewhere adults, to a very much higher
degree than children, have a *right* to be treated as free
agents who know what they are doing and who do it of their
own will; we may add that to a much higher degree than
children they are in fact likely to exercise this right
and to demand (either by active assertion or by passive
resistance and abstention) that educators and educational
providing bodies shall in their actual practice treat them
as free agents with ideas and a will of their own; and we
may note with some satisfaction, though hardly with com-
placency, that in England and certain other Western democracies it has so far proved possible to provide educational opportunities for adults which really do uphold
the character of education as a free commitment voluntarily undertaken by the educand, at least to a much higher
degree than has been achieved (or, pace Illich, is perhaps

inherently possible) in the case of children and adolescents.

There is, I think, no need for us to dwell at any
length on the third of the specific 'task' criteria of an
educational process. We have seen that we rightly require
of any process of education that it shall be under some
measure of conscious control throughout. This is more
than simply requiring that the educator (who may, of
course, be one and the same person as the educand) shall
have a general intention of educating. In addition we
require that each of the successive learning situations
to which the educand is exposed shall be subject to some
degree of conscious planning and contrivance, not
abandoned to the promiscuous interplay of random forces.
As a project of developing persons in their personhood, an
educational activity must be subject to continuous direction by the personal, however discreet and unobtrusive
its superintendence may in practice be. At every stage,
therefore, it must be presided over by clear and definite
educational designs, and as it advances its achievements
must be continuously open to responsible review and evaluation. A teacher who merely escorted his students to a
cathedral, museum, or art gallery, where he allowed them
to wander aimlessly around, could scarcely be described as
conducting an educational activity if he had made no
serious attempt to prepare his students for their visit
and made no attempt to assess its value with them after-
wards. Of course there is always some measure of contrivance, however pathetically vague and exiguous it may
be, in any situation where there is at least a general
intention that people shall be educated. Someone has
presumably at some stage decided that a cathedral or a
museum or an art gallery may be visited, but not a
gambling casino or a billiards saloon or a bowling alley.
Even when an assembled group of students is simply told,
'Discuss!', or 'Relate to one another!', without further
preamble (perhaps without even this preamble), faintly
beating its wings at the back of their minds will be the
surmise, however tentative, that some special response,
however dimly conceived, is expected of them by someone,
for some reason. However, in totally unstructured discussions, completely free encounter groups, and other non-
directive situations, the degree of concerted intelligent
design is often so very low and so very remote that to
regard such situations as satisfying our criterion of
'conscious control' would really be little more than an
empty courtesy. I am not suggesting that an educational
process ought to be under continuously tight control by
the teacher. Indeed, as we shall shortly see, this would
be contrary to what we require a properly educational

process to be. But in a properly educational process there is on the part of someone, teacher or students, some significant degree of intention to use each specific learning situation for some specific learning purpose connected with the overall purpose of the whole ongoing process. It is not enough that students should in a general way be aware of and assent to the broad *kinds* of situation in which they find themselves during the period of their education. Each specific situation itself must be to some degree framed to make a definite contribution towards achieving the distinctive purpose of the whole process in which it is an ingredient. The more frequently and completely this comes about, the more fully can the process in question be thought of as a properly educational process. And we are, I think, entitled to suppose that it is more likely to come about, the maturer the participants in the process. As a matter of empirical fact, adults who are faced by a comparatively structureless and ambiguous situation are more likely than are children to bring clear expectations into the situation, to impose patterns upon it, to transcribe upon it their own educational resolves and aspirations, and generally to shape it in ways that invest the whole situation with a stable and distinctive set of meanings or purposes. And as a matter of ethical principle, this is what we have both the right and the obligation to presume that they will do. Once again then, we can, I think, reasonably claim that the processes of teaching and learning in which adults engage ought to be regarded, on both empirical and ethical grounds, as in general more likely to satisfy one of the key requirements of a bona fide process of education.

The fourth of the specifically 'task' criteria of an educational process which we have propounded embodies the requirement that it should involve some kind of an encounter between persons. Directed as it is to 'the making of persons', a process of education should bear internal witness to the values which it sets out to promote, and thus we rightly require that every educational situation should at least to some degree partake of the nature of a meeting between free conscious selves who are willing and able to respond to each other with some measure of openness and sensitivity in an atmosphere of partnership and shared concerns. If, for example, we feel that the broadcasts, tutorials, counselling sessions, and summer schools of the Open University are what make its courses much more than just highly sophisticated and thorough correspondence courses, this is only partly because these forms of personal encounter between teachers and taught are, as a matter of psychological fact, conducive to more efficient learning; it is also because we feel it to be

intrinsically appropriate that processes which we propose
to dignify by the name 'educational' should have a personal not an impersonal character and should therefore
include the possibility of meaningful personal relations,
not exclude personal relations altogether. (17)

To speak of 'personal relations' is to speak of the
characteristic kinds of relations which can and ought to
hold only between free conscious selves each of whom is,
first, a centre of awareness reaching out to and mirroring
reality (including the reality of other selves and, in
self-awareness, his own distinctive reality);   second, a
separate *individual,* an idiosyncratic and indeed logically
unique point of view on the world, *from* which it is
mirrored, grasped, valued, and responded to;   and third, a
locus of those special rights and duties which are conse-
quential upon being the kind of being that is not only *in*
the world but also capable of consciously relating himself
to the world and in fact under a continuous necessity of
doing so.   If one man is to treat another as a 'person' -
that is, to recognize him as the bearer of at least the
minimum rights integral to that status - he must at least
have for him what Kant called 'respect', an active and
principled sense of the other's inherent dignity and
worth.   Morally, this means that he must at least regard
him as someone whose interests have to be given due consideration, not ignored or belittled;   as someone who has
free will and is therefore morally accountable for his
actions, not a zombie or a machine;   and in both these
fundamental senses as an equal of himself, a 'moral
equal', neither inherently his inferior nor essentially
his superior.   However, one man may treat another as a
person without there being, properly speaking, a personal
relation between the two.   For a personal *relation* to
exist between two people, there must at least be *mutual*
respect, expressing itself in the ethically fundamental
ways just described.   Now clearly, a teacher of children
is morally bound to treat his pupils with this kind of
respect, since this is the very minimum to which they are
entitled.   But it does not follow that he will be treated
with respect in return, and indeed it will be unreasonable
for him to expect this if his charges are very immature.
Mature or immature, he must treat them as persons.   But it
is only if they are relatively mature that they will be
able to recognize and respond to, in their teacher and in
their fellow pupils, what he recognizes and responds to in
them.   It is only if a class is relatively mature that its
members will be able to enter into anything that can
properly be called 'personal relations'.

A class of adults, on the other hand, is made up of
students who are necessarily deemed to be mature, and we

are therefore justified in presuming that its members
normally *will* be able to conduct themselves towards one
another, and towards their teacher, with at least the
consistent respect due to each of them as the very minimum
to which they are all entitled as persons. Indeed we are
justified in expecting much more than this from a class of
adults. While mutual respect is the minimum form which
relations between persons can take, the fuller development
of personal relations involves the flowering of such
qualities as forbearance and good humour, sympathy and
active benevolence. Those with whom we have good personal
relations are those with whom we co-operate enthusiastically; they are those to whom we show generosity and affection, and with whom we are bound by ties of mutual
loyalty, reliance, and trust. Since a class of adults is
made up of men and women who are supposed to be mature,
who are supposed to be more fully developed *as persons*
than children or adolescents, with a wider and deeper
understanding of themselves, their fellows, and the world
in which they have to live and work together, we are
justified in expecting its members to do more than just
conduct themselves according to the minimum standards required of relations between persons: we are entitled to
expect that a class of adults will engender and sustain a
network of relations which are more fully and distinctively personal - relations between teacher and students, and
relations among the students themselves - than we can
reasonably expect in the case of a class of
schoolchildren, and that these relations will surpass in
quality and scope the elementary respect on which they are
based and become more akin to the kinds of personal relations we have in mind when we use such words as
'community', 'fellowship', and even 'friendship'. No
doubt classes of adults, like classes of children, can
sometimes sink below the level of the personal, rent by
jealousies and antagonisms, the relations among their
members cheapened and coarsened by petty squabbles and
grudges (although such classes must be extremely rare in
liberal adult education, where class membership is for the
most part voluntary). No doubt, too, classes of adults
may sometimes fail to rise above a level of grey and
leaden formality, their members irreproachably correct but
stiff, reticent, and cautious in their attitudes to one
another and to their teachers. Nevertheless, what we are
entitled to expect in a class of adults, and what we in
fact generally find, is on the whole a greater willingness
to take the other person's experience and insights
seriously as a point of view on life, a quicker and more
perceptive understanding of the other person's difficulties and problems, a greater concern to be fair to every-

one, greater tolerance, tact, delicacy, and attention to
the feelings of others, and in general a greater fastidi-
ousness and considerateness in teacher-student and
student-student relations than we can normally expect to
find in a class of schoolchildren. What we are entitled
to expect, and what we commonly find, is that a class of
adults will prove able to work together with something
more than a basic mutual respect: we expect, and we
commonly find, a measure of active harmony, of mutual
assistance and support, cordial, unselfconscious, and
unforced, which therefore entitles us, I think, to regard
the adult class - to a much greater degree than a class of
schoolchildren - as constituting a real exercise in human
collaboration, and at its best as making up a real fellowship of study.

The fifth and last of the specifically 'task' criteria
of an educational process which we have propounded stipu-
lates that it should involve some kind of activity on the
part of the educand, some degree of personal effort and
self-giving which will ensure that he is a real participant in the working out of his own education, not just a
passive beneficiary of the exertions of others. This requirement is intimately connected with the preceding one.
To enter into anything that can properly be called personal relations with others necessarily involves some kind of
outgoing self-commitment, however meagre and tentative.
And to take part in anything that can properly be called
collaboration, still more a real fellowship of study,
necessarily involves a fairly high measure of enterprise
and personal initiative, since in any sort of positive
collaboration or living fellowship the efforts of one
partner have to be sustained and reinforced by the efforts
of all the others. No doubt student activity and student
effort are very important as means leading to more efficient learning: no doubt, as a matter of empirical fact
in the psychology of learning, a student who explores
archives, performs dissections, or takes part in exca-
vations is much more likely to make significant advances
and hold on to what he has learned than a student who puts
out very little activity of his own in the course of his
studies. But a logically quite separate reason for encouraging active student engagement (and the one with
which we are solely concerned here) is that it is
intrinsically fitting that processes designed to foster a
man's development as a person should themselves respect
and uphold one of the principal attributes of personhood -
namely the capacity to *act*, to freely initiate meaningful
changes in some state of affairs (including the agent's
own state of mind) - and it is intrinsically unfitting
that such processes should in their own nature ignore or

deny this essential attribute of the very personhood which they seek to foster.

Obviously the 'activity' which we require of the participants in an educational process is not just any sort of activity. If it is to count as *educational* activity of an appropriate kind, it has to be purposefully relevant to the specific forms of worthwhile learning which are under way. That is to say, its appropriateness will be determined, not by the energy expended, the enthusiasm displayed, the gratification experienced, or the sense of fulfilment obtained by those taking part (though these are often very good clues that something educationally worthwhile is happening), but by the degree to which student activity is purposefully in keeping with the objective standards inherent in the specific subject which is being studied or the specific skill which is being mastered. A would-be poet in a creative writing class whose activity consisted in indefatigable effusions of bad verse ought not to be deemed an 'active' member of the class in any educationally relevant sense if, in his artistic pride, he made not the slightest attempt to learn from criticism or to identify and remedy his own shortcomings. There are still, alas, very many well-meaning but naive teachers who are perfectly happy to extend a welcome to any kind of student activity, however shapeless and maladroit, in the name of debased conceptions of 'creativity', 'originality', or 'self-expression'. The numerous fallacies to which these terms offer hospitality have been well described by J.P.White, who points out that if we are to speak meaningfully of 'creative' activity we must be able to say of the activity in question that it 'leads to a result which conforms to criteria of value in one domain or another'. (18)   Similarly, real 'originality' involves more than just 'producing something entirely new', since a monkey let loose on a typewriter would be virtually certain to dash off an entirely new string of nonsense syllables;   real originality involves producing something entirely new with at least some degree of awareness of the distinctive novelty of what one is doing, and this entails that one has some degree of acquaintance with existing achievements in one's chosen sphere of activity;   but real originality surely also involves producing something which has some degree of genuine intellectual or artistic merit judged by the objective standards of truth or taste governing the sphere of inquiry or creativity in which it is produced and giving that sphere its distinctive character and meaning. In any case, the kind of originality which counts as educationally worthwhile does not literally require the production of something 'entirely new', but only that something of genuine merit should be produced by

someone who is at least aware that what he is doing is
new to him; thus originality in the sense appropriate to
educational activity does not require a student to produce
some unique and unprecedented discovery, invention, idea,
or insight, but it clearly does require him to possess an
adequate background of relevant knowledge - since the more
he knows of existing achievements the more difficult and
therefore the more praiseworthy it is for him to branch
out in directions which are new to him - and it does
require him to produce work which satisfies objective
standards of value in the sphere of his specific activity.
The same is true of anything that really deserves the name
'self-expression'. There can be no self-expression in a
cognitive vacuum, since the 'self' which a man expresses
is not some absolutely detached and insular 'pure ego',
uncontaminated by external influences, but rather his
awareness of the world in which he finds himself; what
he expresses is his knowledge, beliefs, judgments, perceptions, and feelings *about* the different kinds of
objective reality by which he is confronted; and so the
educational value which we can attach to a student's
efforts at self-expression, not only in literature and the
arts but in every form of human awareness, cannot possibly
be determined without reference to objective standards of
truth and taste which may well oblige us to regard what he
accomplishes as elegant and ingenious but which on other
occasions may oblige us to regard his accomplishments as
commonplace or unimaginative, and perhaps sometimes even
as inept and obtuse.

Of course, in determining the educational value of a
student's activity we also have to take into account the
ability and existing level of attainment of the individual
student whose activity it is. What we should consider a
rather inferior piece of work if done by a gifted student
in an advanced class might reasonably count as a very good
piece of work if done by a somewhat backward member of an
elementary course. However, neither the gifted student
nor the backward student could be meaningfully said to be
doing work that was good, bad, mediocre, promising, disap-
pointing, improving, or in any other way deserving of the
slightest commendation or criticism, if we could not
ultimately appeal to standards or criteria, intrinsic to
the specific kind of work being done and therefore external to the individual students themselves, against
which the performance of each of them could be objectively
measured. We can only say that someone's work is
straightforwardly 'good' or 'poor' in the light of
whatever objective criteria are appropriate to the work in
question. And we can only say that someone's work is

'good for him' or 'poor for her' by appeal to the same
objective criteria, appropriate to the work in question,
since it is only in the light of these objective criteria
that one student can be judged to have done '*better* than
might have been expected' and another to have done '*less
well* than might have been expected'.

While we can and must acknowledge, then, that the educational status of student activity is that of an end in
itself, something to be valued for its own sake as an
integral part of every truly educational process, not just
a highly effective instrument or midwife of learning to be
valued purely for its utility, we do well to remember that
the student activity under consideration has to be of an
educationally relevant kind: it has to be activity *within*
the terms of reference and criteria governing the specific
domain which is being studied. There are, of course, many
different kinds of educationally relevant activity.
Worthwhile student activity may take the form of overt
physical behaviour - sculpting, playing musical instruments, performing chemical experiments, drawing maps, re-
hearsing a play, conversing in a foreign language - or it
may consist in reading, considering, visualizing, reflecting, and other forms of essentially private and
inward activity. But whether the student is engaged in
painting a picture of his own or contemplating someone
else's, in transcribing a mediaeval document or reading
Froissart, in thinking out a philosophical argument for
himself or expounding it to others, the purpose of his
activity, if it is educationally relevant, will always be
to enlarge his awareness (or his fellow students'
awareness) of some thing, event, state of affairs,
process, concept, or dimension of reality which comes
before him as an intrinsically worthwhile object of
knowledge laying just claim to his attention and that of
his fellows. To speak of 'the purpose' of student activity is of course perfectly consistent with recognizing, as
we did a moment ago, that student activity must be
regarded as an educational 'end in itself'. We saw in
Chapter 1 (19) that there are many activities directed
towards purposes which are logically intrinsic to these
activities, in the sense that the concept of some distinctive purpose forms part of the very concept of the
activity in question; and we saw there that 'education'
(like 'haircutting', for example, but unlike 'running')
is a purposive activity of this logical type. Of genuine
student activity, then, we can say both that it counts as
an integral part of any process of education worthy of the
name and so as an educational end in itself, and also that
its value on any given occasion depends on the degree to

which, on that occasion, it fulfils its own nature by
fulfilling the essential purpose of the process of which
it is an essential part.

Now, when we come to examine the levels of student
activity which actually prevail in classes of children and
adolescents and compare these with the levels normally
prevailing in classes of adults, we are bound to recognize, as a fact of experience, that there are many
schoolchildren who, in their classwork and private study,
show themselves to be industrious, enterprising, and
committed, as well as many who can only be described as
apathetic and inert and some who are positively ob-
structive or even subversive. Among the adult population,
too, it is a fact of experience that individuals vary very
widely in their degree of educational zeal and initiative,
from those whose appetite for educational activity seems
to be insatiable to those who seldom rouse themselves to
pursue any serious intellectual or artistic interests and
others who react to the very idea of education with sus-
picion or open hostility. The difference is, however,
that whereas children who are indifferent or hostile to
education are nevertheless compelled to go to school,
adults who have no interest in or liking for educational
activities are normally free to stay away from them and
nearly always in fact do so. Thus, at any rate in liberal
adult education, a teacher of adults at the beginning of a
new session can be much more confident than can, say, a
teacher in a comprehensive school that his classes will
contain no saboteurs and few if any passengers. It does
not follow that all his classes will operate at a high
level of educationally relevant activity, since the
comparatively high motivation of his students may not be
matched by their ability to do work that is in keeping
with the inherent requirements of the subject to be
studied or the skill to be mastered. But it does mean
that he has on the whole a better chance than his
colleague in the comprehensive school of eliciting responses from his students which will become more and more
educationally relevant and worthwhile in proportion to
their growing experience and his own skill as a teacher.

Moreover, we are *morally entitled* to expect a higher
degree of educationally relevant activity from students
who are deemed to be mature men and women. For reasons
which we have already seen, we are entitled to presume a
comparatively high degree of wittingness and willingness
in students deemed to be mature; we are entitled and
indeed obliged to treat each individual adult as in the
last analysis responsible for the shape and direction of
his own continuing education; and we are justified in

expecting supposedly mature students to be capable of
working together on a basis of mutual respect and even
active goodwill and harmony. And it is surely clear that
from men and women who are deemed to be aware of the
nature of what they are freely doing, who are regarded
as ultimately carrying the responsibility for their own
continuing education, and who are supposed to be capable
of collaborating meaningfully with one another and with
their teacher, we are morally entitled to expect - as a
corollary of all these presumptive moral and personal
attributes and competencies - an appropriately high
measure of active and constructive participation in
whatever educational business occupies the classes or
courses of which they are members. The maturer the
student, the more we are justified in expecting him to
view himself as a full member of his class or course, with
all the rights and obligations attendant on this, and to
pull his weight alongside his fellows. The maturer the
student, the more we are justified in expecting him to do
all he can to make a success of the educational enterprise
on which he is embarked.

    In England and some other Western countries these dis-
tinctive expectations have in fact always played a prominent part in both the theory and the practice of liberal
adult education. In England the idea of the adult class
has been traditionally the idea of a co-operative venture,
an active partnership of study, to which the tutor brings
his specialist knowledge of the subject and the students
bring their accumulated experience, their general
knowledge of life, and their many individual insights and
points of view. Everyone has something to contribute, and
something is contributed by everyone. While the tutor's
knowledge of his subject obviously places him in a special
position, he is supposed to be and commonly is in a very
real sense on a footing of moral equality with his
students, many of whom may be older than he is, wiser,
perhaps more sophisticated, and indeed sometimes simply
better educated than he is, although their specialist
knowledge of the subject in hand falls short of his: it
would often in fact be simply absurd for a tutor of adults
to come forward with the manner of someone who has an essentially superior and condescending role to play.
Ideally, and often in practice, the atmosphere in an adult
class is one of shared endeavour, of work done and understanding gained for which every member of the class has to
take some share of the responsibility and receive some
share of the credit. It is the exact opposite of what
Paulo Freire calls 'the banking concept of education' in
which

the teacher teaches and the students are taught, the
teacher knows everything and the students know nothing,
the teacher thinks and the students are thought about,
the teacher talks and the students listen meekly, the
teacher disciplines and the students are disciplined,
the teacher chooses and enforces his choice and the
students comply, the teacher acts and the students have
the illusion of acting through the action of the
teacher, the teacher chooses the programme content and
the students (who were not consulted) adapt to it, the
teacher confuses the authority of knowledge with his
own professional authority, which he sets in opposition
to the freedom of the students, and the teacher is the
subject of the learning process, while the students are
mere objects. (20)

Indeed this description of what we might call 'the teacher
-as-fiend-incarnate', by one of our foremost educational
demonologists, furnishes us with an admirably succinct
account of everything that the typical adult class sets
out *not* to be (and usually succeeds in not being). Thus
the students in a liberal adult education class in this
country are quite likely to belong to a students' organization (the WEA, for example, or a democratically run
Educational Settlement) which actually controls the class
and is perhaps responsible for the very existence of the
class. They often help to settle the topic and work out
the detailed syllabus for their course in consultation
with the specialist whom they have invited to be their
tutor. They often express very definite views about the
learning goals of their course and about the approach to
the subject which they would like their course to take.
If the tutor flouts these views too flagrantly, he simply
loses his class. And above all students in a liberal
adult education class are expected to pull their weight
and take their share in making the class educationally
effective by joining actively in the various kinds of
pursuit which make up the distinctive work of the class.
In a zoology class this may mean collecting and classifying specimens, performing dissections, or observing
animals in their natural habitat. In a local history
class it may mean transcribing mediaeval documents, analysing data culled from probate registers, or drawing maps
to illustrate the progress of agricultural enclosures in
some particular locality. In a literature or philosophy
class it may mean the private analysis and evaluation of
texts, the preparation of papers to be presented to the
class, and informed and critical participation in class
discussion. But whatever the subject it is always possible and always desirable that students in a liberal adult

education class should play their full part, which should
normally be a very large one, in making their class a
purposefully functioning educational unity; and in
English adult education this is a principle which is not
only honoured in theory but also accepted and to the best
of their ability implemented by the great majority of
those engaged in educational practice.

Many of those engaged in adult education as tutors or
students would, I think, unhesitatingly pronounce the
activity of class *discussion* to be by far the most important kind of activity in which the members of an adult
class can take part. This is not just because of the
instrumental value of discussion as a highly effective
means or method of facilitating learning. It is primarily
because, at its best, the kind of discussion in which an
adult class engages lays claim to being something of very
great *intrinsic* value - namely a direct, living encounter
of consciousness with consciousness in face of some
objective reality which it is their common purpose to
explore and understand. (21) At its best it becomes the
kind of authentic educational 'dialogue' so vividly described by Buber: (22)

> It is the extension of one's own concreteness, the
> fulfilment of the actual situation of life, the com-
> plete presence of the reality in which one partici-
> pates. Its elements are, first, a relation, of no
> matter what kind, between two persons, second, an event
> experienced by them in common, in which at least one of
> them actively participates, and, third, the fact that
> this one person, without forfeiting anything of the
> felt reality of his activity, at the same time lives
> through the common event from the standpoint of the
> other.

Of course there are classes where what passes for 'discussion' is nothing like this, but merely desultory,
rambling, and incoherent chatter, screening rather than
revealing the students' relations to, and perspectives on,
the common reality which they have ostensibly gathered to
confront and grasp. But where real discussion takes
place; where a dozen minds are occupied together in
questioning, evaluating, expounding, criticizing, and in
one way or another coming to terms with some poem, historical event, philosophical argument, or sociological
concept which is the continuing focus of their common
attention; where the unspoken premises governing their
transaction are those of completely open but purposive and
reasoned inquiry; and where each individual contributes a
fresh dimension by freely offering his own insights and
interpretations to be thoroughly weighed and considered by

his fellow class members, who feel themselves growing in understanding of the theme before them as the discussion of it unfolds and evolves: then what we are witnessing is surely something which embodies and proclaims the essential spirit of education as a cardinal human undertaking more completely than any other single activity in which it is possible to engage. And it is surely something which, while perhaps possible with children and adolescents, can only ever achieve its full meaning when those who are participating can make their contribution from a certain depth of experience and personal reflection which we can reasonably expect only in students who are comparatively mature. Real discussion - authentic educational dialogue - is, we may claim, one of the crowning glories of all education, and one of the peculiar and distinguishing glories of the education of *adults*.

We have now looked at each of the specifically 'task' criteria - wittingness, voluntariness, conscious control, interpersonal encounter, and active participation - which we demand that any process of study shall satisfy if it is to count as a genuinely 'educational' process, and we have seen that, in each case, experience entitles us and the presumptive maturity of the educands obliges us to regard these criteria as being more fully satisfied in the case of the education of adults. In these respects, the activities of teaching and learning which go on in schools, where trapped pupils often have to be coerced and cajoled into acquiring worthwhile knowledge, sometimes do not bear even a superficial resemblance to genuinely educational activities. No doubt the 'achievement' criterion of education - the acquisition of broad and balanced structures of intrinsically valuable knowledge and understanding - is more consistently satisfied in the school situation, where the operation of a coherent curriculum is intended to ensure that every child leaves school having at least been given some grounding in the main forms of knowledge necessary to the mental equipment of an educated person. Despite many failures, this intention is no doubt in the main broadly fulfilled, and at any rate the average child in school is much more likely than the average student in adult education to be pursuing a broad and balanced range of studies and much less likely to be caught up in purely vocational studies or to be immersed in recreational pursuits of an educationally trivial kind. However, the 'achievement' criterion of education also includes the requirement that the educand should become in some degree *committed* to pursuing and preserving knowledge in all its various forms. (23) An educated man is supposed to appreciate, value, and *care for* the bodies of worthwhile

knowledge into which he has been initiated. And we may
well feel that the processes of study in which adults
engage are on the whole more likely to achieve *this* distinctive educational end than are the processes which go
on in schools (which too often turn out, in this respect,
to have been positively anti-educational).

Moreover, if the 'achievement' criterion of an educational process tends to be more consistently satisfied
in the school situation, this is largely *because* attendance at school is compulsory and *because* the broad
outlines of the child's curriculum are normally worked
out and laid down by the school - in other words, it is
because the 'task' criteria of an educational process tend
to be comparatively played down or ignored. If,
therefore, we want to see what education can *achieve,* when
undertaken systematically and on a large scale, we do well
to look at what is done with children in schools. But if
we want to see what true *engagement in educational activity* is like, we do better to look at the experiences of
mature men and women participating in education in later
life, and especially at the experiences of those who participate in what is conventionally (and rightly) designated as 'liberal adult education', that is, in England,
chiefly the non-vocational work done by university extra-
mural departments and the Workers' Educational Association.

When we assert that the educational experiences of
adults exemplify and convey the true nature of education
as an activity more completely and more vividly than do
those of schoolchildren, this is of course an empirical
assertion about what generally is the case but it is also
a declaration of what we are morally bound and entitled to
presume to be the case. Now, although as a contingent
matter of fact we find that schoolchildren tend to fulfil
most of the 'achievement' requirements of education more
consistently and thoroughly than adults, if we accept that
as a matter of moral principle they cannot reasonably be
expected to fulfil the 'task' requirements of education to
any very high degree - because of their presumptive immaturity and because of the lower moral expectations built
into the concept of 'immaturity' - it plainly follows that
in the nature of the case we cannot ever reasonably expect
children to meet the *full* requirements of an educational
process to a high degree. (Individual children or classes
of children may in fact do so, but we are not morally
entitled to expect them to do so.) With adults, however,
the case is crucially different. Adults *can* reasonably be
expected to fulfil the 'task' requirements of an educational process to a high degree, and since it is merely

a matter of contingent fact (not a presumptive limitation rooted in the very nature of adulthood) that they are less likely to fulfil the 'achievement' requirements of education to the same high degree, we can therefore say of adults, and only of adults, that there is *nothing* which, in the nature of the case, makes it unreasonable to expect *them* to meet the *full* requirements of an educational process to a high degree.

Now, this amounts to saying that adults, and only adults, can reasonably be deemed capable of rising to the full demands of education. In fact, they seldom do so. In fact, children sometimes do so. But the greater maturity which we necessarily ascribe to the adult entitles us, indeed obliges us, to *regard* him as being generally capable of undertaking more, partaking of more, initiating more, sustaining more, and - other things being equal - capable of altogether doing and being more than we can reasonably expect or require of the average child or adolescent, whether his sphere of choice and action is life in general or whether it is those dimensions of life in which he is seeking to develop himself in his being as a person, that is, to educate himself. It is in the years of immaturity that human beings are *made* to engage in education. But only in the years of their maturity can we ever say that what they are engaging in is really *education,* since it is only in the years of maturity that we can really regard education as having become in the fullest sense possible. And since only the possible can ever be actual, it is only in the years of maturity that we should ever expect to find educational processes actually becoming - in the spirit as well as in the substance - everything that they inherently ought to be. It is only in the years of maturity that we should ever expect to find processes of education in the fullest sense actually taking shape and coming to pass.

Adult education and society

Part IV

Concepts of educational justice   8

In every civilized society education is widely recognized
to be something of very great value. By many people it is
recognized to be something abundantly worth pursuing for
its own sake. By still more people it is seen as a cornu-
copia from which all kinds of benefit, private and public,
may be made to flow: some see in education the path to
personal economic and social advancement, the ladder to a
higher income or at least to higher status, while others
see in it a powerful lever of social change or perhaps an
essential stabilizing force giving massive support to the
maintenance and transmission of the established order of
things. Whatever special value is attached to education
by particular individuals or groups, however, one fact is
obvious to all. It is inescapably obvious that the level
of education which people actually attain is something
which in every society varies considerably - in some
societies, enormously - from individual to individual and
from social group to social group. In every society, as
well as people who are rightly thought of as highly educated or reasonably well educated (in terms of the general
educational standards of the society in question) there
are usually large numbers of people who are rightly
regarded as quite poorly educated and many others whose
level of education is so low that (in terms of prevailing
standards) it is often considered reasonable to refer to
them simply as 'uneducated'.

Now, whenever something admitted to be of great value
is perceived to be unevenly distributed it is desirable,
and in any case inevitable, that fundamental questions
should be raised about the manner of its distribution and
in particular about the principles of fairness or justice
by which its distribution ought to be governed. Within
the adult population of our own and other civilized societies the level of actual educational attainment varies

strikingly from individual to individual and also from one
social group, section, or class to another. Within the
adult population of our own and other civilized societies
the degree of ongoing educational activity, the degree to
which different individuals and groups avail themselves of
such facilities as are provided for their continuing education, varies still more strikingly. It is both inevitable and desirable, then, that we should at some stage try
to establish what is involved in and what we are committed
to by the notion of 'educational justice', and that we
should go on to examine the ways in which our general
principles of educational justice ought properly to be
framed and brought into focus when we come to apply them
to the education of adults in particular. It is,
therefore, to these questions that we shall now turn.

The word 'justice' belongs to a gallery of ethical
terms, along with words like 'freedom' and 'democracy',
which have such extreme generality of meaning (not to say
vagueness), and which at the same time convey such powerful moral approbation, that they are endemically liable to
be used, and abused, in a bewildering variety of sometimes
incompatible senses. Needless to say, it is *distributive*
justice with which we are here alone concerned, but it is
in fact the notion of distributive justice - whether
applied to education, economic issues, or any other sphere
of human interest - that gives rise to most of the ambiguities and difficulties which typically bedevil and
frustrate our innocent attempts to determine what is
'just' and what is 'unjust' in most of the matters that
concern us. If the bare concept of 'justice' in itself
conveys no more than the idea of giving people what is due
to them, the notion of 'distributive justice' has only a
slightly less meagre content and in itself conveys no more
than the idea of giving people their *rights*. (Whereas a
man's 'rights' are discretionary claims, which he is
always free to waive if he chooses, that which is 'due' to
him may sometimes be rightfully enforceable upon him, as
in the case of lawful punishment, for example.) And of
course, merely to know that in giving a man his rights we
are acting justly, and that in denying him his rights we
are acting unjustly, is to know very little of practical
use unless we also know what it is that he has a right to
and how his right to it can in practice be upheld.

Since it is solely with distributive justice that we
are here concerned, for brevity we can from now on con-
veniently use the single word 'justice' on the understanding that, unless otherwise specified, it will always
in fact be distributive justice that we have in mind.

The concept of justice is always recognized to be

closely associated with, and is sometimes mistakenly
identified with, the concepts of 'impartiality' and
'equality'. Certainly the just man has to be impartial,
at least when his actions affect people's rights. Some
moralists would argue that the concept of impartiality
does not strictly apply to certain domains of purely
private taste and initiative - the contrasting of
friendships, for example, the giving of presents, the
choosing of a spouse, and so on - where the concepts of
'rights' (and therefore also of 'justice') would seem to
be quite inoperative and out of place. But clearly where
people's rights are concerned, the just man is under a
binding obligation to act impartially, that is, not to
show favour to any individual or group. This, of course,
amounts to saying that he is under a binding obligation to
uphold the rights of all *equally,* and indeed it is fairly
obvious that the moral principle of 'treating people impartially' and the moral principle of 'treating people
equally' are essentially one and the same moral principle.
Whether expressed in terms of impartiality or of equality,
however, it is important to notice that the principle in
question is a purely formal one, which does not of itself
prescribe any one particular course of action rather than
another in any concrete moral situation. Indeed, its
abstract formality is almost that of a logico-mathematical
principle, since in effect it simply enunciates the tautological proposition that, ceteris paribus, any moral situation 's' defined by the presence and operation of moral
rights 'r' and therefore morally demanding a form of
conduct 'c' is equivalent to any other moral situation 's'
defined by the presence and operation of moral rights 'r'
and therefore morally demanding the form of conduct 'c'.
It is not surprising, therefore, that justice should
involve more than respect for the principle that people
should be treated equally or impartially. After all, it
is possible for a man to be impartially unjust. While
seeking no sort of selfish advantage from his treatment
of his children, a Victorian father might with stony
impartiality deny each and all of them various things to
which as children we should consider they had a right (the
right to engage in imaginative play, for example), and in
such a case we should certainly accuse him of acting unjustly towards his children although we could not accuse
him of any kind of partiality, since he would be showing
no favouritism and his unjust treatment of his children,
we have postulated, would not be intended to further his
own private interests or gratify his own private desires
(with which his misguided policy of harshness might even
be in conflict). Such a man would be scrupulously ap-

plying the principle of equality of treatment to all of
his children, but he would nevertheless also be acting
unjustly towards all of them.

Treating people equally may in a sense be a necessary
condition of just action, then, but it is certainly far
from being a sufficient condition. The concept of
justice, we have said, is the concept of giving people
their *rights*, and therefore it is here, in the giving to
people of what they are morally *entitled to*, that we have
to locate both the necessary and the sufficient conditions
of just action. In giving Smith what he is entitled to,
we are fulfilling the necessary condition of acting justly
towards him, since it would be solely in refusing him what
he was entitled to that unjust action towards him would
consist. And in giving Smith what he is entitled to, we
are fulfilling the sufficient condition of acting justly
towards him, since there is no more that can be required
of us if all we are seeking to do is what is required of
us by simple justice. We ought not to say that 'treating
Smith equally with other bearers of the same rights' is
also necessary, as a *second* condition, if our treatment
of him is to count as just, because this purely formal
requirement is *already* built into the concept of giving
Smith 'what he is entitled to' (which of course is and
must be exactly the same as the entitlements of people
whose entitlements are exactly the same as his). When we
said above that treating people equally was a 'necessary
condition' of just action, we added 'in a sense',
therefore, because as a purely formal condition it would
be unnecessary and in some circumstances misleading to
state it, as it were, in a separate clause, as if it were
an independent and supplementary condition embodying fresh
requirements of a substantive kind.

The principle of equality, then, is a necessary condition of every just act only in the same trivial sense
that the laws of logic, for example, are necessarily
presupposed by every true statement. If, nevertheless,
men's attention is so often held and their emotions are
so often aroused by issues of equality and inequality,
this is, I suggest, partly because in practice the
treatment meted out to Brown and Robinson is often rightly
regarded as furnishing a good clue to the kind of
treatment to which Smith is entitled, and partly also
because the portions awarded to Brown and Robinson in fact
often determine the kind of portion which remains available to be awarded to Smith. The part played by considerations of equality in arriving at just solutions, I
suggest, when not purely logical or formal, will always
be found to be evidential or causal rather than constitutive or substantive.

Of course, it would be wrong to underestimate the importance even of purely formal principles in arriving at moral decisions. The principle that '2x3=3x2' may not exactly be heavy with momentous truth, but any book-keeping which broke this elementary arithmetical rule would have proved itself to be impossibly bad book-keeping. The principle of equality represents, if we may so put it, the arithmetic of justice. When two people who are acknowledged to have precisely the same rights are treated differently with regard to the subject-matter of these rights - when, for example, one man is paid £100 and another £200 in respect of the same service, or when one employee is granted three months leave and another six months leave in respect of the same industrial injury (all other relevant considerations being presumed to be equal) - then we can be quite sure that an injustice has been done to at least one of them.

The trouble is that all other relevant considerations seldom are equal. And to treat people exactly alike who are in fact different in some relevant respect is to create a situation which is every bit as unjust as the situation created by treating people differently who are in fact exactly alike. Indeed, very often one and the same unjust action can be correctly described in either of these superficially different ways. When the starving are considered to have a right to larger rations than the already well-nourished, one and the same unjust act of discrimination against Peter can be described equally correctly by saying that starving Peter has been given no larger rations than well-nourished Paul or by saying that he has been given smaller rations than starving Patrick and Pamela although he is admittedly no less starving than they are. The principle of distributive justice is often expressed, cryptically but appropriately, in the formula that equals should be treated equally and unequals un-equally. We are obliged to treat Peter, Patrick and Pamela equally with one another but we are not obliged to give well-nourished Paul equal treatment with his starving neighbours in respect of the size of his rations. The equality of treatment demanded by justice, we are often told, does not mean *uniformity* of treatment.

Now this is manifestly true. And yet it is only a half-truth. Equality of treatment *does* mean uniformity of treatment - when it is uniformity of treatment to which the parties concerned have a right, that is to say, when they have exactly the same rights. It only does not mean uniformity of treatment when the parties concerned have no right to uniform treatment, that is, when they do not have exactly the same rights. The fact is that words like 'equality' and 'uniformity' are systematically ambiguous. Sometimes the qualification 'just' is understood, and sometimes not. When it is understood that we are speaking only of a *just* equality of treatment, clearly inequality of treatment is bound to be unjust. But clearly when we are speaking of literal or factual equality (equality in respect of the actual sums of money paid, equality in respect of the actual periods of leave granted, equality in respect of the actual amounts of rations allocated, and so on), inequality of treatment may or may not be unjust, depending entirely on the rights of the parties concerned. Similar considerations apply to words like 'discrimination' and 'privilege'. Unless the qualification 'unjust' is understood, the assertion that someone has been discriminated against leaves it an open question as to whether an act of injustice has been committed. It is just to discriminate against the lazy and the self-assertive. It is just to discriminate in favour of the humble and the hard-working. Whether we consider some discriminatory act to constitute fair or unfair discrimination will depend entirely on what we consider to be the rights of the parties concerned. The question which we always have to answer, then, and the only question which we have to answer in order to establish what is the just course of action in any moral situation, is this: To what can the various people involved be correctly judged to have a right?

Before we consider whether and in what sense people can be said to have rights in the domain of education, it will be as well, I think, if we first pause to take note of some important logical features of the concept of 'rights' in general.

First, there is the relation between rights and duties. Logically, whenever Smith can be correctly said to have a right to something, there must be some party or parties whose duty it is to ensure that Smith obtains whatever it is that he has a right to. The party in question may be a particular individual or body, as when Smith has a right to the wages owed to him by his employer or employers. Or it may be society in general, as when a man has a general right to have his property protected against theft. Or it may be anyone who happens to be suitably placed to carry out the duty in question on the occasion that it arises, as when the victim of a road accident has a right to the active assistance of anyone who happens to be passing. But the idea of someone's possessing the right to something logically incorporates the idea of *some* party

or parties, particular or general, actual or hypothetical,
to whom there attaches a correlative duty. The converse,
however, is not true. It is not the case that the idea of
someone's having a duty logically incorporates the idea of
some party or other to whom there attaches a correlative
right. A man has duties to himself (the duty to develop
his talents, for example), but it would not make sense to
ascribe to him 'rights against himself', since in such a
case the party against whom the 'right' was held would be
in a position to waive the right and this in itself is
obviously enough to nullify it as a right. Some moralists
would argue that it does not make sense to ascribe
'rights' to animals, although we undeniably have duties
towards them. And most moralists would accept that we
have what are sometimes called duties of imperfect obli-
fation, that is, duties which are in varying degrees less
than rigorous in the sense that it would be in varying
degrees inappropriate to exact them compulsorily from
those whose duties they are, and which therefore do not
give rise to anything we can properly call rights: thus
although men have a general duty to contribute to charitable causes at least sometimes and in some measure, since
we have a general duty to show concern for those in need,
no individual or body has a 'right' to be the recipient of
charity (nor does the whole class of the needy have such a
right), since if an individual, body, or class has a right
to something what they have a right to clearly cannot be
regarded as 'charity'. Every right generates a correlative duty, then, but not every duty generates a correlative right.

That this is so will be evident from a consideration of
the second general feature of the concept of a 'right' to
which we shall draw attention. When we say that Smith has
a right to something, we are saying not only that he has
a moral claim to it but also that his moral claim is of a
kind which it would in principle be reasonable for him to
enforce, and for us to help him to enforce, against those
on whom he has the claim. Of course, there will be
circumstances which will sometimes make it in practice
inappropriate or unreasonable to enforce a man's rights.
Moreover, we must bear in mind that there are many different forms which enforcement can take besides direct coercion, and whether it is in principle reasonable to
enforce this or that species of moral claim is in any case
very much a matter of degree: it is obviously more
reasonable to force an employer to pay his employees the
wages he owes them than to force passers-by to render assistance to the victims of a road accident, although obviously the enforcement of the latter duty is by no means

unreasonable. Be that as it may, there clearly are many
duties the performance of which it would in principle be
reasonable to enforce, and there are also many duties the
performance of which it would not in principle be reasonable to enforce. Although we have a duty to show some
sympathetic interest in the problems worrying another
person (even a comparative stranger), for example, this
is hardly the kind of duty which it would be appropriate
to try - directly or indirectly, by coercion or inducements - to force people to perform, since the value
of the sympathy to the person receiving it would largely
vanish if it were not sincerely and therefore freely
given. There are many other considerations which can make
it intrinsically inappropriate or unreasonable to enforce
the performance of some duty, but obviously where the
value of the dutiful action is largely dependent on the
quality of the intentions governing it this will generally
be in itself a conclusive reason against enforcing its
performance. When we judge that it would be in principle
unreasonable to enforce the performance of some duty,
then, we are judging that the duty in question is not of
a kind, or of a degree of importance, which generates
anything that can be properly called a correlative
'right'. But when we judge that it *would* be in some
degree intrinsically reasonable to enforce the performance
of a given duty, what we are judging is that any moral
claims generated by the duty in question are of a kind,
or of a degree of importance, which does merit their being
accorded the status of rights.

Third, we need to bear in mind that conflicts of rights
can and do frequently occur. An employee's right to the
wages owed to him by his financially ailing employer may
conflict with the rights of his employer's creditors to
receive payment for the goods and services which they had
supplied to him. Since some rights are more important
than others, when this happens the more important right
will override the less important (at least to some extent,
namely to the extent that there is a difference in importance between them). Of course, there is a sense of
the word 'rights' in which it must always be morally wrong
to deny a man his rights, and in this sense of the word it
is obvious that a 'conflict of rights' is logically impossible. If the word 'right' is taken to signify what a
man is morally entitled to after everyone's moral claims
have been duly weighed and compared and a just balance
struck, obviously a conflict of rights in this sense
simply cannot occur. However, if - as we typically do -
we apply the word 'rights' to general types or categories
of moral claim rather than to the specific moral claims

which emerge victorious from the clash of moral claims in
specific situations, then it most certainly makes sense
to speak of a conflict of rights and it is lamentably
common for such conflicts to occur. Nothing of substance
hinges on our choice of expressions, as long as we are
clear about the distinctions which these are intended to
mark. Having defined a right as a species of moral claim
which it would in principle be reasonable to enforce, we
can properly draw attention to the fact that in practice
it may happen that two or more parties may possess such
claims in circumstances which render it impossible to meet
all of them in full, and in such a case we can properly
say that there are claims which it would in principle be
reasonable to enforce - that is, rights - but which in
practice it would not be reasonable to enforce in full,
since the result of doing so would be the infringement of
other rights which we also consider to make serious and
binding claims upon us, and thus we have to conclude that
some kind of mutual adjustment or harmonization is called
for.

Fourth, rights may be either positive or negative in
character - that is, they may be rights to some definite
measure of active assistance (so-called 'welfare rights')
(1) or they may be rights of non-interference (or 'liberties'). Accordingly, the duties which they impose may be
duties of active intervention or they may be duties of
passive acquiescence, and plainly it is essential that we
should be clear about what kind of duty is entailed when
we ascribe some given right to someone. When we say that
all men have a right to work, for example, are we saying
that society has a duty to ensure that everyone has the
means and opportunity to work, if necessary by providing
work for him to do, or are we merely saying that it is
unfair to prevent or deter people from doing work which
they are willing and able to do? Are we demanding intervention, or are we protesting against interference? When
we say that people have a right to a home (at least in the
sense of some kind of permanent accommodation which is
private to them), we are obviously saying that they have
a right to be given some sort of active assistance to
acquire a home. Equally obviously, when we say that
people have a right to smoke, we are not implying that
they should be actively helped to acquire the materials
of smoking, but only that they should ordinarily be
allowed to smoke as they please without hindrance or
molestation. Of course, there are many different ways and
degrees in which people can be actively assisted, ranging
from direct provision to discreet guidance and encouragement; and there are many different ways and degrees in

which people can be actively prevented and deterred,
ranging from forcible prevention to gentle dissuasion and
indirect discouragement. No doubt the refusal to help,
advise, or encourage can sometimes operate as a sufficient
deterrent, and no doubt abstaining from interfering with
someone's efforts can sometimes amount to providing them
with the object of their efforts. We may accept that in
practice the kinds of steps needed to implement what we
have called people's positive rights are not always
markedly different from the kinds of steps needed to
implement what we have called their negative rights.
Nevertheless, whatever *measures* may as a matter of empirical fact prove to be needed to secure a man's rights, the
nature of *that to which* the man in question has a right is
what must first of all be determined, and in settling this
essentially ethical question it is obviously necessary
that we bear in mind the distinction between having a
right to the beneficent exertions of others and having a
right simply to be or do for oneself what one chooses to
be or do for oneself without let or hindrance.

The fifth and last feature of the concept of 'rights'
to which we shall draw attention is that a man's rights
are from his point of view *discretionary* claims, which
must in principle be granted if he chooses to press them
but which no one can properly force him to press. While
I have a right to demand that my employer shall carry out
the promises which he freely made to me, I am at liberty
to release him from any or all of his promises to me if I
so choose. A 'right' which its possessor could be properly compelled to exercise would no longer be a *right:* its
nature would be that of a duty, and indeed its nature
would clearly be that of a duty of the rigorous and
bindingly obligatory type. Although there are no doubt
rights which their possessors morally *ought* to exercise
(a man's right to take measures to keep himself in good
health, for example), if we are to speak of a 'duty' to
exercise such rights this will be at most a 'duty of
imperfect obligation', the performance of which it would
normally be inappropriate - indeed morally wrong - to
enforce. Except in the case of a conflict of rights, no
one can have a right to demand that I shall exercise my
rights. Except when the rights of others are thereby
jeopardized, my refusal to exercise my rights can never
be correctly described as unfair or unjust. To have a
right to something is to have a morally enforceable claim
to it, which, however, I may or may not choose to enforce,
as I and I alone decide. Every possessor of rights, we
may say, has the right to decline to exercise his rights.

Now that we have seen what we are logically committed

to when we assert that someone has a right to something, we are in a position to consider whether and in what sense people may be correctly said to have rights in the domain of education. It is, I think, easier to identify the general grounds on which people can be said to have a right to education than it is to establish precisely what the scope and limits of their educational rights are. It is fairly obvious, for instance, that the educational rights of children are mainly grounded in the principle that, since a child does not choose to be born, those who are responsible for summoning him into existence have a binding duty to help him to become more fully and completely that which they have summoned him into existence to be: that is, they have a duty to foster his growth and development as a person, and it is the bindingness and gravity of this duty towards the child which justifies us in describing his claims to education as 'rights'. Since our concern here is with the educational rights of adults, we need not trouble ourselves about the identity of the party or parties against whom the educational rights of children are properly asserted (the relative obligations of parents and society, for example). (2) In the case of adults, we may assume, whatever educational rights they may possess represent claims which they are entitled to press against the society to which they belong (or against any agencies to which society might choose to delegate its responsibilities). And the general grounds on which adults may be deemed to possess educational rights, and on which society may be deemed to have definite educational duties towards its adult members, are on the whole fairly clear. Among the most grave and binding duties of any society is its duty to preserve its members and to assist them in their efforts at self-preservation. But equally grave and binding is its duty to help them become fuller, better people, to help them make the most of their opportunities of life so that they do not just barely exist as persons but become more fully and intensely alive, more fully and intensely aware of the world in which they find themselves alongside their fellows, and thus more fully and intensely *real* as conscious selves and living personalities. A just society cannot remain indifferent as to whether its members are lifeless machines, docile languorous animals, or living, active, wakeful, and intelligent human persons. To its children it owes a particular duty. But to its adult members, too, it has educational duties of the utmost seriousness, based ultimately on the general moral principle that we have an obligation to help our fellow men to make the most of themselves and to reach the highest level of humanity and

of personal worth that they are capable of attaining.
This obligation, powerful enough in the case of an individual's relations to his fellows, is in the case of a
society's relations to its members a duty of the most
basic and inescapable kind. Of someone who is earnestly
striving to make himself into a truer, fuller human being,
more reasonable, more perceptive, with a wider range of
insight and a greater depth of understanding, we can say
not only that it is strongly desirable that he should be
actively helped but that he has a positive *right* to be
encouraged, guided, and helped and that a society which
remained indifferent to his needs would thereby be
declaring itself indifferent to the deepest personal good
of its members. Of a society which was indifferent to the
development of its members as persons - still more of one
which (like some actual societies) was systematically
hostile to this objective - we would surely be bound to
say that, in this major respect, it was showing itself to
be very much less than a just society. (3)

   Moreover, there is such a thing as a man's right to
know. A man has a right to be told those truths which are
genuinely of direct or indirect concern to him, and in
some circumstances leaving him deliberately in ignorance
of the truth amounts to the same thing as deliberately
lying to him. Our duty to tell the truth is a duty to
tell the whole truth as well as nothing but the truth.
Whether suppressio veri actively misleads those who have
a right to know the truth suppressed or whether it can
merely be accused of wilfully keeping them in ignorance,
in either case an obligation of a grave and binding kind
is being violated and an act of injustice committed. Of
course, there are many truths which do not concern us,
directly or indirectly, and which we therefore have no
right to be apprised of. There are many truths concerning
others which are of a purely private character and which
rightly remain confidential to those concerned and perhaps
their closest associates. But the knowledge which it is
the proper business of education to communicate is clearly
of public and indeed universal concern: it is knowledge
of the workings of the physical world, knowledge of human
society, of our common past, of logical and moral principles, and in general of the myriad things, events,
processes, relationships, and concepts which make up the
objectively accessible world in which we live alongside
our fellows and which we, along with them, are entitled
to explore, contemplate, appreciate, and enjoy. Everyone
surely has a right to know who he is and where he is, what
kind of a being he is and what kind of a situation he
finds himself in. That is to say, he has a positive right

to be given this knowledge if it is already known by
others, not just a negative right to acquire this
knowledge if he can, without active obstruction by others.
Those who possess this knowledge surely have a positive
duty to communicate it. The general knowledge of public
concern which a society possesses, then, it surely has a
positive duty to transmit to its members, and it is on
this intellectual obligation owed by a society to its
members that the adult's right to continuing lifelong
education may surely be held in part to rest.

Some people might try to argue that educational activity in later life, while no doubt very admirable and well
worth encouraging, cannot really be regarded as something
for which society has a binding *duty* to make provision but
rather ought to be viewed as something of essentially
private interest and significance which individuals ought
to pursue for themselves at their own expense, possibly in
co-operation with like-minded individuals by means of
voluntary and self-supporting associations formed for this
purpose. At most, some people might argue, the public
provision of liberal adult education is something which is
highly commendable and desirable, if public resources will
stretch so far after all the real obligations of society
to its members have been met; but at most it is a work of
supererogation on the part of society, and surely not
something which people are entitled to demand from their
society as a right. Now, assertions like these are very
commonly made, and when supported by an all too easily
compiled selection of sufficiently tendentious examples -
courses on bridge, golf, motor car maintenance, soft toy
making, millinery, and so on - they often enjoy a high
measure of plausibility. However, what such assertions
backed up by such examples in fact reveal, I suggest, is
that those who make them either have a total misconception
of what the liberal education of adults is really about or
have totally failed to grasp the crucial part which education, properly so called, can play in shaping a man's
whole life-experience and investing it with immensely
greater meaning and worth. We have already pointed out
and indeed emphasized (4) that courses on bridge, flower
arrangement, dressmaking, and so on, whatever their general social or therapeutic value, are normally of such scant
educational value that they can seldom be seriously
regarded as 'educational activities' properly so called
(in fact they seldom are by those who attend them) and
certainly not as exercises in liberal adult education.
And so, when we claim that adults have a moral right to
continuing lifelong education, we are of course by no
means claiming that they have a moral right to be provided

with golf coaching or with help in making their own hats
or dresses or maintaining their own cars. What we are
claiming is that they have a moral right to be actively
aided in their efforts to extend and deepen their
knowledge and understanding of themselves and others, and
of the wider world in which they and their fellows live,
and thereby to become fuller and more complete human
beings. What we are claiming is that a society which
deliberately left some of its members mentally undeveloped
and ignorant when they were hungering for greater
awareness and understanding would be in this crucial
respect a positively unjust society, for it would be
deliberately allowing some people to go through life
narrowed and diminished as persons, with a poorer capacity
for experiencing and grasping life in all its facets than
they might have had; it would be deliberately allowing
some people to spend their whole lives on a lower level of
consciousness, on a lower plane of being as persons than
they might have attained, and by this act of social denial
it would be committing one of the most deadly of all forms
of social injustice. Grown men and women who are seeking
deeper and richer insights, more systematic and varied
knowledge of the human condition, and wider spheres of
mental activity and achievement, surely have a *right* to
expect the highest measure of assistance in their endeavours from the society to which they belong. It was
Sir Winston Churchill, in a memorable and much-quoted
statement in the House of Commons, who declared: (5)

There is, perhaps, no branch of our vast educational
system which should more attract within its particular
sphere the aid and encouragement of the State than
adult education. How many must there be in Britain,
after the disturbance of two destructive wars, who
thirst in later life to learn about the humanities, the
history of their country, the philosophies of the human
race, and the arts and letters which sustain and are
borne forward by the ever-conquering English language?
This ranks in my opinion far above science and technical instruction, which are well sustained and not
without their rewards in our present system. The
mental and moral outlook of free men studying the past
with free minds in order to discern the future demands
the highest measures which our hard-pressed finances
can sustain. I have no doubt myself that a man or
woman earnestly seeking in grown-up life to be guided
to wide and suggestive knowledge in its largest and
most uplifted sphere will make the best of all the
pupils in this age of clatter and buzz, of gape and
gloat. The appetite of adults to be shown the foun-

dations and processes of thought will never be denied
by a British Administration cherishing the continuity
of our Island life.

We consider ourselves entitled to assert, then, that
the educational obligations of society to its adult
members represent a positive and ongoing duty of the most
serious and binding kind. But perhaps we ought also to
emphasize here that it is not only society which has educational duties. Every individual adult also has duties
in the domain of education. Each of us has a duty to take
what steps he can to make himself a wiser, better person,
and if a man neglects to foster his own development as a
human being, if he neglects the opportunities offered to
him to gain new perceptions and insights and advance in
knowledge and understanding, we are bound to consider that
in this important respect he is a morally poorer being
than his neighbour who hungers and thirsts after every
truth, great or small, in which he hopes to find something
that will help him to become in some degree a more fully
aware and more fully responsive person. However, when we
say that a man has a duty to continually reach out after
continually higher levels of education and that he is a
better man for doing so, we must not be taken to imply
that this duty is of the rigorous and bindingly obligatory
type which it would be right to exact forcibly from anyone
who will not discharge it voluntarily. A man's efforts to
improve himself would lose all their moral value if they
were made unwillingly and merely as a result of pressure
or coercion. In any case, it would be wrong to force any
adult to take part in the work of formal and officially
provided classes and courses, since he might well judge
(and might sometimes rightly judge) that the level or type
of work being done in such courses as were officially
available and conducted by the teachers officially appointed was completely irrelevant to his personal educational needs; and as we saw in Chapter 7 an adult is
fully entitled to be guided by his own judgment in this
matter. The individual adult has duties in the domain of
education, then, but they are not the kind of duties which
give rise to rights against him on the part of society.
They are duties of imperfect obligation. While every
adult ought to exercise his educational rights in full,
it would be wrong for other people to force him to exercise them even in part. Society may suggest, advise,
prompt, encourage, appeal, remonstrate, and exhort. But
if it in any way *constrains* a man to perform his educational duties, it does so at the cost of doing violence
to their character as educational *rights*.

We must now turn to what is surely the most important and certainly the most difficult and complex of the questions that face us. What precisely are a man's educational rights? What precisely is it that an adult is entitled to in the domain of education?

To this question two completely different types of answer may be offered. First, it may be suggested that people have a right to attain some specific level of educational *achievement*. Some absolute level of attainment may be specified, whether high or low; or the level of attainment to which a man is entitled may be fixed in relation to whatever educational levels are in fact being attained by his fellow members of society at that particular time. Alternatively, it may be suggested that what people have a right to is some specified share of the *resources* - the educational materials and equipment, the knowledge and skills of sympathetic teachers, and so on - which are in one way or another, and in varying degrees, necessary if a person's education is to be systematically advanced.

Now, the suggestion that people have a right to attain some specified level of educational achievement is intelligible, I think, only if we suppose that it is possible for a man's educational advancement to be secured for him entirely by the actions of others. To say that a man has a right to something, we have seen, logically implies that someone else has a duty to provide him with that thing, and this in turn implies that it is possible for the latter to provide it. If it is quite impossible for me to perform some service for my neighbour, I cannot meaningfully be ascribed a 'duty' to perform it and my neighbour cannot have a right to require it of me. A man may have a right to be treated for an incurable disease, but it would be nonsense to say that he had a right to be cured. Thus it is only if it is possible for a man's teachers to secure for him a given level of educational attainment that he can be meaningfully described as having a 'right' to that level of attainment.

If everything that has been said so far about the concepts of 'education', 'teaching', and 'learning' is accepted, however, we are clearly bound to conclude, not only that it would be educationally inappropriate, but also that it is in fact *impossible* for a man's teachers to do any such thing. Teaching, we have seen, is not the 'bringing about' of learning if by this is meant that the learning done is wholly attributable to certain measures taken by the teacher, since it is only if a man responds to the teaching he is receiving that learning will take place. (6) The teacher is the 'external proximate agent'

who stimulates learning but does not literally cause it to
occur. The decisive act in the learning process, as we
earlier saw, must emanate from the will of the learner.
(7) But what this clearly entails is that no teacher can
possibly give a guarantee of educational achievement to
his pupils, since the achievement sought depends in large
measure on the efforts of the pupils themselves. And from
this it clearly follows that his pupils, or those who
desire to be his pupils, cannot meaningfully be ascribed a
'right' to any fixed or given level of educational attainment, in whatever way supposedly determined. A man
cannot have a right to reach some given level of educational attainment defined in absolute terms, whether
conceived of as a personal minimum level specific to him
or whether laid down as a general minimum level for
everyone. Even if the level of attainment to be reached
is pitched extremely low, the most skilled and consci--
entious endeavours of a man's teachers cannot ensure that
he will reach it, for without his active collaboration
their endeavours will be wasted. Nor can a man have a
right to reach some given level of educational attainment
defined in relative terms, that is, by reference to the
actual levels of attainment reached by other members of
his society, whether what he is supposed to be entitled
to is exact parity with others or whether (for whatever
reason) he is supposed to be entitled to a level of educational attainment in some fixed degree higher, or in
some fixed degree lower, than the average level of attainment actually reached by other members of his society
at the time in question. To grant a right to Smith to
reach whatever level of attainment will actually be
reached by Brown - or at any rate the right to reach some
level fixed by specific reference to that actually attained by Brown - would (if it could be put into effect)
obviously be deeply unfair to Brown: it would set all
Brown's efforts at naught, since his finest efforts would
only bring him some fixed measure - perhaps higher, perhaps the same, perhaps lower - of what Smith was being
generously guaranteed, granted, and presented with freely
and as a matter of course. But in any case Smith *cannot*
be guaranteed a level of attainment which will be related
to that actually reached by Brown, unless of course we are
prepared to take whatever measures may be necessary to
check, restrain, or nullify the educational endeavours of
Brown himself. And the measures that would be necessary
to achieve this end would be quite certainly abhorrent and
almost certainly impracticable. The measures that would
need to be taken to ensure that Smith's general level of
knowledge, understanding, insight, taste, and skill was

continuously maintained in some definite relation to that
of Brown, never deviating from this to any significant
degree for any significant period of time, would obviously
involve nothing less than the continuous superintendence,
planning, and control of the thoughts and experiences, and
therefore of the interests, activities, and relationships,
not just of Brown but of *both* men in every department of
their daily lives, since the toleration of unlicensed
personal initiatives of any kind would mean tolerating the
various discrepancies in general mental attainment to
which these would so often lead. Consider what would have
to be done if this concept of educational 'justice' were
to be enforced throughout a whole society. People who
shared the same keen interests would often have to be
prevented from associating, in case their association
awakened talents and perceptions which would set them in
some uncovenanted fashion above their uninterested
fellows. People who had no common interests would have
to be driven together, to develop skills and forms of
understanding which they had not the slightest wish to
acquire. Many would have to be held back, chafing and
embittered, while others were pushed forward, reluctant
and uncomprehending. In fact a totalitarian society would
be the sine qua non of this kind of educational engineering. The whole of society would have to be turned
into one big schoolroom, with perfect discipline imposed
upon everyone from above (except, of course, for the élite
few who would function as the schoolmasters).

Anyway it is, I think, extremely doubtful whether Smith
could be guaranteed a level of mental attainment comparable to that of Brown even if it was intended to bring this
about by crushing Brown down to whatever level seemed
commensurate with Smith's ultimate ceiling of attainment.
If society cannot definitely guarantee to elevate the
minds of its members, neither can it be absolutely sure
of its power to curb, constrain, and crush them. But
since policies of 'positive discrimination' against the
intelligent and the energetic cannot be definitely assured
of success, clearly no one can be meaningfully said to
have a 'right' to a level of educational attainment which
only the successful and wholesale implementation of such
policies could possibly guarantee.

Moreover, if education is essentially the development
of persons in their personhood, to say that someone had a
right to some given level of educational attainment (in
whatever way defined) would be to say that he had a right
to become a person of a certain kind, that he had a right
to achieve for himself a certain personal stature or
inherent personal worth. However, it is surely manifest

that no one can have a 'right' to become an intrinsically higher kind of person. We have to make ourselves better, by effort, self-discipline, and constant upward striving. The most that we have a right to is to be given some measure of help upon our way.

Thus it is not to any specified level of educational achievement, I think we may conclude, but rather to some specified share of educational *resources* that the adult must be deemed to have a right. It is to classrooms, laboratories, specimens, tools, equipment, books, and (above all) teachers and their teaching skills that he has a right, not to some prefigured quality of mind, not to some definite measure of insight, knowledge, and judgment, which in the end he may or may not attain whatever the resources placed at his disposal.

Theoretically, it might seem, every adult might be credited with a right to some absolute amount of educational resources, for example some fixed quantity of educational materials and some definite sum of teaching time, expertise, and effort. In practice, however, it is obviously impossible for a society to guarantee to each of its adult members a fixed sum of educational resources, since the total amount of resources which any society can physically afford to make available for adult education will be likely to vary from one period to another, perhaps even from year to year, and the total amount of resources which can in practice be made available for adult education is something that obviously varies enormously from society to society. (If what people in general were supposed to be morally entitled to was some absolute amount of resources for their continuing lifelong education, it would be hard to see why this absolute amount should be fixed at a higher level for an Englishman than for a Sudanese, as obviously it would in practice have to be. The rights pertaining to members of comparatively rich societies surely do not differ in kind from those pertaining to members of comparatively poor societies.) In practice, then, people in general simply *cannot* be guaranteed any given absolute sum of resources for their continuing education, and from this it follows that they cannot even in theory be credited with a 'right' to some definite amount of educational resources specified in absolute terms. Thus what every individual adult does have a right to, it seems clear, can only ever be some appropriate *share,* and neither more nor less than that share, of whatever overall resources a society finds that it can reasonably devote to the business of promoting the education of its adult members.

Now, unless there turn out to be special reasons for

assigning to this or that category of adults a somewhat
higher or lower share of the socially available educational resources, the share of resources to which any individual adult is morally entitled will, it would seem, be
exactly equal to the share to which every other adult is
morally entitled. Of course, the type of resources to
which one man may properly lay claim will often be very
different in character from the type of resources to which
his neighbour may properly lay claim. One man will need
access to a chemistry laboratory, while another will need
tuition in the use of a musical instrument. A common
measure will therefore be needed for comparing and
equating their respective claims, and - given that we
have excluded the criterion of educational benefit or attainment for all the reasons that we have just seen - it
is hard to see how this common measure can be anything
other than the comparative overall *cost* of meeting their
different claims, no doubt expressed ultimately in our
society (indeed, presumably in most societies) in
straightforward monetary terms. Not everyone will in fact
claim the full share of educational resources to which he
is entitled, thus enabling the shares of all those who do
claim their full entitlement to be proportionally
augmented. However, unless there are good reasons to the
contrary, it would seem that simple justice can only consist in recognizing every adult's moral *right* to a simple
and literal equality in the apportionment of the available
resources, and it will then, we may conclude, have to be
left to those responsible for organizing the provision of
adult education to translate this general principle into
detailed and regular practice as best they can.

But is an exactly equal division of resources what educational justice does in fact dictate? May there not in
fact be good reasons in justice for apportioning the resources available for continuing lifelong education
differently in different cases?

It can, I think, easily be shown that most of the
reasons commonly advanced in favour of a differential
distribution of educational resources are strictly irrelevant to questions of educational *justice* and would lead to
situations which might in various ways be thought of as
desirable but which, viewed in terms of what people are in
fact entitled to, could not properly be regarded as fair
or just. When it is argued, for example, that resources
should be directed to those joints or sinews in the social
organism where they will best serve the health or improve
the efficiency of the whole organism (it might be by supposedly reducing racial tensions, or it might be by supposedly removing misunderstandings between capital and

labour, or it might be by supposedly promoting any other
theoretically laudable social, economic, or political
objective), it will often be clear that policies are being
envisaged which will in fact subordinate people's educational rights to considerations of perhaps urgent but
probably limited and transient social utility. (8) Even
when such policies do not involve tailoring the content of
courses to this or that social, economic, or political
objective - and so destroying them as properly *educational*
courses - they at least involve directing educational resources away from those who want and value them to those
who do not necessarily either want or value them; that
is, they subordinate the production of educational good to
the production of other varieties of social good and so at
least result in manifest educational injustice, which
because of the great importance of education in the whole
quality of people's lives may well amount to one of the
most grievous forms of social injustice also.

A differential distribution of educational resources
might be advocated on the ground that resources ought to
be distributed according to people's *needs*. Those whose
educational needs are greatest, it might be urged, ought
to have the greatest share of whatever resources are
available. The trouble with this suggestion, which as a
verbal formula sounds so reasonable, is that there is more
than one way of construing the term 'need' and that in any
case, however we construe it, in seeking to determine a
man's rightful share of educational resources by reference
to what he needs we are covertly and by implication
ascribing to him a right to reach some predetermined level
of educational *attainment* - and this is something to
which, for the reasons we have already seen, no man can
in fact be correctly said to have a right. Perhaps it is
most natural to consider 'those whose educational needs
are greatest' to be those members of society whose
existing levels of education are the lowest. But if it
is then claimed that the educationally needy in this sense
have a 'right' to be helped to achieve some stipulated
educational norm, we must, I think, take issue with this
tendentious and misleading way of putting the matter.
Since no one has a right *to achieve* any stipulated educational norm, no one has a right to receive some definite
measure of help which is computed and weighed out *in terms
of* achieving such a norm. As R.F.Dearden has pointed out,
to speak of a 'need' at all is necessarily to refer to
some norm or standard which is not in fact being achieved,
(9) and we may add that the only possible way in which
someone's need could be measured for the purpose of supposedly assigning to him his rightful share of educational

resources would be by establishing what resources would be needed to ensure that the individual in question actually achieved the norm or standard in question. Thus any proposed distribution of educational resources on the basis of people's educational 'needs' is logically rooted in the assumption that what individuals essentially have a right to is not some portion of educational resources after all, but rather some notional level of educational attainment, to which (it is supposed) they can assuredly be led if only the amount of resources necessary for this can be accurately calculated. (10)

Another and very different interpretation of what constituted a fair distribution of educational resources might be that resources should go to those - whoever they might be - who would thereby be helped to make the greatest educational *progress*. 'Educational progress' might be construed in absolute terms, in which case the two steps forward taken by dull John would count for pro- portionally less than the four steps forward taken by bright James; or it might be regarded as essentially relative to the existing mental status of the educand, in which case the shorter distance covered by John might well be thought to represent 'greater progress' than the more extensive ground covered by James. In whichever way construed, this general mode of distributing educational resources might in some circumstances operate in favour of the more able and better educated and in other circum- stances in favour of the less able and less well educated, but we can, I think, be tolerably sure that in one way or another it would nearly always result in a decisively uneven distribution of some kind. Of course, this is not in itself an objection. However, what surely does invali- date any such simple cost-benefit account of educational justice is that it manifestly rests on the assumption that the relevant educational benefits can be accurately pre- dicted and automatically transmitted to those supposedly entitled to them. And so, like an analysis in terms of educational 'needs', an analysis in terms of educational 'progress' covertly implies that what people really have a right to is some notional level of educational *attainment* which we can guarantee for every educand if only we do our homework thoroughly. The implication is, once again, that it is not really after all a share of the available resources but rather some predetermined level of educational achievement to which every adult is in the last analysis supposed to have a right, and, once again therefore, such an analysis must be rejected if we are correct in our assertion that a given level of educational achievement is precisely that to which in the nature of the case no one can be properly said to have a 'right'.

It would seem, then, that a just distribution of the resources for continuing lifelong education would require that whatever resources are available be shared out (among all those adults who choose to claim them) on a basis of strict and literal equality. It would seem that when it is a matter of distributing those resources of society which can help individuals to grow in awareness, in knowledge and understanding, and so to develop as persons, no man's rights ought to be regarded as greater or smaller than anyone else's.

This general conclusion we can, I think, accept - at least, subject to two important qualifications, which we had therefore now better state.

In the first place, there will obviously be some adults who arrive at the state of adulthood without having received their full share of educational resources during their childhood and adolescence. This may be because during their schooldays they did not even receive what a fair judge, taking account of all the relevant circum-stances then prevailing (including the pupils' own express or presumed desires), would have considered them to be then entitled to. Or it may be because they are the kind of 'late developers' whose educational interests do not fully blossom until they are mature men and women. No one is to be blamed if an idle and incurious fourteen-year-old, whom the best efforts of his teachers cannot awaken from his settled indifference, is quite properly denied resources which are instead diverted to his more active and enthusiastic fellows. But the fourteen-year-old himself, who at that age can hardly be judged as if he were a fully responsible moral agent, may one day become a man of forty who keenly regrets his adolescent insouci-ance and intensely desires to make up for lost time. Of course even a fourteen-year-old has to take some degree of responsibility for what he does (or omits to do), and when he at last reaches maturity it would be unreasonable for him to expect to avoid the consequences of his earlier actions (or inaction) altogether. Nevertheless, if we grant that it would be no less unreasonable to require him to bear the full consequences of errors made when he was still little more than a child, we will clearly have to grant that as an adult he is entitled to at least *some* measure of preferential treatment in the allocation of educational resources by way of compensation for the re-sources which he failed to take up during his schooldays. (11)

Second, in every society there will be many adults who from one cause or another are prevented from taking up and enjoying the full share of educational resources to which

they are entitled.   Those who live in remote rural areas,
the elderly and the infirm, shift-workers, housebound
mothers of young children - in every society the list of
those who are liable to be in some measure deprived of
their rightful opportunities to engage in continuing
lifelong education will nearly always be very heterogeneous and very long.   Of course we are not suggesting that
everyone whose physical, economic, or social circumstances
are in any way whatsoever disadvantageous can be properly
regarded as 'educationally deprived' and therefore as a
suitable candidate for compensatory treatment.   We need to
distinguish between those whose inability to participate
fully in continuing lifelong education is attributable to
circumstances over which they have little or no control
(most hospital patients, for example) and those who have
debarred themselves from systematically pursuing their
further education by exercising their own free preferences
(men who work overtime in order to acquire a more ex-
pensive car or to enjoy a luxury holiday, for example).
And we need to distinguish between adverse circumstances
which may directly and in themselves prevent certain
adults from availing themselves of educational opportunities which are otherwise generally accessible (certain
types of physical handicap, for example) and circumstances
which, while undoubtedly in a clear sense adverse, do not
of themselves directly prevent a man from taking up the
share of educational resources to which he is entitled
(for example, a relatively low income, which in itself is
no barrier where access to educational opportunities is
free or virtually free and which indeed in such conditions
ought to make the opportunities offered seem all the more
attractive).   When all the proper distinctions are drawn,
however, it is clear that there will remain in every
society a body of adults who can be granted the equal
share of educational resources to which they have a right
only if society is prepared to meet the higher overall
costs which, for one reason or another, unavoidably arise
in the special circumstances in which they find themselves.   Educational justice, such cases therefore remind
us, may indeed consist in ascribing to every adult the
right to an equal share of the available educational resources - books, teachers, equipment, and so on;   but in
order to make this right effective (and therefore logically and morally incorporated within it) this or that adult
or group of adults may well need extra facilities of
various non-educational kinds - special accommodation or
transport, for example, or more flexible administrative
arrangements;   and so, while in their strictly educational
content the educational rights of adults remain literally

and exactly equal, expressed in terms of the fluctuating
financial outlay involved they will often appear to be
(and in these terms actually will be) for various reasons
and in varying degrees unequal for different individuals
in different circumstances.

Of course, if two men are given exactly equal shares of
the available educational resources, the levels of actual
educational attainment to which they rise with the help of
these resources will almost certainly differ and may well
differ very strikingly, even if both men start out from
exactly the same educational level. As we saw in Chapter
7, every adult must ultimately be allowed to determine for
himself the general shape and direction of his own continuing education by constructing his own personal curriculum from among the wide range of options available to
him, but if this principle is upheld obviously one man may
make educational choices which from the point of view of
his overall educational progress are extremely sensible
and educationally productive while his neighbour may make
curricular choices which are by comparison ill-judged and
educationally wasteful. And even when both men make extremely apt and sagacious curricular choices, one of them
may go on to exploit his chosen share of resources more
creatively, purposefully, or energetically than the other,
responding to the teaching he receives, for example, with
greater flair, enthusiasm, or determination and so deriving proportionately greater educational benefit. However, if we are correct in maintaining that educational
justice is about the fair distribution of resources not
about equalizing or otherwise adjusting and regulating
levels of attainment, the fact that two men prove to be
of unequal educational attainment clearly does not of
itself in any way denote that any sort of educational
injustice has been committed.

To this it may be objected that, given equal educational opportunities in the sense just defined, two men
starting out from the same educational level may make
equally sensible curricular choices and apply themselves
to their chosen educational undertakings with equal
purposefulness and zeal but may nevertheless end up with
palpably unequal levels of attainment because one of them
happens to be held back by disadvantageous factors over
which he has no control and for which he himself cannot
therefore be held responsible - perhaps a culturally im-
poverished background or perhaps simply inferior natural
ability attributable ultimately to an inferior genetic
endowment. Would not this be injustice, and does not the
disadvantaged individual have a right to have his disadvantage removed or at least, if it cannot be removed, to

receive compensation in the form of a comparatively higher
share of resources than that to which his neighbour is
entitled? If adults are to enjoy a genuine 'equality of
educational opportunity', must not all relevant educational barriers be removed or at least equalized (not so that
an impossible equality of educational attainments can be
secured but so that everyone gets the same start and a
man's eventual attainments therefore reflect only what he
himself, by his own efforts, has managed to achieve); and
does not a comparatively poor cultural background or the
possession of a comparatively poor brain represent a very
real and highly relevant kind of barrier to educational
success?

Objections like these have, I think, considerable validity when it is the educational rights of children that
are under consideration. However, here it is specifically
and solely with the educational rights of *adults* that we
are concerned, and once again we must surely distinguish
between the ways in which this or that moral principle may
apply to those still in the condition of childhood and the
ways in which the same moral principles apply to men and
women deemed to be mature with all the rights and obligations pertaining to that status. A child of ten growing
up in a home without books or other forms of access to
worthwhile knowledge, surrounded by mindless chatter and
perhaps even actively discouraged from taking an interest
in any kind of serious learning by his family and his
neighbourhood friends, can hardly be held responsible for
the cultural handicaps weighing upon him and we rightly
demand that the relative disadvantage from which he
suffers should be taken into due account by those responsible for his schooling. But this is not how the
matter stands with a man of forty, who must surely be held
responsible for the priorities he establishes if he
prefers beer to books, if a football match takes precedence over a symphony concert on his car radio, and if
he chooses to spend his time in the undemanding company of
the mentally shallow, eagerly joining them in their
pursuit of the superficial and their absorption with the
trivial - the more so when he lives in a society with free
public libraries, museums, and art galleries, with a whole
host of other cultural activities permanently on offer to
him at a comparatively low cost, and with formal and in-
formal adult education facilities permanently on offer to
him at a purely nominal cost. In a culturally open
society the fact that a man has to spend thirty-five hours
a week among philistine and uninterested colleagues in
office or factory, or that the houses or flats by which
his home is surrounded are occupied by philistine and un-

interested neighbours, in no way prevents him from pursuing his cultural and educational interests in the wider
community in those large portions of his life which are
his to spend as he pleases. Unless we are going to
obliterate the moral differences between the child and the
adult, we must expect the adult to be capable of taking
charge of his own private life; we must treat him as essentially an autonomous agent; and clearly, this being
so, it cannot reasonably be demanded of us that we compensate him for the existence of those aspects of his life-
situation which will adversely influence the course of his
continuing education only if, and to the extent that, he
himself permits them to do so.

The time to compensate someone for his culturally deprived background is when he is at the mercy of his
background, that is, when he is a child. Obviously, it
is only if he has not already received adequate compensation for his early cultural deprivation during his years
of schooling that a man is entitled to receive compensation for this during his years of maturity, and - equally obviously - there must at last come a time when full
compensation must be judged to have been given. The same
applies to any educational compensation to which an individual is entitled in respect of the inferior genetic
endowment with which he starts out. Whereas the brain of
the six-weeks-old infant is what it is almost entirely
because of genetic factors which are totally outside his
control (as are, for the most part, such environmental
influences as may have already begun to be operative in
the infant's life), we are bound to regard the brain of a
sixty-year-old adult as embodying, to a very much greater
degree, the influence of a long and complex train of environmental factors which, moreover, we are entitled to
think of as having been in some significant measure under
his control and for which, therefore, we are entitled to
expect him to take some significant measure of responsibility. Of course in practice it is extremely difficult,
perhaps impossible, to offer any very reliable assessment
of the relative importance of original genetic endowment
on the one hand, and of the individual's subsequent life-
experiences and life-activity on the other hand, in producing the kind of brain of which, at some given stage of
his life, a grown man finds himself the possessor. What
in general we can be sure of, however, is that the younger
the individual the less he can be held responsible for the
kind of brain that he has, and the older the individual
the more we must hold him responsible for the kind of
brain that he has, since his brain is what it now is in
large part because of the life that he has chosen to lead,

the activities in which he has chosen to engage, and the
experiences to which he has chosen to expose himself.
Thus the time to compensate comeone for his inferior
genetic endowment is during his early years, when native
inferiorities assert themselves most clearly. And obviously there must at last come a time when full compensation for this must be judged to have been given, since
obviously a man cannot go on receiving compensation indefinitely and immeasurably for what was originally only
a finite and theoretically measurable handicap. It is,
then, only if (and to the extent that) a man has not
already received adequate compensation for his initial
genetic handicaps during the years of his childhood and
adolescence that he is entitled to claim and receive some
due measure of educational compensation for these when he
reaches the condition of adulthood. Compensatory education, for whatever reason demanded, is clearly not to
be thought of as an intrinsic and permanent element in
continuing education, but rather as a finite duty to be as
rapidly as possible discharged so that those who have a
right to it may be restored, as soon as possible, to that
fair equality with others which is their true and basic
educational right.

We have seen that a commitment to educational justice in
no way commits us to securing an absolute equality of
actual educational attainments for every adult member of
society. For many different and perfectly valid reasons
an educationally fair society may well contain people who
are highly educated and also people who are poorly educated, people with a high level of knowledge, taste,
judgment, understanding, and insight, and also people who
are ignorant, vulgar, foolish, uncomprehending, and blind.
In an educationally fair society there may, for instance,
be many adults who do not in fact take up and utilize that
portion of educational resources to which they are entitled and which their society makes freely available to
them, and who are very much the worse for their failure to
do so. However, there are limits to what an educationally
fair society can do about this. The concept of a 'right'
is the concept of a morally enforceable claim which its
possessor is free to enforce or not to enforce, as he and
he alone chooses. We cannot insist that a man shall
exercise his rights. We can exhort him to do so, we can
do our best to ensure that he is fully acquainted with
what they are, we can remove whatever practical obstacles
may lie in the way of his exercising them - but if we set
out to *ensure* that he exercises his rights (whether by co-

ercion, moral pressure, propaganda, or by any other means
presupposing that we in our wisdom are entitled to take
his decisions for him), then what we are in effect declaring is that we do not really regard his claims in the
character of *rights* at all but rather as duties of perfect
obligation which we on our part are entitled to exact from
him: we are in effect asserting *our* rights *against him.*
In requiring or constraining a man to exercise his
'rights' we are in effect denying him his rights no less
than if we were preventing him from exercising them. It
cannot be too clearly emphasized that policies which are
designed to ensure, by hook or by crook, that everyone
exercises his educational rights actually represent forms
of educational *injustice,* that is, they are actually a
violation of people's educational rights, no less than
policies which in one way or another obstruct or prevent
people from taking up and enjoying the educational resources to which they are entitled.

Naturally, educated men and women hope that those amid
whom they live their lives will also value education and
pursue it as something supremely worthwhile. However,
while it is entirely fitting (and indeed laudable) that we
should want our fellow men to be constantly seeking to
improve their level of education, we certainly cannot be
ascribed a *right* to have fellow creatures whose educational attainments and motivation bear some specific relation
to our own. The assertion of such a right against one's
fellow man would amount to the denial of *his* rights. Our
neighbour has a right to remain ignorant of that which we
take joy in knowing, he has a right to disdain that which
we value, and he has a right to reject that which we offer
to him. He has a right to abide by his own valuations and
to reject ours, and thus to reject our estimates of what
would best foster his development as a person. If what we
are offering him is something of great intrinsic worth
which would in fact contribute greatly to his development
as a person, then it is of course deplorable that he
should reject it. But he is an adult, and in treating him
as such we have to acknowledge that ultimately the decision is his to make and the responsibility is his to
carry. There are many things which it may be highly desirable that a man should do but which it would nevertheless be wrong that other people should force him to do,
and a man's participation in educational activity is
surely just such a thing. Anyone who denies this must
really stop talking about educational 'rights'. He may
talk if he chooses about promoting his neighbour's educational 'wellbeing' (although when we bear in mind the
'voluntariness' criterion of an educational process

properly so called, even this way of putting the matter
must be suspect to us); but he really must not claim to
be giving his neighbour his educational 'rights'. And so
- since justice consists in giving people their rights -
he must not claim to be promoting educational 'justice'.
We have to recognize that justice, like freedom, may well
require the sacrifice of other things admitted to be of
great value. Social justice may sometimes be gained at
considerable cost in terms of such other things as prosperity or social harmony. And educational justice may
sometimes be upheld only at the cost of tolerating a
certain amount of educational apathy. Certainly, we
cannot assume that in an educationally fair society there
will always be a high level of educational attainment and
of ongoing educational activity throughout the entire
adult population. All we can assume, since this is all
that can properly be accomplished in the name of justice,
is that in an educationally fair society every adult will
be given his rightful *opportunity* to take part in educational activity and to improve his general level of
educational attainment at every successive stage of his
life.

It is logically impossible to force a man to exercise
his rights. However, it is logically possible - and
indeed it is often our positive duty - to encourage him to
do so. Of course, there are many kinds and degrees of
force, from direct and irresistible coercion down to what
we should probably prefer to call very strong social, economic, or emotional pressure; and there are many kinds
and degrees of encouragement, ranging from gentle and
unstudied exhortation to those unusually vehement or
thorough kinds of incitement or persuasion (perhaps ac-
companied by the offer of definite material inducements)
which most of us would probably also want to categorize as
forms of social, economic, or emotional pressure. No
doubt it will often be very difficult to draw a clear line
between acceptable and unacceptable kinds and degrees of
pressure, between honest if somewhat officious encouragement on the one hand and inveiglement, bribery, or moral
bullying on the other, and no doubt when a clear line can
be drawn there will often be a strong temptation to over-
step it. By far the most apt and morally unambiguous way
of encouraging a man to exercise his educational rights
(once all the practical obstacles in the way of this have
been removed) is obviously to set before him, as vividly,
truthfully, and explicitly as possible, the precise nature
of *that to which* he has a right, in the conviction that if
this is done with sufficient energy, patience, and perseverance, a rational being will increasingly come to see

and feel the irreplaceable value and unique importance of
the opportunities for continuing growth and betterment as
a person which are his for the taking. By far the most
appropriate and acceptable way of encouraging people to
take part in educational activities, in other words, is
to *teach* them what educational activities really are and
what they mean for the life of the individual and for
society. This kind of 'education about education' is of
course not easy, as is shown by the very limited success
which has greeted the many attempts at educational pio-
neering made by organizations like the Workers' Educational Association and the educational centres movement, which
in so many respects might have seemed so well adapted to
the demands of missionary work with educationally uncom-
mitted adults. Educating people about education is
certainly more costly, more time-consuming, more arduous,
and - at least in the short run - less reliably efficacious than simply arranging to conscript them (firms
sending their employees off for a week or a month 'on a
course', for instance) or offering extrinsic inducements
of one kind or another (certificates and diplomas, for
example). All this shows, however, is that in the sphere
of adult education, as in most spheres of human endeavour,
the undertakings which are most meritorious are those
which call for correspondingly greater effort and imagination and are attended by correspondingly greater risk.
(12)

Before we finally leave the subject of educational
justice, one possible source of misunderstanding perhaps
needs to be removed. We have said that educational
justice consists in giving a man his full educational
rights, and these we have seen to consist (other things
being equal) in an equal share, along with his fellows, of
whatever resources are socially available for continuing
lifelong education. Educational justice, we have said, is
essentially about the distribution of resources, not about
men's relative levels of educational attainment. However,
it may be as well to emphasize that the educational rights
of which we have been speaking throughout this whole discussion of educational justice have of course been what we
earlier called men's 'positive' rights, that is, their
rights to some relevant measure of active assistance, not
just passive acquiescence, from other people or from
society as a whole. And we must not forget the existence
of what we earlier called men's 'negative' rights, namely
those rights in respect of which a man is entitled to do
or refrain from doing some action without obstruction or
molestation from others. For while a man cannot indeed be
said to have a positive right to any particular level of

educational attainment whatsoever, he can most certainly
be said to have the negative right to reach *whatever* level
of educational attainment he chooses to set himself - that
is to say, any deliberate attempt to hinder or prevent him
from rising to some new height of knowledge, understanding, and insight to which he would otherwise rise by
his own efforts and enjoying only his own fair share of
the available resources must always be stigmatized as
deeply perverse and unjust, however high his present educational level may be.   Whereas a man exercising his
positive educational rights will normally be using up some
definite amount of educational resources and thereby reducing the amount of resources that remain available to
others, a man's increase in knowledge, understanding, and
insight does not and cannot of itself reduce or in any way
adversely affect whatever levels of knowledge, understanding, and insight other people have attained or hope
to attain.   In one sense of educational justice, then -
the only one with which society need normally concern
itself directly, and therefore the one on which we have
concentrated here - justice in the domain of adult education is concerned with ensuring a fair distribution of
the *means* whereby adults may continue to grow and develop
as full living persons.   But we must never forget that
there is another sense of educational justice, one which
is more directly concerned with the *ends* of education and
which requires of society only that those who are striving
to develop their being as persons should not be arbitrari-
ly prevented or deterred from doing so and that those who
have already made some significant progress in this direction should not be discriminated against simply for
having achieved what all education sets out to achieve.

Education for democracy　9

In the last chapter we were concerned with the principles
of justice which determine the individual's rightful share
in whatever provision is made by his society for the continuing education of its adult members. We did not
venture to discuss the principles of justice which a
society ought to observe in determining what proportion
of its overall resources it ought rightfully to devote to
this whole form of educational provision, and indeed it
would be extremely difficult, if not impossible, to lay
down any very definite or exact rules by appeal to which
this latter question could be settled, since there are so
many different and rapidly changing demands on a country's
resources and the degree of priority to which continuing
lifelong education is entitled will necessarily vary according to the varying influence of the many different
kinds of factor which go to make up the sum total of a
country's fortunes and prospects. The share of its resources which can rightfully be devoted to the liberal
education of adults when a country is at peace with its
neighbours and enjoying great domestic prosperity, for
example, will nearly always be very much higher than when
that country is facing a dire and imminent military threat
or when it is in the depths of a severe economic de-
pression.

However, if education has the immense significance for
the lives and personalities of grown men and women which
we have ascribed to it, we may at least assert with some
confidence that the claims of adult education ought
normally to be placed very high indeed on any society's
scale of priorities, and certainly very much higher than
they are in fact placed in the priorities of any country
in the world today. No matter how apparently enlightened
and progressive any actual society we care to look at may
be, we invariably find that in its social priorities the

education of its adult members is consistently placed far
below the health of its adult members, for example, or the
education of its juvenile members. In an ideal society,
which would recognize that education is not just an
initial and temporary ingredient but something of continuing and permanent importance in the life of a human being,
and which would assess education at its true value, that
is, in terms of 'the quality of life which it inspires in
the individual and generates for the community at large',
(1) we should confidently expect a very different set of
priorities to be established.

We have already seen (2) that in the sphere of education society has a positive duty of the most binding
kind towards each of its members as an individual. Clearly, the discharging of its obligations towards individuals, which it owes to them in virtue of various general
moral principles which we have already noted, in itself
constitutes an amply sufficient reason for making regular
and substantial provision for adult education. However,
many people have also considered adult education to be
something which a wise society ought in any case to
promote because of the unique contribution which it can
make to the wellbeing of society itself. Traditionally,
and rightly, British adult educators have attached great
importance to what they have usually called the 'social
purpose' of adult education. Often 'social purpose' is
contrasted with 'personal development' as an objective of
adult education; sometimes it is assumed that these two
objectives are absolutely distinct in kind and must
therefore be to some extent in competition with each
other; and it will, I think, be found that those who tend
to make this assumption also tend to give the higher priority to the social objective. Thus the '1919 Report'
refers to 'the twin principles of personal development and
social service'. The adult educational movement, it says,
'aims at satisfying the needs of the individual and at the
attainment of new standards of citizenship and a better
social order'. The Report goes on, 'In some cases the
personal motive predominates'; but it adds, 'In perhaps
the greater majority of cases the dynamic character of
adult education is due to its social motive.' (3)

Now, phrases like 'social purpose', 'social relevance',
and so on, are crucially ambiguous. They may be intended
to express the conviction that education is a powerful
instrument or *weapon*, something waiting there to be *used*
by us in our efforts to bring about this or that supposedly desirable social change. Or they may be intended to
express the conviction that education, and in particular
adult education, forms a necessary *part* of, or is an es-

sential *ingredient* in, the kind of society and social life
which the speaker considers to be the most desirable and
the most worth trying to bring about. The social value
ascribed to adult education may be instrumental and extrinsic, or it may be constitutive and intrinsic.

For those who passionately believe in the desirability
of some given social objective there will no doubt always
be the greatest temptation to demand that the resources of
adult education be utilized as an instrument or weapon in
its service. And no one, I think, would seriously wish to
dispute that adult education can in many ways make a notable contribution, perhaps an indispensable contribution,
to the remedying of many specific social problems and to
the general betterment of our social life - for example,
in helping to create better industrial relations, helping
to alleviate racial and religious conflicts, helping to
improve the quality of family life, helping to smooth the
transition between work and retirement, helping to promote
higher standards of health and hygiene, helping to reduce
environmental pollution, and in countless other ways
helping to make the world an altogether better place to
live in. However, it is one thing to acknowledge that
adult education can incidentally make a notable contribution to the accomplishment of many worthwhile social
purposes. But it is quite another thing to view adult
education as essentially or primarily an instrument to be
utilized in the service of such purposes. This latter
conception of adult education is clearly fraught with
danger, not only to the deepest values of adult education,
but also to the deepest values of society itself. Dis-
cussing true and false versions of educational 'relevance', Israel Scheffler states the issue with admirable
clarity: (4)

> The notion that education is an instrument for the
> realization of social goals, no matter how worthy they
> are thought to be, harbours the greatest conceivable
> danger to the ideal of a free and rational society.
> For if these goals are presumed to be fixed in advance,
> the instrumental doctrine of schooling exempts them
> from the critical scrutiny that schooling itself may
> foster.... The fact is that the larger society that
> the school is said to serve at any given time cannot
> be taken for granted as providing an ultimate end. It
> must itself be judged worthwhile by reference to the
> rational standards and the heritage of critical values
> to which the school bears witness.

Although it is the education of schoolchildren that
Scheffler has in mind, his comment applies no less forcibly to the education of adults. To view adult education

as an instrument for the attainment of some favoured
social purpose is to treat that social purpose as a given
and unquestioned starting-point, as an original and basic
datum by reference to which teachers and students ought
constantly to be framing their activities, and as the
central and overriding criterion by reference to which
their achievements must ultimately be evaluated. But
there are and can be no social objectives which are so
manifestly just or benign that their desirability is absolutely beyond question. The integration of different
racial groups to form one single community? A greater
degree of equality between the sexes? More harmonious
relations between employers and employed? In every
society we shall find rational and informed people who
utterly reject these as goals for their society, and we
shall always find many others who by no means regard such
goals as wholly desirable in every respect. There is and
can be no social objective which is so *indisputably* desirable that its pursuit can be ordained and laid down as
canonical for everyone engaged in education. (5) If
problems of race relations, sexual equality, or industrial
relations are to be studied in ways that entitle us to
consider such studies truly 'educational', they will involve a critical review of ends as well as means, a re-
examination of values as well as facts, and a systematic
testing and challenging of official assumptions not a
docile acceptance of them - all of which makes it utterly
impossible that adult education, properly so called,
should ever be made to function as the biddable servant of
any particular social outlook or as the pliant instrument
of any particular social policy.

The impossibility in question is of course a logical or
conceptual impossibility, not just a factual or practical
impossibility. Built into the concept of 'education' is
the concept of certain distinctive purposes - those which
we have characterized as 'the development of persons in
their personhood' - and thus processes of teaching or
learning which are not under the jurisdiction of these
purposes simply do not count as processes of 'education'
They may be *called* processes of education. But calling
two different things by the same name does not magically
convert them into the same thing, and if ever two things
were different in kind surely equipping a man to look at
a social problem freely and critically from every relevant
viewpoint and equipping a man to play a predetermined role
in a predetermined policy for resolving that social
problem must be counted as two things which are radically
and crucially different in kind. And indeed the briefest
examination of the content and design of 'socially useful'

and 'socially relevant' courses will generally make the
comparatively narrow and educationally unambitious character of the knowledge and skills fostered by such courses
pretty incontestably visible. Of course we are by no
means suggesting that courses which show farmers how to
use animal foodstuffs more economically, which help young
couples to manage their household budgets more skilfully,
or which encourage motorists to drive more carefully, are
not well worth devising and providing or that they do not
deserve the active support of those groups for whom they
are intended (unless, that is, they are devised and conducted - as they sometimes are - in ways which have the
effect of actually making it *harder* for those who participate in them to approach the personal or public issues
involved in an independent, impartial, and critical
spirit). But we are certainly suggesting that the
provision of courses of these kinds, with their limited
and severely utilitarian terms of reference, cannot seriously be regarded as forming any very significant contribution to the *education* of society's adult members;   and
clearly we are also suggesting that the misguided attempt
to justify the provision of adult education by appeal to
its social utility can only end up by furnishing a justification for sundry exercises in training, instruction,
guidance, exhortation, or propaganda which in fact need to
be sharply distinguished from adult education, which ought
never to be confused with adult education, and which may
well be to some extent in competition or even in conflict
with adult education.

No doubt courses which are designed to promote more
efficient farming or safer roads may incidentally impart
forms of knowledge and understanding which are intrinsically worth acquiring. And no doubt courses which are
designed and provided simply as courses of liberal education can incidentally help to improve the quality of
family life or to promote higher standards of health and
hygiene in the community at large. But in each case it is
the fundamental purpose of the course which determines its
true nature and which will therefore finally settle its
scope and limits and prescribe its content and its methods
of approach. Courses closely geared to a specific and
preappointed social objective can never aspire to fulfil
the achievement criterion of a truly educational process
unless they burst asunder their preappointed limits and
pursue the issues which they raise, of whatever kind, in
a liberal and unfettered spirit. And courses which are
genuinely free, open, and generous in aims and spirit -
that is, courses which involve processes of education
properly so called - can by no means be safely relied

upon to produce those social consequences, and only those
social consequences, which an unwise society may rashly
require and expect of them.

Fostering someone's development as a person involves
fostering in him all the virtues and skills which are
proper to his status as a rational being. It involves
fostering in him a respect for, and an ability to engage
in, the distinctively rational activities of free inquiry,
free discussion and debate, and free and searching if also
responsible and constructive criticism and questioning.
The desire to form objective and impartial judgments, and
the capacity to form such judgments, are morally if not
logically inseparable from the concept of personhood, and
thus any education which is worthy of the name will equip
men and women to make a fair and fearless assessment, not
only of this or that particular scheme for improving
society in this or that particular respect, but of the
very nature of the society in which they live, its deepest
and most widely held values, and the kinds of personal and
if society itself, with all its institutions and established practices, must duly appear before the tribunal
of reason and submit itself to critical examination and
objective judgment, there can never be any question of
education passively conforming to the assumptions and requirements of the society within which it operates. And
for precisely the same reasons, education can never serve
as the instrument of any class, section, party, or
pressure-group within the wider society. It is the
business of education to probe and shed light in every
corner, sometimes to the grave discomfiture of partisan
and sectional interests. Moreover, just as education must
subject every aspect of existing society to merciless
scrutiny, so it must subject every proposal for changing
society, whether put forward by private groups and
sectional interests or by the accredited representatives
of society as a whole, to the same intense, ongoing,
critical scrutiny, without ever surrendering or bending
into any sort of final acquiescence or relaxing into a
sympathetic posture of easy benediction. It cannot be
part of the purpose of education either to vindicate the
status quo or to advocate social change, whether gentle
and piecemeal or radical and sweeping. The commitment of
education is to knowledge, understanding, insight, in
whatever social directions these may happen to point. The
commitment of education is always and necessarily to *the
truth*, wherever it may lead.

Adult education, then, cannot take sides on any social
question. The knowledge and understanding spread by adult
education will often have direct social implications, to

which the teacher may and should draw attention. And
he may be unable to help being aware that the knowledge
which he is honestly and objectively communicating for
its intrinsic cognitive value in fact bears witness
(as it sometimes does) to the rightness of one particular
solution to this or that social question or even (in some
ways, and in some degree) to the rightness of one
particular social outlook or overall social philosophy.
However, he must not allow himself to be influenced in
his teaching of what he knows to be true and educationally worthwhile by his awareness of its probable social
consequences, and of course - given that he observes
this principle - the fact that what he teaches happens
to favour one side of some social question rather than
another in no way impugns a teacher's essential impartiality any more than a cricket umpire's impartiality is
impugned by the fact that his ruling on some issue
happens to favour one side rather than another, as
indeed in the nature of the case it is anyway nearly
always certain to do.

We earlier stated that phrases like 'social purpose'
and 'social relevance' can be understood in two quite
different ways when applied to education. If they are
intended to express the conviction that adult education
can be usefully and legitimately employed in the service
of specific social causes or of society in general, as a
tool or instrument to be used as its employers think fit,
we may now declare that the education of adults has and
can have no 'social purpose' or 'social relevance' in this
narrowly utilitarian sense. (6) On the other hand, such
phrases may be intended rather to express the conviction
that adult education is an intrinsic *element* or essential
ingredient in any society that is genuinely worth building
and preserving - that is, an essential feature or constitutive part of the completed edifice not just one of the
tools with which it is built or one of the weapons by
which it is preserved. But when this is so, we are obviously being presented with an altogether different concept
of the social value of education. And in this much more
radical and far-reaching sense we may certainly assert,
and indeed must vehemently insist, that the education of
adults fulfils a most vital social purpose and is always
of the keenest social relevance. ·For we may surely claim
that any society which can be regarded as desirable by
free and rational beings will be one in which the distinctive values of education, and the distinctive qualities of educated people, will permeate and enlighten
every aspect of social life. And thus the continuing education of its adult members, its citizens, throughout the

whole of their lives as citizens is, we may further claim,
an absolutely indispensable element in the ongoing life of
any free and rational society. A continuing concern for
the education of its citizens must be integral to the
ideals and practice of any society that assents to the
Kantian vision of every man rightfully enjoying the dignity and autonomy of a law-making member of a rational
kingdom of ends. It is part of the very life-blood of the
tolerant, pluralistic, open society described by Karl
Popper, who reminds us that, like fortresses, the institutions of a free society need to be manned. (7) And it
is inseparable from the idea of democracy in that wider
sense in which, according to Dewey, 'a democracy is more
than a form of government; it is primarily a mode of associated living, of conjoint communicated experience'. (8)

If we subtract the idea of an educated citizenship from
the idea of 'democracy' (which, we must never forget, is
the rule of the *people*, that is, the rule of *persons* not
of things or fiends), what we are left with is the idea of
mere 'ochlocracy', the rule of the mob, of the crowd-fiend
or the crowd-thing on the moods of which communists and
fascists can play and on the back of which they can
eventually climb to power. As Richard Wollheim points
out, education, like toleration, is one of the essential
not one of the accidental attributes of a democracy. (9)
No doubt P.A.White is right in claiming that logically
'there could be beings, in other respects like men, except
for the possession of certain innate ideas and capacities
constituting the knowledge of how to operate a democractic
system' and that for such beings any kind of preparation
for life in a democracy would be quite unnecessary. (10)
However, Mrs White concedes that, as a matter of empirical
fact, *human* beings do always need some sort of education
for democracy or at least it is always very much in the
public interest to ensure that they be given such an education; and we might well feel that even this way of
putting it involves a serious understatement of the true
position. For it is surely the case that the very notion
of a 'human being', as distinct from a superhuman being,
incorporates an admission of moral and mental imperfection
and thus *logically* requires from us the admission that any
particular human being will necessarily be less than
perfect at the task of living together in society with his
equals. Moreover, any being recognizable as human will
continue to be imperfect. Throughout the course of his
whole life, therefore, it will always be meaningful for
any man, however morally and mentally advanced, to aspire
to a somewhat better understanding of society, a deeper
insight into his social duties and rights, a sharper

awareness of the claims and interests of others, and a
fuller, surer grasp of important social and political
issues: in other words, it will always be appropriate
and desirable that he should be given the opportunity to
carry on his social and political education, as a continuing process which has and can have no natural term or
definitive end. (11)

A concern for the continuing education of its citizens
is, then, one of the essential attributes of a democracy.
To speak of a 'democracy' at all is to speak of a form of
social life in which all adults are treated as political
equals, and this in turn means that every adult has the
right and the duty to take at least some part in making
the decisions which shape the life of his society and
build up its identity. In a democratic society every
adult is entitled, and is expected, to take at least some
part in forming the public mind. Democracy, we may say,
is essentially about consultation: it is essentially a
commitment to open discussion and debate, to the free
exchange of views on public questions. A democratic
society is a society in which people's opinions count, a
society in which people's judgments are respected and
taken seriously. But this presupposes that people have
opinions to express and that they are capable of forming
judgments which deserve to be taken seriously. A democratic society is not only concerned with the counting of
heads: it must also be concerned with what is in the
heads that are counted. Since what Smith thinks is supposed to *matter,* it really does matter that Smith should
think. We saw in an earlier chapter (12) that a man's
thinking is really 'thinking' only to the extent that it
matches up to the requirements of rationality; and we may
note here, therefore, that if the judgments and opinions
of its citizens are the very stuff and substance of democracy it is clearly essential to the existence of a democracy that all its citizens should really 'judge' and
'form opinions', not just mouth slogans, bandy platitudes,
or shelter behind the popular prejudices and uncriticized
myths of party or class in order to evade the responsibilities of rational choice. The democratic citizen has
to take part in forming the public mind; he cannot allow
himself to form part of a mindless public. But judgments
and opinions are only 'judgments' and 'opinions' to the
extent that they are based on knowledge, not mere habit or
feeling, and to the extent that they are reasoned and
thought out by those who hold them. The public only has a
'mind' to the extent that it is a knowledgeable and
rational public. And so education in general, and the
education of its adult members in particular, must be
recognized as central to the very concept of a democracy.

Democracy is the attempt to institutionalize or give
political form to the principle of rationality in the
conduct of social relations. It follows that education,
which when true to itself acts as the voice of reason
among men, upholding its standards and teaching its procedures, must be regarded as one of the chief ingredients
or components of the democratic ideal. 'Without education in the sense of a training in the interpretation of
evidence and the development of an understanding of the
issues involved, democracy cannot even begin, says K.H.
Lawson, (13) and in stating this he is stating a logical
truth not an empirical generalization based on our observation of the workings of actual democracies. Like liberty of thought and expression, the education of its citizens ought not to be regarded as a sort of luxury with
which a democratic society may or may not choose to adorn
itself, but rather as a morally necessary requirement
which a society has to fulfil if it is even to qualify as
a 'democratic society' in the first place. If, as
Scheffler reminds us, a democratic society by definition
has to be 'open' in the sense that 'there is no antecedent
social blueprint which is itself to be taken as a dogma
immune to critical evaluation in the public forum'; (14)
and if, as Peters puts it, 'all political decisions are
moral decisions "writ large"', involving many issues which
are essentially 'matters of judgment, not computation';
(15) then clearly any society which is to count as democratic will need to create and maintain the conditions for
permanent public scrutiny and discussion of all public
questions, and in so doing it will (among other things)
clearly need to ensure that its citizens are *free* to pass
judgment on public questions and also that they are *competent* to pass judgment on them. Civil liberties are of no
use to people who exist in mental darkness.

Of course to insist that social and political decisions
involve value judgments as well as technical judgments (on
economic questions, for example) should not be taken to
imply that only the value judgments need be taken by the
citizen body while the technical judgments can be safely
left to the appropriate experts. As we saw in Chapter 5,
it is in the practical application of moral principles in
themselves easily identified to the changing and ambiguous
details of concrete human situations that our real moral
difficulties arise, and in our actual moral judgments the
general moral principles to which we assent can hardly
ever be rendered meaningful other than in and through the
living texture of human actions and reactions, attitudes,
traditions, expectations, and physical, personal, and
social circumstances in terms of which they get their

whole substance and reality.   Intelligent value judgments
cannot be made by people who are ignorant of the relevant
facts.   Thus while we may agree with P.A.White when she
states that the 'value judgment element' in public policies 'cannot be calculated by experts', there is some
danger in too readily agreeing with her accompanying
observation that in working out, for example, the value of
the gross national product 'there are certain highly
technical points which *are* matters for expert calcu-
lation'. (16)   Ideally, the citizen of a democracy *ought*
to be able to follow every process of reasoning which
bears upon any social decision for which he morally
carries some share of responsibility.   If in fact large
numbers of ordinary people prove unable to follow some
complex piece of statistical analysis which is relevant to
some major economic decision, for example, those entrusted
with power in the state are under an imperative obligation
to bestir themselves to take whatever steps may be necessary to rectify this situation before they presume to act
in the name of those by whose ultimate authority their
acts have to be legitimated.   Admittedly this obligation,
while imperative, can never be regarded as literally absolute.   Its gravity and bindingness will always be a matter
of degree and will depend, first, on the degree to which
the technical issue is unavoidably bound up with and
directly relevant to the social decision;   second, on the
degree of actual intellectual difficulty inseparably attaching to the technical issue itself;   and third, on the
relative urgency of the need to reach a decision of some
sort.   Nevertheless, whatever good reasons there may often
be in practice for tolerating a certain amount of public
ignorance, we should never allow ourselves to forget that
to the extent that the public is unable to understand
public decisions, to that extent our society is simply
failing to function as a democracy and in fact simply does
not exist as a 'democracy'.   It is only to the extent that
its citizens are attentive and comprehending that a democracy can really be said to have awakened and to have
come alive.

We do not deny that the notion of a delegative democracy, in which the people trust their chosen leaders to take
wise decisions on their behalf, is a perfectly meaningful
one.   But it obviously needs to be distinguished from the
more thoroughgoing concept of democracy, in which every
citizen is deemed to be personally involved, albeit
perhaps at several removes, in the collective process of
public decision making;   and it is with this purer and
more radical concept that we are alone concerned here.   It
is presumably this concept of democracy which the '1919

Report' acknowledges when it declares that 'there is
latent in the mass of our people a capacity ... to rise
to the conception of great issues and to face the difficulties of fundamental problems when these can be visual-
ised in a familiar form', (17) and which the Russell
Report also acknowledges when it emphasizes the need for
'social and political education of very broad kinds, designed to enable the individual to understand and play his
part as citizen, voluntary worker, consumer'. (18)
Needless to say, however, both Reports go on almost
immediately to envisage and recommend forms of 'leadership
education' of the very kind that would be intrinsically
incompatible with the concept of a democracy deemed to
consist of free rational beings each of whom is capable of
making up his own mind on public questions with adequate
knowledge and full responsibility. Thus the Russell
Report advocates courses 'in which those with potentialities for leadership (including opinion-leaders) can dis-
cover themselves and try themselves out'. (19) And the
'1919 Report', alleging that 'the great mass of a people
in the modern industrial world cannot study Blue Books or
become close students of history, geography, or economics'
and that therefore 'they only require teachers and leaders
whom they can trust', even goes so far as to state that
'here, as always, the successful working of democracy
depends upon people recognising "the natural aristocracy
that is among any body of men".' The Report adds that
'the thoughtful and studious, who will naturally lead the
opinions of their fellows in mine, factory, or shop, can
never be more than a few thousand'; but fortunately education can help 'the millions of the rank and file ... to
recognise those natural leaders'. (20)

It is surely only very much faute de mieux that we
could possibly consider such naked forms of leadership
education as in any way constituting an education for
democracy. Indeed to the extent that they are necessary
or appropriate, to that extent the society which they
serve confesses itself to be less than a democracy. No
doubt the educational provision of any democratic society
ought to ensure that its members of parliament, local
councillors, trade unionists, magistrates, and other
public officers are adequately prepared for their public
functions. But the paramount educational obligation of a
democracy is manifestly to ensure that its sovereign body
of citizens, to whom its public officers must always be
accountable and in whose name they must ultimately act,
are in general ready and fit to shoulder their more
diffuse but weightier and more solemn burden of responsibility. For while the quality of its public officers may

normally furnish a pretty reliable working index of the
political health of a democracy, it is obviously to the
quality of the whole citizen body's interest and participation in social decisions that we must in strictness
look for the necessary and sufficient condition of a democratic society's political health, since it is in this
that its very existence as a democracy consists.

Now, it would be quite mistaken to suppose that the
quality of a democratic citizen's interest and participation in social decisions depended on the quality of his
social and political awareness only. Social and political
education undoubtedly occupy a special place in the
building up of the democratic mind. The democratic
citizen undoubtedly needs to know how the great institutions of democracy have developed historically, how they
work today, and how he can play his part in helping them
to continue to work; he ought to be capable of reflecting
critically on the ethical foundations of democracy and of
comparing it intelligently with rival systems; and he
clearly ought to have some understanding of the ways in
which such vital assets of any democracy as press freedom
and an independent judiciary make an indispensable contribution to his own and others' liberty and security. But
he must also be helped to acquire the virtues and general
qualities of moral concern which ought to distinguish the
citizen of a democracy - a due regard for other people's
interests and wellbeing, a sincere tolerance of those who
may disagree with him, a respect for the reasoned and
orderly settlement of disputes, an active sense of justice
and fair play, a willingness to stand up and be counted, a
willingness to accept responsibility, and the many other
general habits of mind and moral commitment without which
the institutions and traditions of democracy would be no
more than a dead letter. The democratic citizen needs an
education in democratic morality. Moreover, if democracy
is the attempt to give political form to our ideals of
rationality in the conduct of social relations, every
democratic citizen clearly ought to have some kind of education in practical rationality, equipping him not only
with the virtues but also with the skills distinctive of
a rational being, and above all the skills required for
those central processes of clear and coherent reflection,
balanced judgment, and articulate communication which are
the very heartbeat of a democratic society.

This amounts to saying that what every democratic
citizen needs, if democracy is to work, is a sound liberal
education. And ultimately this can only mean a *full*
liberal education. Nothing less is needed for life in a
democracy. Social and political decisions are not taken

in a cognitive vacuum: they always have a content, a
subject-matter, and the potential subject-matter of social
and political controversy and debate in a democracy, and
in any civilized society, is as wide and deep as human
life itself. The more civilized the society, the more its
members need to be capable of making informed and discriminating judgments on all the subjects which ought to
be of interest to civilized human beings, since the more
civilized the society the more such subjects will tend to
appear among the items of public business calling for some
kind of social policy decision to be consciously taken
(even although the wise decision, as will no doubt often
be the case, may in the end be to leave the matter to the
free initiative of private individuals). The life of a
civilized community does not revolve wholly around such
things as housing, transport, food, fuel, health, personal
incomes, social insurance, industrial investment, and so
on. While the efficient production and fair distribution
of material goods and services must obviously figure
prominently among the public concerns of any society, we
do not expect a civilized society to equate 'quality of
life' with 'material standard of living', and the more
civilized the society the less importance we expect it to
attach to purely material achievements once a reasonable
minimum of physical wellbeing has been secured for all its
members. We expect a civilized society to be interested
in its own past and in the past of other societies, preserving that which has come down to us from earlier times
and promoting a fuller understanding of the values, the
aims, the attainments, and the ways of life of our
ancestors and of all those who have come before us in
experience of the human condition; we expect the members
of a civilized society to be interested in their natural
environment, the ground beneath their feet, the seas by
their shores, and the skies above their heads, not only
for any material benefits to be discovered and exploited
but chiefly for the truths, the glimpses of other realities, and the many forms of beauty to be found therein;
we expect a civilized society to be capable of discerning
and appreciating good art, good music, good literature,
and in its public policies to demonstrate that it has both
the will and the taste to protect and foster the highest
standards of artistry and craftsmanship in every field of
creative endeavour; and - perhaps most important of all -
we expect a civilized society to protect and encourage its
members in their desire to interpret and evaluate their
common human experience, in their desire to seek some kind
of overall meaning in their lives and to work out for
themselves where they stand on all the urgent ethical,

philosophical, and religious issues with which every reflective person has somehow to come to terms. In short,
the business of a civilized society is civilization. But
this being so, it needs civilized men to conduct it. And
when a civilized society is (as all truly civilized
societies are) a *democracy*, it needs nothing less than a
whole population of civilized men if its proper business
is to be transacted fittingly and well. Thus the idea of
a liberal education, we may say, forms an essential part
of the idea of a liberal democracy. (21) Of course, if a
liberal education were something that could be imparted to
a man once and for all in the days of his youth, this
would so far merely constitute an argument for giving a
liberal education to children and adolescents as a preparation for what awaited them. But we must surely reject
any such notion of a definite end and term to a man's education. Knowledge continually advances, and the savant of
yesterday becomes today's ignoramus; moreover, the wisest
of us is never omniscient and is therefore always in
principle capable of further learning, development, and
growth; and in any case any man who has become in any
measure *really* 'educated' will necessarily regard his own
educational progress as something to be continuously promoted without halt or limit, inseparable as it will have
come to be in his eyes from his personal worth and dignity
and indeed from his very identity as a person. Unless it
makes adequate and regular provision for the continuing
liberal education of its citizens as a permanent feature
of their lives, we may conclude, a society which is
aspiring to realize itself as a democracy will be manifestly failing to meet one of the fundamental requirements
which every society logically *has to* meet if it is
rightfully to count as a 'democracy' in the fullest sense
of the term.

This conclusion is surely reinforced when we remember
the distinctive 'task' criteria which any educational
process properly so called must satisfy and when we remember that these criteria are satisfied most completely
and dependably in the case of educands who are mature men
and women with all the moral and personal attributes and
competencies of maturity. (22) In any process of liberal
education we are entitled to suppose that those taking
part are doing so wittingly, voluntarily, and actively,
and that the whole process represents a free coming
together of conscious selves, a meeting and interaction
of persons. But this is precisely what we are entitled
to expect of democratic processes in their truest and
fullest sense. Processes of liberal education are the
very mirror of the democratic process at its best. And,

as we have amply seen, it is only in the liberal education
of adults that - in the nature of things - we can expect
to find processes of education attaining their definitive
realization. It is in the liberal education of its adult
members, its citizens, that democracy can behold itself in
its clearest and most appropriate mirror. The concept of
the educational experience as a free meeting of moral
equals bent on a common task is at the heart of all liberal adult education, and to all who share in it, we may
therefore claim, this experience, with all the demands
which it makes on the individual to respond with tolerance
and candour to the interests and insights of his fellows,
ought in itself to constitute a rich and living education
in democracy.

We have now, I think, sufficiently clarified the sense
in which the education of adults can, and the sense in
which it cannot, be rightly expected to make an important
contribution to the wellbeing of the society by which it
is supported. Education cannot - without ceasing to *be*
'education' - allow itself to be used as an instrument in
the pursuit of non-educational ends, however socially
necessary or desirable these may often admittedly be. We
do not deny that, if and when there occurs some set of
circumstances which make it inescapably necessary or even
on balance objectively desirable to employ the teaching
resources of the community in the service of some extrinsic social, economic, or political goal, the high
claims of education may in these circumstances have to be
justifiably subordinated to what is judged to be a still
higher moral imperative; but we must insist that when
this happens the nature of what is happening needs to be
frankly recognized and the processes of teaching and
learning involved need to be clearly and emphatically
distinguished from processes of education in the correct
sense of the term, no matter how closely they may outwardly resemble these, lest the gravely mistaken impression be
created that the community in question is fulfilling its
educational obligations when what it is really doing is
fulfilling obligations of an entirely different kind. The
sole contribution which the education of adults, properly
so called, can rightly be expected to make to the wellbeing of any society is to make that society a better educated society. And we may surely claim that in making
this contribution it will always be contributing something
inestimably precious for which there can be no equivalent
or substitute. In contemplating the idea of a society of
educated men and women, who remain throughout their whole
lives eager to deepen their knowledge and understanding
and who are constantly striving to improve their standards

of taste and skill, we are surely contemplating the idea
of something pre-eminently worth building and preserving
for its own sake, quite irrespective of the many other
forms of social good which as a matter of contingent fact
are likely to accrue to a society composed of educationally active men and women (and which may legitimately be regarded as a gratifying by-product or bonus albeit never as
part of the *purpose* of their educational activity).

The sole and sufficient task which the education of
adults can rightly be called upon to perform in the
service of a democracy, therefore, consists simply in
making that democracy a better educated democracy, and
thus in making it more truly and fully a *democracy*. If we
are right in claiming that the degree to which a society
is able to realize itself as a democracy depends above all
on the quality of its people as people - that is, as
active, thoughtful, perceptive, autonomous, rational and
responsible selves or persons - it follows that education,
understood in its most fundamental sense as the making of
persons, can be quite literally described as democracy in
the making. But the making of persons and so the making
of democracy is an undertaking which in the nature of the
case can never be finished or complete; it is a moving
frontier which always can be and ceaselessly demands to be
pushed forward towards fresh horizons which constantly
beckon us; it is an enterprise on which we need to be
continuously engaged. In any society that is genuinely
striving to realize itself more truly and fully as a democracy, then, the education of its members will not be
regarded as something which as a matter of course ought to
be brought to a fitting close and put aside when childhood
and adolescence are over, but rather as an activity and a
commitment which for every member of society ought as a
matter of course to be continuing and lifelong. In the
highest interests of society itself, as well as in the
deepest interests of each of its members as an individual
human person with a life to build and an identity to
create, a democracy which rightly sees itself as permanently in the making will rightly see in the liberal education of its adult citizens a permanent and welcome
challenge and a permanent and welcome necessity.

Notes

CHAPTER 1   ADULTHOOD AND EDUCATION

1   R.S.Peters, What is an Educational Process?, in R.S.
    Peters, ed., 'The Concept of Education', London,
    Routledge & Kegan Paul, 1967, p.1.
2   G.A.Beck, Aims in Education: Neo-Thomism, in T.H.B.
    Hollins, ed., 'Aims in Education', Manchester,
    Manchester University Press, 1964, p.122. The phrase,
    'the making of persons', must not of course be taken
    to mean the *creation* of persons. A new-born child is
    a person, and we may loosely describe a man as a 'com-
    pletely uneducated person' without (even loosely) im-
    plying that he is really as yet a non-person. A very
    poor specimen of personhood is still a person in a
    sense in which stocks and stones are not (see footnote
    5, infra). Education must therefore be thought of as
    the building-up in someone of an identity which he
    already possesses in at least some minimum degree -
    the nourishment and cultivation of a seed which obvi-
    ously must first of all exist in order to *be* nourished
    and cultivated.
3   R.S.Peters, 'Ethics and Education', London, Allen &
    Unwin, 1966, p.31.
4   Supra, p.14.
5   To this account of the defining purpose of 'education'
    it might be objected that the enlargement of a man's
    awareness is only one aspect of his overall develop-
    ment as a person, and that what we are doing amounts
    in practice to devolving upon this one aspect all the
    prestige and authority which we have illegitimately
    purchased by a professed allegiance to the more
    comprehensive and morally much more powerful and
    significant concept of the development of personhood.
    Clearly, this objection can be adequately answered

only by unpacking the concept of 'the enlargement of
awareness' and demonstrating that, in one way or
another, it really does embrace everything that we
should want to include in the concept of 'the development of personhood' (whilst embracing nothing that we
should want to exclude from this latter concept).
Part Two of the present book will, I hope, demonstrate
precisely this - both indirectly, by its general
purport, and also directly, on the various occasions
when this specific issue will have to be explicitly
confronted (see, e.g., pp.67-74, infra). Here, however, it might be as well to stress at least one very
basic point - namely, that the concept of a 'person'
(as we are employing it) is *both* a descriptive *and* a
normative concept (though we are mainly interested in
its normative employments). Descriptively, the
concept of a 'person' is one and the same with the
concept of a 'centre of awareness'. Thus a new-born
child is already a person. But to speak or think of
the *development* of a person - of his becoming 'more
fully developed as a person' or 'more fully a person'
- is immediately to acknowledge the normative dimension which is built into the concept of personhood.
It is in this sense that we think of the mother as
being more fully a person than her new-born child.
Now this is so, I suggest, because the concept of 'the
development of the individual as a person' is one and
the same with the concept of 'the enlargement of the
individual's awareness' and because, while 'awareness'
itself may be a straightforwardly empirical concept,
to speak or think of the *enlargement* of awareness is
necessarily to acknowledge the operation of normative
criteria whereby what is empirically merely an
addition to or extension of someone's awareness is
deemed worthy of counting as an enhancement or 'enlargement' of his awareness. Thus a mother's learning
something of the emotional needs of very young
children would surely count as an 'enlargement of her
awareness' in a sense in which her merely learning,
say, that her child had a mole on his elbow surely
would not. Clearly, the enlargement of awareness
which we are identifying with the development of
personhood is no mere additive process but above all
a process of transforming, deepening, refining, and
enriching the individual's perceptions, feelings,
insight, and understanding, and of putting him in
touch with reality in all its most significant and
worthwhile forms. Built into the concept of 'the enlargement of awareness', then - and hence built into

the concept of 'the development of persons', given
that this is really the selfsame concept - is the
logical requirement that various pertinent judgments
of *value* shall be made. We may appropriately describe
these as judgments of *intrinsic cognitive value*. The
most important of these will be examined in Part Two,
especially Chapter 3 (but see also, e.g., pp.157-8 and
179-93, infra).

It might be as well to add here that it is only
persons (in the descriptive sense) who can be guilty
of forsaking or betraying their status as persons (in
the normative sense). It is *people* who act brutishly
and daemonically. It is only a conscious being who
can endeavour or pretend to be unconscious or who can
try to debase or disfigure his consciousness. As
Sartre has taught us in his remarkable analysis of
'bad faith', it is only a 'pour-soi' which can try to
become a thing or pretend that it is already only a
thing.

6 For a task-achievement analysis of 'education', see
   R.S.Peters, What is an Educational Process?, in R.S.
   Peters, ed., op.cit.

7 Supra, p.14.

8 Supra, p.4.

9 Supra, p.5.

10 See supra, p.28.

11 Report by a Committee of Inquiry appointed by the
    Secretary of State for Education and Science under
    the Chairmanship of Sir Lionel Russell, CBE, 'Adult
    Education: A Plan for Development', London, HMSO,
    1973, para.47.

12 Ibid., paras 58.1 and 58.3.

CHAPTER 2   LIBERAL ADULT EDUCATION AND ITS MODES

1 P.H.Hirst, Liberal Education and the Nature of
   Knowledge, in R.D.Archambault, ed., 'Philosophical
   Analysis and Education', London, Routledge & Kegan
   Paul, 1965, p.115.

2 Ibid., pp.113-16.

3 J.Lowe, 'Adult Education in England and Wales: A
   Critical Survey', London, Michael Joseph, 1970, p.23.

4 In the autumn of 1919, the Adult Education Committee
   of the Ministry of Reconstruction presented its
   lengthy and closely reasoned Final Report to the Prime
   Minister. The scope of this report, its searching
   discussion of the place of adult education in a free
   society, and the sense of high purpose by which the

whole report is animated, have combined to make it a classic document in the history of adult education. In 1956 an abridged version, with an introduction by R.D.Waller, was published under the title 'A Design for Democracy'.

5 'A Design for Democracy: An abridgment of a report of the Adult Education Committee of The British Ministry of Reconstruction, commonly called "The 1919 Report", with an introduction, "The Years Between", by R.D. Waller', London, Max Parrish, 1956, p.72.

6 See infra, pp.46-8.

7 M.V.C.Jeffreys, 'The Aims of Education (Glaucon)', London, Pitman, 1972, p.88.

8 Loc.cit.

9 Report by a Committee of Inquiry appointed by the Secretary of State for Education and Science under the Chairmanship of Sir Lionel Russell, CBE, 'Adult Education: A Plan for Development', London, HMSO, 1973, paras 58.3 and 213.3.

10 Ibid., para.213.3.

11 Ibid., para.58.3.

12 Ibid., para.213.3.

13 Loc.cit.

14 Supra, pp.22-4.

15 See supra, p.16.

16 Mary Warnock, Towards a Definition of Quality in Education, in R.S.Peters, ed., 'The Philosophy of Education', London, Oxford University Press, 1973, p.116.

17 Ibid., p.117.

18 See infra, pp.199-203.

19 See supra, pp.20-1.

20 See infra, pp.85-94.

21 Arguably, however, the idea of an absolute and exclusive specialist is not even a logically possible idea.

22 In defending the objective of educational breadth and comprehensiveness I have not drawn upon the argument, which is frequently met with, that it is only by encountering and, as it were, sampling many different forms of knowledge, experience, taste, and skill that an individual can put himself in a position to make a rational and informed choice of the kind of mental and cultural life he would ultimately like to build for himself and the kinds of ingredients he would ultimately like it to have. This argument tends to be advanced in discussions of the education of children and adolescents, and in these contexts it is often clear that education is being regarded very much as something temporary and of its nature preliminary.

However, the concept of education with which we are
operating here is one which makes education par excellence the kind of activity in which a man can and
ought to engage throughout the whole of his life
because he sees it as something intrinsically and
therefore permanently worthwhile and indeed as the
principal vehicle of his continuing mental and cultural development. And it is, I imagine, fairly clear
that the scope of an education deemed to be continuing
and lifelong cannot be appropriately settled by appeal
to principles which imply that education consists in
being *introduced* to or *initiated* into worthwhile forms
of experience and skill. One cannot go on 'sampling'
the (finite) range of worthwhile forms of experience
and skill for ever. And so the scope of *adult* education, I suggest, needs to be decided on quite a
different basis and by appeal to quite different considerations (viz. what is of permanent value and
permanently worth pursuing and enjoying).

23 See supra, pp.38-9.
24 See infra, pp.179-81.
25 See infra, pp.195-218.
26 See infra, pp.188-95.
27 Lowe, op.cit., pp.29-30.
28 Ibid., p.25.
29 'A Design for Democracy', p.59.
30 Loc.cit.
31 Supra, p.32.
32 'Adult Education: A Plan for Development', para.58.1.
33 See infra, pp.100-2.

CHAPTER 3   THE COMMUNICATION OF KNOWLEDGE

1 P.H.Hirst, Liberal Education and the Nature of
   Knowledge, in R.D.Archambault, ed., 'Philosophical
   Analysis and Education', London, Routledge & Kegan
   Paul, 1965, especially pp.128-31.
2 Ibid., pp.128-9.
3 It is sometimes claimed that 'a little knowledge
   gained by one's own efforts is better than a quite
   large amount of knowledge acquired from others'. It
   is difficult to know where to begin in sorting out the
   confusions with which statements like this are
   riddled. Let me therefore simply make the following
   three points. First, the intrinsic value of a piece
   of knowledge does not vary in accordance with variations in the manner of its acquisition. What our
   speaker must really have in mind, therefore, is I

suggest no more than the platitude that it is better
to have the ability to do something in a certain way
(find something out by conducting one's own investigations) than not to have that ability. This leaves
it a completely open question whether the value of
having and using the ability to acquire what is admitted to be only a little knowledge by one's own
efforts *outweighs* the difference between the value of
that little knowledge and the value of the quite large
amount of knowledge which might otherwise have been
acquired. I suggest that in general it conspicuously
does not. Second, statements like the above derive a
large part of their specious force from their pointed
insinuation that self-conducted inquiry, because of
the greater initiative and effort supposedly involved,
is *morally* superior to learning directly from others.
But learning about birds from books, teachers, and
courses can and sometimes does require much more real
initiative and effort than is required for amateur
birdwatching. Moreover, we must not forget that the
self-directing inquirer who figures in this particular
educational controversy is presumed to have at least
acquired his knowledge of the techniques of inquiry by
learning directly from others. And in any case we may
well doubt whether a deliberately large expenditure of
comparatively unproductive effort really is morally
superior to a lesser expenditure of effort made by
someone who rightly believes this to be more genuinely
productive of results. Third and lastly, let us admit
that someone who learns by direct encounter with the
phenomena rather than by means of books, teachers, and
courses may thereby acquire knowledge which is more
'alive' both in the sense that it is more vividly
impressed upon his mind and also in the sense that it
stimulates in him a keener appetite for further
learning. However, let us also take note that this
is merely a contingent consequence, not a logically
necessary feature, of this kind of learning. Whether
this highly desirable state of affairs actually comes
about, and the degree to which it comes about, in
practice depends on very many different factors, not
least on the specific aptitudes and temperament of the
learner. For John the experience of actually observing an osprey alight in her nest, coming as the
reward of many hours of skilful and patient endeavour,
may constitute an unforgettable and permanently inspiring educational event. But for James, gifted
perhaps with a keener imagination and a more self-
fuelling enthusiasm, the whole rich spectacle of wild

birdlife, native and exotic, may rise up time and
again with equally compelling and inspiring vividness
even although it is presented to him for the most part
only indirectly and by the mediation of books and
teachers.

4   See supra, p.79.

5   For the reason given we willingly acknowledge that an
adequate understanding of the procedures of inquiry
undoubtedly has great *instrumental* cognitive value
(which must therefore be added to the comparatively
limited degree of intrinsic value earlier mentioned).
And perhaps we should draw attention here to two
further reasons, one rooted in contingent and alter-
able social circumstances and the other rooted in
necessary and unalterable educational principle, which
make it in different ways desirable that students -
and adult students in particular - should acquire at
least some understanding of the instrumentalities of
inquiry. First, in most societies the provision of
liberal adult education tends to be on an extremely
limited scale, so that unavoidably the continuing
higher education of many if not most men and women is
something which they largely have to undertake for
themselves; to the extent that this is so, it is
desirable that they should be equipped to conduct and
direct whatever types of research and investigation
may be needed for this purpose. However, we should
not exaggerate the range and degree of special skills
which are in practice needed for this. The self-
directing student of English history, for example, has
much greater need of general bibliographical and
information retrieval skills than he has need of the
special skills involved in, say, the analysis of
probate inventories or parish registers. Second,
there are certain procedural aspects of the pursuit of
knowledge of which everyone has to have some grasp if
he is to be capable of thinking and acting *reasonably*.
We shall see in Chapter 4 that a reasonable man ought,
for example, to have at least some understanding of
the broad nature of inquiry, of what counts and what
does not count as evidence in different areas of
inquiry, and of the different criteria of validation
and proof which are applicable in different forms of
human knowledge and experience. We shall also see in
Chapter 4 that reasonableness is *intrinsically* good.
In this case, therefore, it is intrinsically good that
a man should possess a set of skills which are themselves of primarily instrumental value. (There is no
contradiction in this. It is usually the case that

the work a man does in his job is also primarily of
instrumental value, but we grant that the conscientious spirit and the sense of service which some men
bring to their work are nevertheless qualities of
great *intrinsic* worth (see supra, pp.43-4).)

Clearly these two reasons for promoting some understanding of the instrumentalities of inquiry are
fundamentally different in kind. As a society grows
in enlightenment it may make increasing provision for
liberal adult education, thus rendering the first
reason increasingly inoperative. We may hope that
society will not *always* be blindly grudging with
regard to the education of its adult members. But it
will always be the case - since human beings will
always be mentally and morally finite - that the development of *reason* in men can and ought to be systematically fostered, since greater reasonableness will
always be something supremely worth fostering for its
own sake.

6 Report by a Committee of Inquiry appointed by the
Secretary of State for Education and Science under the
Chairmanship of Sir Lionel Russell, CBE, 'Adult Education: A Plan for Development', London, HMSO, 1973,
p.xi. Perhaps sensing disaster, the Report immediately qualifies this inane but at least admirably clear
statement by adding: 'provided that those engaged in
it develop a greater awareness of their own capacities
and a more certain knowledge of the totality of their
responsibilities as human beings'. The arbitrary
choice of these two particular stipulations is not
further clarified. However, their vagueness is
perhaps intended to leave readers with the impression
that the original bold declaration has been sensibly
qualified and yet, somehow, in spirit, not really
qualified at all.

7 It does not follow that things evil, degraded, or
repulsive have no cognitive value. Environmental
pollution, sexual perversion, and the careers of
tyrants obviously do have high cognitive value. But
equally obviously, our *main* interest in such things is
instrumental, and we want to understand them mainly in
order to avert them or bring them under control. In
so far as slums, sadism, and Stalin possess *intrinsic*
cognitive interest in their own separate right (which
they clearly do), this is, I think, entirely attributable to their high degree of 'cognitive richness'.
Granted an equivalent degree of cognitive richness,
however, we would, I am sure, consider palaces,
personal relationships, and Pericles to have a very
much higher degree of intrinsic cognitive *value*.

8   Supra, p.85.
9   See supra, pp.7-10.
10 See supra, p.61.

CHAPTER 4   THE ADVANCEMENT OF REASON

1   It is particularly important to be clear about the
    difference between educational activities and other
    intellectual or cultural activities such as scientific
    research or artistic creation. Unlike the scientist
    or the artist, who sets out to discover new truths or
    express new insights, the educator sets out to develop
    his pupils by transmitting truths which are already
    known or insights which have already been expressed.
    In so far as an astronomer or a poet is engaged in
    astronomical investigations or the writing of poetry
    (i.e. in so far as he is *practising* as an astronomer
    or a poet) he is not engaged in *transmitting* an under-
    standing of astronomy or poetry. And in so far as
    what a man is engaged in doing is the teaching of
    astronomy or poetry, he is not engaged in advancing
    the astronomical knowledge of mankind or adding to
    mankind's poetic heritage. Of course a man can do
    both types of thing at once and indeed often by
    carrying out one set of operations only; of course
    both the activity of teaching and the activities of
    intellectual and artistic origination can fructify
    each other; but to say that two things can be done
    simultaneously, or that they can fructify each other,
    is thereby to acknowledge that *two* distinct things are
    in question, that we have to do with two things, not
    one. To speak of 'educating', 'advancing scientific
    knowledge', and 'promoting new art', is to speak of
    activities which are logically quite distinct. Thus,
    even if someone were to argue that the concept of
    'promoting reasonableness' was logically contained in
    such concepts as 'advancing scientific knowledge' or
    'fostering the development of art', and that these
    latter activities were obviously intrinsically
    worthwhile, he would still not have furnished us with
    an *educational* justification for promoting reasonable-
    ness in children and adults. But in any case to argue
    in this way would surely be highly implausible. The
    connection between the spread of reasonableness and a
    society's advances in knowledge or artistic abundance
    is manifestly causal and contingent, not conceptual
    and logically necessary. There is no logical contra-
    diction involved in the idea of a society advancing in

knowledge or art by means which involved a partial
rejection of reason, by mechanical means, for example,
or by the imposition of thought-control, or by a fe-
licitous reliance on serendipity.   However, if in fact
reasonableness is regarded as merely a means to an
end, and is thus ascribed no separate value in its own
right but simply used or discarded according to its
contingent utility, we cannot claim that it is being
regarded as a fit object of strictly educational
endeavour.   And so we must conclude that, if the
diffusion of reasonableness were justifiable only as
a strategy for advancing knowledge and promoting art,
whether supposedly as an integral part of this general
end or whether merely as a means to this end, it would
be without any strictly educational justification at
all: it might be undertaken by educators, but they
would not be functioning as educators in undertaking
it.   (Exactly similar objections apply to arguments
which attempt to justify the diffusion of reasonableness as an educational objective by appealing to its
social, political, or economic utility.)

2   Epictetus, 'Discourses', Book II, Chap.25 (That Logic
is Necessary).

3   There is of course an extremer type of irrationalist
who *is* apparently prepared to resign any claim to
validity in his thinking and discourse.   I am not
thinking so much of the consciously 'absurd' philosophy of someone like Camus in his 'Myth of Sisyphus'
(since he speaks there of an absurd 'reasoning') as of
Dadaists like Tristan Tzara or nihilists like Max
Stirner, whose cult of unreason was explicitly em-
braced as an act of deliberate intellectual frivolity.
See R.W.K.Paterson, 'The Nihilistic Egoist: Max
Stirner', London, Oxford University Press, 1971, pp.
286-310, for a discussion of what might be called
absolute irrationalism.   Ridiculing every philosophy
that demanded to be taken 'seriously', Stirner did not
exempt his own.   Irrationalism, he willingly tells us,
ends up by advocating and practising 'not thought, but
thoughtlessness' and by reducing all things - including at last its own assertions - to utter meaning-
lessness.   Clearly, irrationalists of this radical
stamp do not call for a refutation, since they do not
put up any meaningful assertions to *be* either con-
firmed or refuted.   They are simply not in the
business of putting forward ideas.

4   There is no reason why the study of logic should be
confined, as it in fact is in most systems of education, to students of high intelligence at a fairly

advanced stage of their education. The study of logic
- at least in the form of 'clear thinking' - can be
profitably undertaken at any intellectual level, as
F.D.Maurice rightly affirmed:

> The reasons which I gave for the wonderful popu-
> larity of Abelard's lectures at Paris in the
> twelfth century, will be a sufficient defence for
> me, when I plead for offering instruction in Logic
> to our working classes. If I supposed I should be
> introducing them to a new subject, to one apart
> from all their previous thoughts and habits, I
> should be obliged, by the maxims which I have laid
> down, to reject it from our circle. But since the
> workers speak and think and reason, they are all
> logicians in embryo: what they want in this, as in
> other cases, is to be taught what they are doing,
> to have their minds set in order about their own
> operations. I am far from sure that the person who
> undertook this task, knowing what it signified, and
> with a resolution to avoid pedantry, might not make
> his lessons popular as well as very profitable. I
> do not indeed anticipate a return of the middle age
> frenzy. I do not suppose that if Mr Mill announced
> a lecture on Universals at Drury Lane Theatre or
> Exeter Hall, there would be an instant rush for
> front boxes, and that tickets would be unprocura-
> ble. But the working man who has been used to
> vagueness often manifests such a delight in dis-
> covering lines and distinctions which were always
> existing, and which he had not perceived, as the
> student, tired of these lines and distinctions, and
> longing to fill them up with actual forms, cannot
> appreciate. Everything shows what a blessing each
> may be to the other. (F.D.Maurice, 'Learning and
> Working', ed. W.E.Styler, London, Oxford University
> Press, 1968, pp.141-2)

5 See supra, pp.5-7.

CHAPTER 5   THE MORAL EDUCATION OF THE ADULT

1 S.Kierkegaard, 'Purity of Heart is to Will One Thing',
   trans. D.Steere, London, Fontana Books, 1961, p.166.
2 J.-P.Sartre, 'Being and Nothingness', trans. H.E.
   Barnes, London, Methuen, 1957, p.462.
3 See R.S.Peters, 'Reason and Compassion', London,
   Routledge & Kegan Paul, 1973, pp.36 ff.; and R.S.
   Peters, Freedom and the Development of the Free Man,
   in J.F.Doyle, ed., 'Educational Judgments', London,
   Routledge & Kegan Paul, 1973, pp.127 ff.

4   R.M.Hare, Language and Moral Education, in Glenn
    Langford and D.J.O'Connor, eds, 'New Essays in the
    Philosophy of Education', London, Routledge & Kegan
    Paul, 1973, p.164.

5   J.S.Mill, 'Utilitarianism, Liberty, and Representative
    Government', London, J.M.Dent, 1910, p.33.

6   A stock objection to theories which ground our value
    judgments in feelings, in intuitive responses, or in
    what Max Scheler called the 'emotional a priori' (see
    'Der Formalismus in der Ethik and die materiale
    Wertethik') is that our feelings and emotions vary so
    widely according to purely subjective influences that
    no kind of public and objectively valid system of
    values could possibly be based upon them. There is
    no space here to discuss this objection at any length.
    However, since it might well seem to invalidate the
    whole project of moral *education,* we shall briefly
    consider the relevance of this type of objection when
    we come to look at the question of the *justification*
    of moral education later in this chapter (see infra,
    pp.146-8).

7   Many moralists would want to restrict the application
    of the expressions 'moral choice' and 'moral action'
    to those choices and actions which affect the distri-
    bution of good and evil in the universe to *some sig-
    nificant degree*. There is obviously much to be said
    for this linguistic stipulation, provided it is
    recognized that in this case the difference between
    moral and nonmoral choices and actions *is* merely a
    difference of degree not of kind.

8   Supra, pp.119-20.

9   R.F.Dearden, Autonomy and Education, in R.F.Dearden,
    P.H.Hirst and R.S.Peters, eds, 'Education and the
    Development of Reason', London, Routledge & Kegan
    Paul, 1972, p.461.

10 See supra, p.125.

11 See supra, pp.26-8.

12 This is not to deny that constraint and coercion may
    play a part in bringing someone into a situation where
    he may then freely respond to the moral values placed
    before him. No doubt this has a place in the edu-
    cation of children, convicted criminals, and some
    inmates of mental institutions, although surely seldom
    if ever in the education of normal adults enjoying the
    liberties of citizens.

13 L.A.Reid, 'Philosophy and Education', London,
    Heinemann, 1962, p.107.

14 See supra, p.104.

15 F.D.Maurice, 'Learning and Working', ed. W.E.Styler,
    London, Oxford University Press, 1968, p.140.

16   Hare, op.cit., p.161.

17   I hope that my emphasis on the place of a wide general
     knowledge of the objective world in anyone's moral
     education will not be misconstrued as an attempt to
     reduce moral knowledge to factual knowledge. I have
     already drawn attention to the distinction between
     ascriptions of value and descriptions of empirical
     fact. See supra, pp.130-1, where, however, I also
     pointed out that values do not float about in a vacuum
     but in an important sense *depend on* or *inhere in*
     facts. Loyalty and envy, for example, are objective
     human attitudes which can be scientifically investi-
     gated by psychologists and imaginatively explored by
     novelists, and it is precisely by virtue of the fact
     that a man's conduct displays one of these attitudes
     that we can correctly judge it to be 'admirable',
     'contemptible', 'meritorious', 'blameworthy', or in
     some other way morally good or bad. It is hard to see
     how we could even begin to form any judgments of value
     if we had no knowledge of the objective features of
     the world in which values reside. Presenting these
     features of the world for moral scrutiny and conscious
     evaluation by the educand is, I suggest, the dis-
     tinctive and central task of moral education.

18   Perhaps two points ought to be made in passing, to
     remove possible sources of misunderstanding. First of
     all, it might seem as if a definition of moral edu-
     cation in terms of the development of intrinsically
     good qualities (all in one way or another qualities of
     awareness) would have the effect of merging 'moral
     education' with 'education' in general. Now, there is
     undoubtedly a sense in which all education, conceived
     as the development of persons, *can* be thought of as
     the 'moral' development of persons, since education *is*
     directed to a person's overall betterment and there *is*
     a crucial normative dimension in the concept of a
     'person'. However, we have already seen that some
     human qualities are of very much greater intrinsic
     value than others - thus love and a sense of justice
     are vastly more important qualities in a person than,
     say, wit and good taste - and we have also seen that
     there is much to be said in favour of restricting the
     term 'moral' to those choices and actions, and
     therefore those personal qualities, which affect the
     distribution of good and evil in the universe to *some
     significant degree* (see supra, p.134 and footnote 7).
     It is thus entirely reasonable, and in accordance with
     widely established usage, to restrict the application
     of the expression 'moral education' to the development

of those qualities which are recognized to be among
the very highest attributes of personhood (mainly
those which involve our attitudes to others). However, the linguistic question is, I suggest, of no
great importance, provided we always bear in mind that
the difference between 'moral education' in the
stricter sense and education in general is merely a
difference of degree not of kind.

Second, if the development of qualities like love,
tolerance, compassion, fairness, and so on, really is
of such supreme value and significance, it might seem
to follow that we ought to be devoting nearly all our
educational resources to moral education in the
stricter sense and relegating the acquisition of
scientific, mathematical, historical, philosophical,
and other forms of knowledge not just to a secondary
but to a decidedly marginal place in everyone's education. However, this self-evidently absurd conclusion would follow only if intrinsic value were per
se equivalent to educational value. But we have seen
that the educational value (or intrinsic *cognitive*
value) of a form of knowledge depends on, among other
things, the *scope* and *certainty* of the knowledge which
it distinctively offers us. And in *these* respects the
educational value of mankind's scientific knowledge,
for example, is conspicuously *higher* than that of such
moral wisdom as we believe ourselves to have attained
(see supra, pp.86-94).

19 See supra, p.32.

CHAPTER 6   TEACHING AND LEARNING

1 This stipulation has to be made because a man can only
be said to 'know' that so-and-so is such-and-such if
he has *adequate grounds* for his true belief that so-
and-so is such-and-such. A man could not be said to
have 'acquired the knowledge' or 'learned' that salt
dissolves in water if he arrived at this true belief
by spinning a coin, by being hypnotized into believing
it, as a result of seeing sugar dissolve in water and
mistaking this for salt, as a result of processes of
physiological maturation, or as a result of any other
cognitively irrelevant or inadequate process or
processes. Naturally, there is room for disagreement
as to what counts as a relevant perception or a well-
grounded inference.

2 A thoroughgoing behaviourist will argue that the
learning of truths also needs to be analysed in terms

of the modification of behaviour. He may go on to
argue that behavioural changes brought about in ways
not involving relevant perceptions or inferences on
the part of the learner (by the administration of
drugs, for instance) must nevertheless be counted as
'learning'. Significantly, he is much more likely to
say that a man's behaviour has been modified than that
a man has modified his behaviour. And he may even be
prepared to include under 'learning' behavioural
changes signifying *reduced* efficiency (for instance,
a child 'learning' to stammer as a result of mal-
treatment). The more sweeping types of behaviourism
need not be discussed in our analysis of 'learning',
for it will already be evident that they increasingly
tend to part company with the established meaning of
the word 'learning' and to give it an idiosyncratic
meaning of their own. In ordinary correct English a
child cannot be said to 'learn' that London is the
capital of France. A behaviouristic psychologist who
spoke about the 'learning' of falsehoods would simply
not be speaking about what the rest of us are speaking
about when we speak of people learning things.

3 R.S.Downie, Eileen M.Loudfoot and Elizabeth Telfer,
   'Education and Personal Relationships', London,
   Methuen, 1974, p.42. Admittedly, the writers claim
   (p.1) to be concentrating on teaching 'in the sense
   which designates one kind of occupation' rather than
   on teaching as a generic activity. Even so, however,
   the characterization is unduly restrictive, since
   there are many professional teachers (e.g. driving
   school instructors) who cannot be thought of as
   engaged in 'the creation of educated men'.

4 Israel Scheffler, Philosophical Models of Teaching, in
   R.S.Peters, ed., 'The Concept of Education', London,
   Routledge & Kegan Paul, 1967, p.120.

5 Thus, while we agree with Mrs Helen Freeman (Helen
   Freeman, The Concept of Teaching, 'Proceedings of the
   Philosophy of Education Society of Great Britain',
   vol.VII, no.1, January 1973, pp.7-25) that teaching
   implies learning, we do not agree with her when she
   denies that teaching is an activity in which people
   intentionally engage. We do not dispute that the word
   'teaching' is indeed often used to signify what
   happens when, for example, Peter's behaviour or
   conversation provides listening and observant Paul
   with new knowledge or skills although this formed no
   part of Peter's intention for Paul or for anyone else.
   We have already emphasized the ambiguities and inconsistencies with which ordinary usage is fraught, and

we have also emphasized that nothing of substance
hinges on how we choose to use the *word* 'teaching',
or any other word, provided we are clear about the
idea which the word is being used to express on any
given occasion. Nevertheless, there are good reasons
for preferring to use the word 'teaching' in its
stricter sense (as we shall do), logically incorporating an *intention* that learning shall take place.
For this does appear to be the paradigm sense of
'teaching', and other uses to which the word is put
do seem to be erosions, progressive attenuations, of
its full and central meaning. If Peter can 'teach'
Paul something unintentionally, perhaps even when he
is unaware of the very existence of Paul or of anyone
else who is likely to be learning from him, we shall
have to say that one man can 'teach' another although
there may be nothing remotely resembling *communication*
between them. Why should we not go on to say that
Peter can 'teach' Paul something of which he, Peter,
is himself *ignorant* (as when Paul learns by observing
Peter's mistakes)? Why should we not go still further
and say that animals, or for that matter inanimate
physical objects, can and do 'teach' Paul all manner
of useful and interesting things (cows or clouds, for
example, 'teaching' him about the conditions which
precede rain)? Obviously, the further we move away
from the logically primary sense of teaching, in which
it is an activity engaged in intentionally, the more
our use of the word will tend to take on the character
of a metaphor. It is noteworthy that Mrs Freeman
herself suggests (op.cit., p.22) that 'more attention
should be paid in schools to what is unintentionally
taught', so implicitly acknowledging the *desirability,*
at least, of bringing fortuitous and unintended
learning under the conscious jurisdiction of responsible teaching intentions.

6 Thus not everything a teacher does is *teaching*. In
trying to create a pleasant and friendly classroom
atmosphere, or in trying to ensure comfortable physical conditions for adults who are tired after a day's
work, or in trying to foster a sense of common purpose
in a group of students who are strangers to one
another, a tutor of adults is not teaching but rather
trying to establish the *conditions* in which effective
teaching can take place. Such activities are of
immense importance, but it does not help to confuse
them with the teaching activities which they are
designed to facilitate.

7 This requirement is needed to distinguish the activity

of teachers properly so called from the related but quite distinct activities of people like librarians or film projectionists, for example, who are not obliged to possess themselves the knowledge which nevertheless they are most certainly engaged in disseminating.

8   See M.Heidegger, 'Being and Time', trans. J.Macquarrie and E.Robinson, Oxford, Basil Blackwell, 1967, p.171 and pp.264-5.

9   See especially 'Republic', 518b-c, and also the whole allegory of the Cave. Of course it is not teaching in general that Plato has in mind, but rather those kinds of teaching which can be correctly thought of as truly educating the learner. And of course there are other elements in what Plato calls 'the true analogy' besides the metaphor of vision, not all of which are uniformly acceptable. The metaphor of the teacher 'turning round' or 'wheeling round' the soul of the learner, for example, conveys far too mechanical an image and makes the role of the learner seem far too passive.

10 Scheffler, op.cit., p.128.

11 Scheffler also alleges (loc.cit.) that the insight model of teaching, with its specifically cognitive emphasis, cannot easily be stretched to cover the teaching of habits and attitudes. However, this allegation can be thought to have some force only if we overlook the cognitive stipulations written into the concept of 'teaching'. If a man's habits or attitudes are changed by measures which completely by-pass relevant mental activity on his part, we must not say that these changes have been produced in him by 'teaching'. But if a man's habits or attitudes change by reason of some set of relevant perceptions or inferences which our teaching measures have stimulated him to make, we cannot deny that *the part played by teaching* has been that of fostering insight. (Of course, as we have already stressed, the measures taken by the teacher can never of themselves bring about the appropriate kind of change in the learner. His own free initiative and active collaboration are also necessary - and clearly we must not count these in with the 'teaching' or include them in our analysis of 'teaching'.)

12 Perhaps we should note here that in practice we tend to speak of John 'teaching' James only if what John communicates to James is intended to *sink fairly deeply in*. There are many things which we tell people, narrate to them, show them, or explain to

them, which we do not think of ourselves as 'teaching' them. But when John *teaches* James something, he firmly intends that James shall really *learn* it; that is, he firmly intends that James shall become *fully and clearly* aware of it, and probably also that he shall *remain* aware of it for some relatively lengthy period of time.

CHAPTER 7   THE USES OF MATURITY

1   See supra, pp.39-44.
2   Moreover, a difficulty arises about the correct description of courses where the ultimate actual content is significantly different from the specific overt content. If a course on stamp-collecting offered by an evening institute is judged to have serious educational value because it widens students' geographical and historical knowledge and deepens their understanding of other societies and cultures (and is judged *for this reason* to merit its place in the evening institute programme), is it not disingenuous to put this course forward as a course on 'stamp-collecting'? The stock answer would be that to present such a course in its true colours would be to deter many potential students from enrolling and that it is better to educate by stealth than not to educate at all. The validity of this answer will be considered when we come to examine the 'task' criteria of an educational process, especially the criterion of wittingness (see infra, pp.198-9). Here we need only note that where the ultimate actual content of a course is claimed to be significantly wider than its specific overt content, this claim can and ought to be empirically tested in a number of obvious ways. For instance, do the stamp-collecting students who are supposed to have now acquired worthwhile geographical and historical knowledge evince a serious interest in courses *specifically and overtly* on geographical and historical matters when such courses are offered by the evening institute on a subsequent occasion?
3   See supra, p.46.
4   Not only is it possible for processes of education to go on alongside or subsequently to processes of training: as a matter of contingent fact the provision of certain types of training is often highly desirable (even sometimes indispensably necessary) if a man is to receive an adequate education. Training in the efficient use of works of reference, cata-

logues, calculating machines, laboratory equipment, in
the efficient handling of specimens, and so on, may be
of the utmost importance in different areas of a man's
education, if he is not to fumble and flounder among
the cognitive materials by which he is confronted. Of
course, in these and most other instances the content
of the training process is of purely instrumental
value, and for this reason alone we should want to
distinguish between such processes and the properly
educational processes to which they are ancillary.
However, we also speak of a man being 'trained' to
speak fluent German or 'trained' to identify the work
of the Flemish masters, and in these instances, where
the knowledge acquired is undoubtedly of considerable
value in its own right, it is clear that our reason
for withholding the accolade of 'education' is that
the learner's attention is being tightly channelled
towards a comparatively narrow set of learning objectives and that the wider dimensions of language
studies or art studies are therefore being deliberately neglected (usually because they are deemed to be
unnecessary for the specific tasks which the trainee
is being specifically equipped to carry out). This in
fact is our real basis for differentiating between
training and education. What essentially differentiates a process of training from a process of education
is this deliberate restriction and compression of the
trainee's awareness, which is focused tightly on some
comparatively limited set of operations temporarily
disconnected from their wider cognitive setting.

5   People *can* submit wittingly to indoctrination, and in
fact this is a depressingly common phenomenon, observable in many religious and political circles,
where the faithful gather to lap up the pure milk of
the word and to learn new ways of confuting the devil,
and where bewilderment and consternation would reign
if it were even hinted that the devil might not be
wholly black. The political or religious zealot or
fanatic may be uncomfortably aware that there are
other sides to the question, but the last thing he
wants is to be induced to consider them, for he would
much rather forget the very existence of serious
alternatives to his own sweet creed. He may be
seeking some kind of reassurance; he may come to the
indoctrinator because he wants nagging doubts
painlessly removed; he may want to develop his
exegetical, apologetic, or polemical skills in the
service of the cause: but what he does *not* want is
knowledge. We saw in Chapter 4 (see supra, p.110)

that a 'reasonable' man is a man who has an active
commitment to the idea of knowledge as something which
ought to be prized in and for itself. We might say,
therefore, that the willing victim of indoctrination
is the paradigm of the unreasonable man. He is a
familiar figure. The willing victim of the indoctrinators is the man who *does not want to know*.

6   It might be objected that teachers who have themselves
been indoctrinated (someone teaching economic or political theory in Soviet Russia, for instance) cannot
be regarded as indoctrinating their pupils *intentionally,* since such teachers will sincerely consider the
validity of the beliefs or attitudes which they are
transmitting to be beyond question and so it will just
never occur to them to go out of their way actively
and systematically to disfavour rival beliefs or
attitudes, which they will simply and as a matter of
course pass over and neglect. The answer to this
objection is that if the teachers in question are
wholly ignorant of the existence of serious alternatives to the beliefs or attitudes which they are
inculcating we cannot regard them as 'indoctrinators'
at all, since what they in fact are (through no fault
of their own, if they themselves have been unwitting
victims of indoctrination) is *very incompetent
teachers;* however, to the degree that such teachers
suspect that there might at least be some kind of a
case to be made in favour of the rival beliefs or
attitudes and yet, surmising this, studiously avoid
investigating the rival case for themselves or dis-
cussing it with their students, to that degree we
should have to say that their foreclosing of the
issues is intentional and to precisely the same
degree, I suggest, we should have to find them guilty
of 'indoctrinating'. (The fact that they are unlikely
to describe what they are doing as 'indoctrinating',
and very unlikely indeed to think of what they are
doing as pernicious, of course only goes to show that
they are either disingenuous or confused.)

7   Antony Flew, Indoctrination and Religion, in I.A.
Snook, ed., 'Concepts of Indoctrination', London,
Routledge & Kegan Paul, 1972, p.114. Flew, however,
uses 'doctrine' to signify a species of beliefs only,
namely false or at best dubious beliefs which are
distinctively bound up with adherence to some ideology
or other.

8   Strictly speaking, of course, processes of indoctrination which instil false beliefs cannot even be
counted as 'teaching' processes. To the extent that

the beliefs which a man has acquired are false, to
that extent he cannot be said to have 'learned'
anything, and to that extent, therefore, he cannot be
said to have been 'taught' anything. No doubt every
teacher innocently imparts some false beliefs to his
pupils, and nothing very much hinges on the question
of whether we should describe the imparting of false
beliefs as 'defective teaching' or as 'failing to
teach'. As a compromise we might refer to the imparting of false beliefs as 'quasi-teaching', in which
case we should have to say that the process of indoctrinating a man with false beliefs was a quasi-
teaching process rather than a teaching process
properly so called. However, since under either name
the process of indoctrination is still not an *educational* process, our main point is not in the least
affected, and therefore for simplicity we shall in
what follows continue to speak of 'teaching processes'
even when (as the context will normally make clear)
the processes in question are really only quasi-
teaching processes.

9   I.A.Snook, 'Indoctrination and Education', London,
Routledge & Kegan Paul, 1972, p.37.

10   Ibid., p.47.

11   See ibid., p.49 and p.107.

12   See supra, p.49.

13   See supra, pp.38-9.

14   See supra, note 2.

15   Some forms of adult education partly depend on the
operation of educationally extrinsic motives. Consider trade unionists on paid day-release study, men
and women in HM Forces and HM prisons for whom attendance at classes may offer respite from routine
duties, the growing body of extra-mural students who
are hoping to be awarded certificates, diplomas, or
other qualifications, and so on. Within such modes
of provision it is no doubt harder to determine the
degree to which students are motivated by genuinely
educational considerations, but from what we have
already said it should at least be evident that the
concomitant operation of non-educational motives in
no way cancels out or reduces the value of whatever
strictly educational motives may be at work in the
situation.

16   See John Olliger and Colleen McCarthy, 'Lifelong
Learning or Lifelong Schooling? A Tentative View of
the Ideas of Ivan Illich with a Quotational Bibliogra-
phy', Syracuse, Syracuse University and ERIC
Clearinghouse on Adult Education, 1971.

17 From the fact that an educational process properly so
called should involve some kind of personal relations
it does not follow that the concept of 'self-
education' has no proper application. Indeed we have
already seen that in an important sense all adult education is ultimately 'self-education', since in the
last analysis it is the individual adult himself who
has to take responsibility for the shape, direction,
and pace of his continuing education. However, in
doing so, we may assume, a serious student will
normally avail himself of public modes of provision -
classes, courses, study groups, and so on - which will
place him in situations where he will be subject to
the disciplines, and receive the stimulus, of interaction with teachers and fellow students. But what
about someone who embarked on a project of 'self-
education' in a stricter sense, someone who sought to
enlarge his knowledge and understanding entirely by
private study without any kind of personal tuition or
exchanges with fellow students? In this connection
three points, I think, need to be noted. First,
everyone has at some time had *some* face-to-face
teaching, even if only as a young child, and in
literal fact, therefore, there is no such person as
the completely self-educated man. Second, the adult
who, having resumed his education, pursues it *entirely*
by private study is in reality an extremely rare
specimen. Third, when a man pursues his further education entirely by private study, this is almost
always because of the operation of some limiting
factor - his personal circumstances perhaps, or perhaps the unavailability of suitable courses - since,
other things being equal, a serious student will
always welcome qualified guidance and ongoing dialogue
with other serious students (not just as extrinsic
aids to learning, like physically comfortable conditions, but as an integral *part* of the educational
process itself). In other words, the serious student
himself recognizes that something vital is missing if
his studies are purely solitary. And what he is
recognizing, I submit, is that they are something less
than 'processes of education' in the fullest sense of
the term. We need not worry too much about what name
should be given to them. Obviously, if they are sufficiently akin to bona fide educational processes in
every other respect, it would be foolish to refuse to
call them 'processes of education'. What is important
is that theoretical recognition should be given to
what everyone recognizes in practice - namely that the

paradigm case of a 'process of education' is one in
which the educand is at least from time to time involved in personal exchanges with others who are also
committed to the educational enterprise.

18   J.P.White, Creativity and Education: A Philosophical
Analysis, in R.F.Dearden, P.H.Hirst and R.S.Peters,
eds, 'Education and the Development of Reason',
London, Routledge & Kegan Paul, 1972, p.135.

19   See supra, pp.22-4.

20   See Paulo Freire, 'Pedagogy of the Oppressed',
Harmondsworth, Penguin, 1972, pp.46-7.

21   See R.W.K.Paterson, The Concept of Discussion,
'Studies in Adult Education', vol.2, no.1, April 1970,
pp.28-50.

22   Martin Buber, 'Between Man and Man', trans. R.Gregor
Smith, London, Kegan Paul, Trench, & Trubner, 1947,
p.97.

23   See supra, p.21.

CHAPTER 8   CONCEPTS OF EDUCATIONAL JUSTICE

1   We shall in fact avoid the commonly used but somewhat
misleading expression, 'welfare rights', for three
reasons. First, to many people in contemporary
England this expression tends to suggest a particular
range of financial and other material benefits (for
example, social security payments) which people are
legally entitled to receive from the State, whereas
we are of course concerned here with a very much wider
class of rights, and with moral rights rather than
legal rights. Second, people may have a right to
positive action from their fellows in respect of other
things besides their 'welfare', unless the term
'welfare' is to be drained of all definite meaning by
being expanded to cover such things as a man's right
to be told by his doctor that he is dying although
this knowledge may distress him, a child's right to
learn at some stage that he is adoptive although the
effects on him of learning this may be unpredictable,
and my right that you shall keep the promise you made
to me although it no longer affects my interests
whether you do so or not. A person's right to education is essentially his right to knowledge, and it
is extremely doubtful whether knowledge should be
regarded as part of someone's *welfare* except in the
trivially elastic sense of the term. Third, a
person's welfare in the more specific and definite
sense - his prospects of happiness, material security,

health, and so on - entitles him to all kinds of non-interference and acquiescence from his fellows as well as positive assistance from them, and it would obviously therefore be logical (although not conventional) to include *both* these types of right under the expression 'welfare rights'. However, this would only cause confusion. We shall therefore opt to speak of 'positive rights' rather than 'welfare rights', where what we have in mind is people's rights to some kind of *active intervention* by their fellows.

2 For a valuable discussion of the nature and basis of children's educational rights see Frederick A.Olafson, Rights and Duties in Education, and A.I.Melden, Olafson on the Right to Education, in J.F.Doyle, ed., 'Educational Judgments', London, Routledge & Kegan Paul, 1973, pp.173-95 and 196-206. Olafson convincingly argues that children's rights to education are properly asserted against the whole preceding generation of citizens in an organized political community, who must be deemed collectively responsible for the existence, and who must therefore collectively take responsibility for the education, of the whole succeeding generation. However, none of this does much to clarify the educational rights of *adults,* with which alone we are concerned here.

3 Obviously we are here postulating a particular view of the functions of society - or, in the language of classical political philosophy, a particular view of 'the ends of the state'. (Where we speak of 'society', we of course generally mean society acting as an organized unity, and of course this ultimately means the state, even although on many occasions the state may delegate its functions to lesser associations, as when the Department of Education and Science entrusts the provision of liberal adult education to officially designated 'Responsible Bodies'.) It would hardly be possible to expound our view of the functions of society in any detail here. However, perhaps the following points ought to be briefly made. First, among the *minimum* functions of society (or the state) is the *guaranteeing of the rights* of all its members, that is, their moral rights as human beings - the right to life, for example, on which rests the duty of the state to protect its citizens. A society which fails to do this is not even a just society. A morally admirable society - which is more than merely a just society - is one which in principle is willing to do much more for its members than just ensure that they get what they are morally entitled to, but what

in practice such a society will undertake and make a
matter of social rather than individual responsibility
very much depends on its circumstances and will
therefore vary from place to place and from time to
time. In some circumstances it will be highly desirable, but in others perhaps most undesirable, that
society itself should undertake, say, the provision of
sports facilities, or that there should be a National
Theatre or state-run holiday homes. Obviously one of
the major considerations which society ought always to
take into account is the immense moral importance, as
something to be greatly valued for its own sake, of
people developing and exercising their capacities of
personal initiative and doing things for themselves.
Second, the rights which society guarantees or assures
to its members may be *either* rights which a man may
have against other assignable individuals or groups
(for example, his right to repayment of debts owed to
him) *or* rights which do not give rise to duties on the
part of assignable individuals or groups but which
must instead be thought of as giving rise to duties on
the part of society at large (for example, a disabled
person's right to at least whatever minimum standard
of living is deemed to be required by considerations
of basic human dignity). In the former case, the duty
of society is to compel or otherwise induce the
assignable individuals or groups to perform *their*
duties; in the latter case, however, it is on *society
itself* that the duty is laid of providing whatever it
is to which its members have a right (a duty which it
may indeed delegate, but never renounce). Third, the
duties which are laid on society itself are ordinary
moral duties which simply happen to be duties the
carrying out of which is the *collective* responsibility
of a very large number of people by virtue of their
belonging to a single organized political unity. The
duties of society to its members are not some ex-
traordinary or occult category of duties which are
borne by some mystical, superhuman entity - 'society'
or 'the state' - which exists as a special kind of
moral being over and above the individual human beings
who compose it. On a desert island the duty of caring
for my disabled fellow is laid exclusively on me if I
am his sole companion in distress; if there are
several other able-bodied men besides myself, the duty
clearly becomes one which we all ought to share
(unless our disabled companion already has special
claims of some sort on one of us); and it remains
essentially the same ordinary human duty when those

among whom it is shared number fifty million and live
in a complex modern industrial community with
constantly evolving social and political institutions.
Fourth, it is our specific claim here (for the reasons
stated in the text) that every adult has a *positive
right* to education, a right which generates a duty on
the part of *society itself;* and from this it follows
that the provision of facilities for the continuing
lifelong education of its adult members is not just
something which a morally admirable society will
undertake in suitable circumstances but something the
withholding of which amounts to a form of actual
social injustice.

4   See supra, pp.180-1.

5   This admirable declaration of principle was made by
Churchill in 1953. Nevertheless, in that year the
British Government's *total grant* to the Responsible
Bodies for liberal adult education was a beggarly
£330,000. Despite the Government's high professions,
in practice the liberal education of adults occupied
(and still occupies) a very low place in its priorities. Of course the gap between principle and
practice in no way detracts from the value of
Churchill's declaration of principle, viewed purely
as a declaration of principle.

6   See supra, p.167.

7   See supra, p.176.

8   The author recalls hearing an academic seconded to
government employment (who has long since moved
elsewhere) telling an adult education conference (on
behalf of his then employers) that university adult
education courses in social and economic studies ought
to have as a paramount educational objective the
creation of a wider understanding of the then
government's prices and incomes policy (which has
been long since superseded and is probably now only
remembered by a handful of highly specialized economic
historians). However, even when the social objective
being pursued is of unquestionable and permanent
importance to very large numbers of people, it will I
think seldom justify the adoption of educational
policies which violate the individual's right to education in the full sense of the term - that is, to
courses of study which are distinguished by cognitive
breadth and balance and which promote the acquisition
of knowledge and skills that are *intrinsically* worth
acquiring. Of course, if and when there really does
occur a direct conflict between the demands of educational justice and the demands of general social

justice, then indeed it is the individual's educational rights that will have to be set aside in order to
fulfil obligations judged to be still more imperative.
But since people's educational rights - which after
all are concerned with the nature of their very being
as persons - must surely be considered to form a very
large and crucial part of their general social rights,
we may I think surmise that in practice it will be
very seldom that educational injustice of this·kind
can be vindicated in the name of social justice.

9 See R.F.Dearden, 'Needs' in Education, in R.F.Dearden,
P.H.Hirst and R.S.Peters, eds, 'Education and the
Development of Reason', London, Routledge & Kegan
Paul, 1972, pp.50-64.

10 An objector might argue that in a modern industrial
society every adult needs to have at least basic
literacy, and that a system which failed to guarantee
at least this to its citizens would be an unjust
system. However, such an objection (while containing
an obvious truth) enshrines a serious confusion of
principle. Since people cannot be 'guaranteed'
something which depends to a significant extent on the
efforts that they themselves are prepared to make,
that to which they have a right cannot be *defined as*
some minimum level of competence in reading and
writing, however much they may 'need' this. But of
course *in practice* any person not mentally subnormal
who gets from society what he *does* have a right to,
namely an exactly equal share of the resources available for the education of adults, will nearly always be
certain of getting more than enough to help him
acquire the basic skills of literacy if he lacks them
and is keen to acquire them. We have seen (supra, p.
239) that he cannot indeed be *guaranteed* this amount
or any other absolute amount of resources, but at any
rate in a modern industrial society - where being
illiterate is perhaps specially disadvantageous - we
can reasonably presume that, given a will to meet its
overall educational obligations on the part of
society, the overall resources socially available for
adult education will often in practice suffice for
this purpose. Even if they did not *consistently* (year
in and year out) suffice for this purpose (as they
surely ought to), this would not affect the issue,
since a man usually has to learn to read and write
only once in his life. Thus we do not for a moment
deny the immense importance of helping illiterate
adults to reach at least a minimum competence in
reading and writing. But it does not follow from

this that they have a 'right to be literate'. What
they have a *right* to is a certain share of the available resources, which in practice will nearly always
suffice to enable every individual to become literate.
The practical outcome is the same, but the *justifying
principle* is crucially different.

11 Fortunately, it is no part of our task here to determine what constitutes educational justice in the
domain of the education of children and adolescents.
Nevertheless, it might be as well to state that in the
author's opinion pretty much the same considerations
apply in determining the rights of children and
adolescents as apply in determining the educational
rights of adults, except that the younger the child
the less capable he must be deemed of making responsible educational choices and the more necessary it may
therefore be for his teachers to disregard his express
desires and to allocate him the kinds and the overall
share of resources which, in their reasoned assessment, he will retrospectively desire to have been
allocated when he eventually comes to man's estate and
can take a rounder and more balanced view of his whole
educational career. (Obviously, the child's actual
school performance will normally be an important
factor rightly influencing his teachers' estimates of
his probable educational evolution.)

12 If people are allowed to remain in virtual ignorance
of what it is that they have a right to in the domain
of education, their educational rights are in effect
being denied and they clearly count as victims of educational injustice. This is obviously an excellent
reason for trying to ensure that the curriculum of
every schoolchild includes a living and serious encounter with every form of knowledge and awareness at
some stage or other, and more particularly with those
forms of knowledge which he is unlikely to have the
opportunity to explore in the course of his normal
daily living and which would otherwise, therefore,
remain largely unintelligible and closed to him.
J.P.White's concept of the 'compulsory curriculum',
which he advocates for closely similar reasons, manifestly does not apply to the education of adults, but
its general application to the education of
schoolchildren could make a significant contribution
to the cause of educational justice in the domain of
adult education (see J.P.White, 'Towards a Compulsory
Curriculum', London, Routledge & Kegan Paul, 1973).

CHAPTER 9   EDUCATION FOR DEMOCRACY

1 Report by a Committee of Inquiry appointed by the
   Secretary of State for Education and Science under
   the Chairmanship of Sir Lionel Russell, CBE, 'Adult
   Education: A Plan for Development', London, HMSO,
   1973, p.xi.
2 See supra, pp.231-5.
3 'A Design for Democracy: An abridgment of a report
   of the Adult Education Committee of The British
   Ministry of Reconstruction, commonly called "The 1919
   Report", with an introduction, "The Years Between",
   by R.D.Waller', London, Max Parrish, 1956, p.149.
4 Israel Scheffler, Reflections on Educational
   Relevance, in R.S.Peters, ed., 'The Philosophy of
   Education', London, Oxford University Press, 1973,
   pp.83-4.
5 Admittedly there are degrees of certainty, and admittedly the desirability of some social objectives
   (e.g. public health) is well nigh indisputable and
   ought not to be seriously contested by any reasonable
   person. However, educators - qua educators - cannot
   possibly allow the merits of any proposed social objective to be settled for them and for their students,
   off stage as it were, by some external and therefore
   educationally irresponsible agency. Moreover, the
   desirability of even the most manifestly desirable
   objective needs to be weighed against the desirability
   of other objectives with which it may in some measure
   conflict (e.g. public health and personal freedom).
   And in any case what the social objective properly
   consists in will always be a question which educators
   cannot possibly put aside in favour of some officially
   approved answer (e.g. does 'public health' demand a
   society of exuberant athletes who are scarcely ever
   ill, or merely a society of men and women most of whom
   are normally healthy enough to do their jobs and look
   after themselves and their families with at least a
   moderate degree of efficiency?).
6 It might be suggested as a compromise that adult education, while preserving its inherent commitment to
   pursue the truth wherever it may lead, could nevertheless be of great service to society by simply agreeing
   to pursue the truth, quite unfettered and unconstrained, in relation to certain themes or topics
   which are acknowledged to be of vital concern to
   society - for example, industrial relations, race
   relations, housing policy, or the treatment of delinquency - where the spread of objective knowledge

would in itself be a socially desirable event. Now, this sort of educational contribution to social wellbeing would undoubtedly be much more appropriate than the sort which would require of adult education that it subserve predetermined social objectives. Nevertheless, before reaching out happily towards such a compromise, we ought to take careful note of two important points which need to be well weighed by anyone trying to establish the true place of education in society. First, to accept such an approach would amount to accepting that many of the themes and topics selected to figure as (ostensibly) part of the continuing education of adults should be selected by reference to social, economic, technological, or political considerations, not by reference to what would in fact best further the education of those involved; and clearly, to the extent that this was so, it would be strictly false, and indeed hypocritical, to describe courses so devised as courses of 'adult education', since built into the concept of education is the requirement that the content of education shall be selected for its intrinsic value as a formative element in someone's development as a person. Second, the selection of themes and topics to be treated could not entirely be regarded as in itself a cognitively impartial activity, for the nature of the selection made could and would often in practice exert some influence on the actual ways in which public questions came to be viewed: thus the very activity of organizing courses designed to create a background of knowledge against which people could better understand some government policy or piece of proposed legislation (a prices and incomes policy, say, or an Industrial Relations Bill) would tend to have the perhaps intentional result of making that particular policy or piece of legislation seem of the deepest importance (whether it was or not) and also of quietly suggesting that an unbiased inquiry into the social issues at stake could confidently take for granted that these issues had been correctly identified and defined by the sponsors of the policy or legislation in question (which might or might not be the case).

7 Karl R.Popper, 'The Open Society and Its Enemies', London, Routledge & Kegan Paul, 1945, vol.I, p.126.

8 John Dewey, 'Democracy and Education', New York, Macmillan, 1916, p.101.

9 R.Wollheim, On The Theory of Democracy, in B.Williams and A.Montefiore, eds, 'British Analytical Philosophy', London, Routledge & Kegan Paul, 1966, p.266.

10   P.A.White, Education, Democracy, and the Public
     Interest, in R.S.Peters, ed., 'The Philosophy of Edu-
     cation', London, Oxford University Press, 1973, p.227.
11   Of course, a man might acquire the knowledge and
     skills necessary for citizenship in a democracy
     without receiving any formal education for this
     purpose, and one could perhaps imagine a successful
     democratic society whose citizens learned all their
     social and political lessons in and through the
     unsuperintended processes of their daily lives. No
     doubt the occurrence and continuance of such a happy
     state of affairs would in practice be most improbable
     and, I think, wholly without precedent. (The ancient
     Greek 'democracies' were hardly democracies in our
     sense.) However, this is not the real objection. The
     real objection is that a society which cared so little
     about the development of its members' ability to take
     part in public affairs that it left this entirely to
     the unsuperintended processes of daily life, in other
     words to pure chance, could not with any accuracy be
     described as a truly and fully democratic society and
     ought not to be so described, however outwardly
     successful and smooth-running it might be, since it
     is surely part of the very concept of a democracy that
     it should be at least in some measure concerned about,
     and certainly not be wholly indifferent to, the actual
     ability of its members to take a full and active share
     in the running of their own society. We may indeed
     grant that there need be no reason in principle why a
     democratic society should not deliberately allow its
     members to acquire democratic understanding and skill
     in and through the processes of daily living rather
     than by means of formal teaching, if it found that the
     former method really did tend to work better - *pro-
     vided that* this was done as a matter of *deliberate
     choice* between alternative methods of learning lessons
     which were consciously recognized and avowed to be
     necessary, provided also that the working of this
     policy was kept under continuous scrutiny (thus not
     leaving the matter to entirely *unsuperintended*
     processes), and provided that the society in question
     remained continuously prepared to intervene actively
     whenever this seemed on balance desirable. A demo-
     cratic society must at least *take some responsibility*
     for its members' progress in democratic understanding
     and skill. At least in this minimum sense, therefore,
     we are surely entitled to claim that education is
     logically written into the very concept of 'democra-
     cy'.

12 See supra, pp.115-16.
13 K.H.Lawson, 'Philosophical Concepts and Values in Adult Education', Nottingham, University of Nottingham Department of Adult Education in association with the National Institute of Adult Education, 1975, p.23.
14 Israel Scheffler, Moral Education and the Democratic Ideal, in Israel Scheffler, 'Reason and Teaching', London, Routledge & Kegan Paul, 1973, p.137.
15 R.S.Peters, 'Ethics and Education', London, Allen & Unwin, 1966, p.298.
16 White, op.cit., p.223.
17 'A Design for Democracy', p.54.
18 'Adult Education: A Plan for Development', para. 58.3.2.
19 Ibid., para.58.3.4.
20 'A Design for Democracy', pp.54-5.
21 This is so, whatever level of civilization a democracy may have attained at any given stage of its develop- ment, and even if it is in fact still at a very low level of civilization. If the education of a democrat involves an education in rationality; and if, as we saw in Chapter 4 (see supra, p.110), a 'reasonable' man is among other things a man who has an active commitment to the idea of *knowledge* as something which ought to be highly valued for its own sake; it follows that the education of a democrat ought always to reach out enthusiastically to the whole of knowledge as its province. Moreover, if 'democracy' is the rule of the *people* not of brutes or things, the development of democrats will necessarily be the de- velopment of *persons*; and again it follows that the true education of a democrat will be one and the same with a true education in general. For these and many other reasons, we are I think entitled to assert that *no* society which fails to promote the *liberal* edu- cation of all its members can be correctly said to have met the full requirements which are logically enshrined in the concept of 'democracy'.
22 See supra, pp.195-218.

Index